Reinventing Work

Inspiring the Next Game: Strategy Ideas for Forward Looking Leaders

BCG Henderson Institute

Reinventing Work

Creating Advantage with Talent Management
and Technology

Edited by
Martin Reeves and Deborah Lovich

DE GRUYTER

ISBN 978-3-11-136956-3
e-ISBN (PDF) 978-3-11-136992-1
e-ISBN (EPUB) 978-3-11-137027-9
ISSN 2701-8857

Library of Congress Control Number: 2024939264

Bibliographic information published by the Deutsche Nationalbibliothek
The Deutsche Nationalbibliothek lists this publication in the Deutsche Nationalbibliografie;
detailed bibliographic data are available on the internet at http://dnb.dnb.de.

www.degruyter.com

Advance Praise for *Reinventing Work: Creating Advantage with Talent Management and Technology*

Each day, we confront the profound influence that technology is exerting on every facet of our employees' work experience. This collection of essays offers a modern guide for navigating the ever-changing terrain of workforce and workplace transformation, all the while ensuring that our people remain at the heart of the discussion.

—**Robin Leopold**, EVP, JPMorgan Chase

Even with AI booming, people remain our greatest asset, upping the competition to attract and retain top talent. Debbie and Martin's collection of essays from the BCG Henderson Institute shakes up the norm, pushing us to rethink the future of work, embrace new models, and establish next generation frameworks for culture and leadership. You'll feel energized to innovate in ways that deliver better business outcomes and inspire your teams – this book's all about sparking fresh ideas and empowers leaders to find that winning edge.

—**Kelly Ann Doherty,** EVP, Chief Administrative Officer, Mr Cooper Group

A fantastic synthesis of cutting edge research out of the BCG Henderson Institute relevant for every HR leader. Combining the best insights from research alongside practical experience with thousands of businesses on the ground, the BCG team highlights the key lessons around attracting, developing and building talent. Key themes around leadership, diversity, AI, and the future of work are blended into the latest research and data. A must read for current and future HR leaders.

—**Nicholas Bloom**, Professor of Economics, Stanford University

Rapid and disruptive change, acceleration of AI and new emerging trends in the workplace is placing human capital at the center of business and board room agendas like never before. This collection of essays offers insights, challenges us to think creatively, and offers guidance on workforce changes. It's a must read for leaders, executives and professionals who are looking for practical insights in navigating the future.

—**Michael Fraccaro**, Chief People Officer, Mastercard

https://doi.org/10.1515/9783111369921-202

While technology has shaped the way we execute tasks and solve problems, people are still our most valuable asset. *Reinventing Work* challenges us to rethink how we look at talent and operating model strategies during the AI revolution. This collection of real-world lessons from BCG's Henderson Institute shows that we can attract the best talent and positively impact people's lives while creating business advantage.

—**Andi Owen**, CEO of MillerKnoll

Harnessing the capabilities of talented people is the key to competitive advantage. But too often, leaders are stuck in outdated management methods even as we undergo technology revolutions and seismic shifts in demographics. Leaders have an opportunity to make work better for people and improve business outcomes — but only if we reinvent how we work. Debbie and Martin's collection of insightful research and practical guidance is essential reading for those looking to lead the way forward.

—**Brian Elliott**, co-founder of Future Forum

Acknowledgments

We would like to acknowledge all of the authors whose work appears on the following pages: David Allred, Jens Baier, Allison Bailey, Vinciane Beauchene, Julie Bedard, Nicole Bennett, David Blanchard, François Candelon, Jean-Michel Caye, Pablo Claver, Rob Cross, Alice de Chalendar, Julia Dhar, Claus Dierksmeier, Sebastian Di-Grande, Karen Dillon, Leila Doumi, Joseph Fuller, Christopher Gentile, Sagar Goel, Ashley Grice, Kateryna Gudziak, Johann D. Harnoss, Jim Hemerling, Marie Humblot-Ferrero, Sesh Iyer, Michael G. Jacobides, Julie Jefson, Adam Job, Georg Kell, Ryoji Kimura, Philipp Kolo, Ádám Kotsis, Orsolya Kovács-Ondrejkovic, Lisa Krayer, Matt Krentz, Nikolaus Lang, Renee Laverdiere, Katie Lavoie, Jean Lee, Deborah Lovich, Hannah Lu Schmitt, Pragya Maini, Justin Manly, Chris Mattey, Colleen McDonald, Madeleine Michael, Gabrielle Novacek, Parneet Pal, Ulrich Pidun, Fanny Potier, J. Puckett, Sana Rafiq, Saran Rajendran, Manjari Raman, Martin Reeves, Ruba Borno, Raffaella Sadun, Rosie Sargeant, Pierre Schatlowski, Anna Schwarz, Nicole Sibilio, Lisa Simon, Nick South, Rainer Strack, Jorge Tamayo, Martin Twesten, Sebastian Ullrich, Nithya Vaduganathan, Judith K. Wallenstein, John Wenstrup, Robert Werner, Hillary Wool, David Zuluaga Martínez, and Ben Zweig. We would also like to acknowledge the broader BCG Henderson Institute community: our Fellows, Ambassadors, and operations teams over the years, who have all made invaluable contributions to our research; our academic collaborators, who have expanded our horizons of new ideas; and our BCG practice area partners, who have collaborated with us on several of these articles.

https://doi.org/10.1515/9783111369921-203

About the BCG Henderson Institute

The BCG Henderson Institute is Boston Consulting Group's think tank, dedicated to exploring and developing valuable new insights from business, technology, economics, and science by embracing the powerful technology of ideas. The Institute engages leaders in provocative discussion and experimentation to expand the boundaries of business theory and practice and to translate innovative ideas from within and beyond business.

https://doi.org/10.1515/9783111369921-204

Contents

Introduction

Martin Reeves, Deborah Lovich

Most organizations' biggest asset is their people. As such, business leaders must make significant efforts to get the best talent – and to get the best out of their workers. This is easier said than done, as a confluence of forces is reshaping all aspects of talent management:

In *recruiting*, a war for talent is raging: According to a 2024 survey from The Conference Board, attracting talent is the number one priority for CEOs, globally – ahead of AI adoption, product innovation, or cost efficiency. Younger generations are displaying new attitudes to work – demanding more flexibility or greater commitments to social and political causes – forcing businesses to adapt. Demographic aging will mean that labor supply issues are here to stay: Across OECD countries, the population aged 15 to 64 is projected to shrink by more than 92 million (or 7%) in the next 25 years.

At the same time, organizations are demanding more and more from their human capital: "Always on"-transformations and the pace at which new technologies need to be adopted put continuous pressure on every person in the organization. As AI powers more parts of daily workflows, human workers need to learn how to efficiently interact with digital agents. To enable this, companies need to fundamentally overhaul how they *train* their people.

Change has also come to how workers are *deployed*, with COVID driving the adoption of flexible and hybrid work. Deskless work – on the frontlines, instead of in the conventional office environment – now makes up about 80% of the global workforce. Companies will need to find ways to make work better for all types of employees, across all work models – while also delivering value for the organization.

Moreover, business leaders must rethink how to *motivate* their workers, as shifts in work models and in perspectives on work have changed what drives employee engagement. In a world awash with data, scientific management – focused on maximizing efficiency and measurement of work – is tempting, but it neglects the human and inspirational aspects of work.

Finally, new approaches to *leadership* are required: For example, the rise of business ecosystems means that leaders can no longer rely purely on hierarchy. They must lead through cooperation and inspiration, rather than through mandate and coercion.

In these turbulent times, CEOs and their entire teams – not just HR – need to rethink how they create a people advantage – going beyond spans and layers, performance management and compensation, or leadership development. This

https://doi.org/10.1515/9783111369921-001

book – collecting recent essays written by researchers at the BCG Henderson Institute, Boston Consulting Group's think tank – helps leaders *reinvent work* by providing a forward-looking perspective on all aspects of talent management.

Chapter 1 discusses *attracting the talent of the future*, providing an instruction set for fundamentally rethinking talent acquisition and setting it up for the modern age. Moreover, it features deep dives into how to attract talent specifically for AI-powered businesses, as well as for how to effectively tap into internal – rather than external – talent pools. Finally, it discusses how to harness the power of migration to expand the talent pool and build a global team.

Chapter 2 focuses on how to *shape winning talent*. It provides evidence of the decreasing half-life of skills and provides a framework for continuous up- and reskilling in times of rapid change – with a deep dive into skills for the AI era. Moreover, the chapter shares innovative ways for meeting the needs of a diverse employee base.

Chapter 3 is about *embracing new models of work*, discussing not only how to embed flexibility into work models – but how to make these work for both companies and their people. Moreover, the chapter discusses how to make work better for the still too often overlooked cohort of deskless/frontline workers. Finally, it provides ideas for how to reshape the HR function around these challenges, and how to scale its impact with digital technologies.

Chapter 4 discusses *building the workplace of the future*. It leverages new insights on what causes stress and fuels burnout – and on what brings joy and purpose – to define a more employee-centric model of work that drives motivation, inclusion, and retention.

Finally, Chapter 5 deep dives into *establishing new models of leadership and culture*. With regard to leadership, it explores new models required for an age of AI and ecosystems, helping leaders to think about how they can get the best out of their teams. On culture, it deep dives into how to create a diverse workplace, and how that can drive productive disagreement and innovation.

The goal of this book is to provide broad and future-oriented perspectives on the multifaceted people challenges companies are facing today. Each chapter not only introduces novel concepts based on years of extensive research but also leverages real-world examples to make their implications tangible and practical for readers. We hope that the insights shared in this book will inspire business leaders to apply innovative and informed thinking toward their biggest asset – their people.

Chapter 1
Attracting the Talent of the Future

40 Ideas to Shake Up Your Hiring Process

Joseph Fuller, Nithya Vaduganathan, Allison Bailey, and Manjari Raman

Many companies today are struggling to hire and retain talent, but more often than not the problem is self-inflicted: They're simply not using a broad enough array of tools, sometimes because they don't even know the tools exist. In this article, the authors list 40 tools – some familiar but underutilized, others unfamiliar and innovative – that can help companies find and keep the people they need to succeed in both the short term and the long term.

Despite challenging economic conditions, companies are still finding it difficult to attract and retain the right talent. That's one of the takeaways from the most recent US Bureau of Labor Statistics report,[1] which showed that job vacancies still remain above 10 million as of November 2022. We've confirmed that trend in our own work: Last August, when we surveyed 800 senior business leaders, more than 95% of them told us that hiring and retaining talent was one of their top three priorities as they strive to deliver on their strategies. However, those needs are not constrained to the short-term: More than two-thirds of the leaders we surveyed reported that filling positions for lower- and higher-wage workers is critical for their organization's ability to compete, both in the next 12 to 18 months and in the next three to five years.

But business leaders are doing very little that's innovative to tackle the talent challenge. When it comes to higher-wage workers, they're relying primarily on two basic strategies: increasing compensation (a fairly obvious approach) and implementing remote/hybrid work models (an unsurprising approach, given the effects of COVID-19). They're doing even less for lower-wage workers: In our survey, fewer than half of respondents reported using even basic levers, such as health care benefits and compensation increases, to attract and retain lower-wage workers.

---

1 https://www.bls.gov/news.release/pdf/jolts.pdf

Note: "40 Ideas to Shake Up Your Hiring Process" by Joseph Fuller, Nithya Vaduganathan, Allison Bailey, Manjari Raman. hbr.org, January 16, 2023. Reprinted with permission. Copyright 2023 by Harvard Business Publishing; all rights reserved.

Acknowledgments: *We would like to thank Colleen McDonald, Partner, and Christina Li, Consultant, both with Boston Consulting Group, for their contributions to this piece.*

https://doi.org/10.1515/9783111369921-002

Much of this is due to a lack of awareness of innovative talent practices. Many of the leaders we surveyed simply did not know what other options were available to them. This, they recognized, was a problem: Less than 20% of them reported their organizations had very mature talent strategies.

So how can you enable more talent innovation and measure its impact? Based on our survey findings, organizations need to use a more expansive portfolio of practices to strengthen their ability to recruit and retain talent. To help, we've identified nearly 40 strategies, which we've organized into seven categories that either strengthen the hiring process or help enhance a company's offer. Some of these practices are familiar but underutilized, and others are newer and more innovative.

Strengthening the Hiring Process

Hiring Campaign and Selection
Many companies rely on traditional recruiting strategies to identify candidates who fulfill a long list of requirements. Finding candidates who tick off every box on the list is not easy – and those few who do are often actually not the right people for the job. By embracing more expansive hiring and selection processes, companies can do a better job of finding the talent that's right for them. Here are some innovative practices to consider:

– Figure out what work *really* needs to get done, and rewrite job descriptions to focus on the skills and specs that matter the most for that work, instead of relying on generic education or experience requirements.
– Seek candidates who match 70% to 80% of the most critical skills for the role – and develop learning curricula to equip them with the remainder.
– Offer "micro-internships" (short-term paid projects) or apprenticeships that reach new candidate pools and allow employers and candidates to assess fit before committing to a full-time hire.
– Host open hackathons to assess talent and facilitate the hiring of candidates in batches.
– Consider candidates simultaneously for multiple open roles if they have a high degree of overlapping skills.
– Leverage tech-based and AI-based talent assessments to screen for technical or interpersonal skills.
– Employ inclusive, gender-neutral language in job descriptions[2] to attract more diverse candidates.

---

2 https://hbr.org/2020/03/write-a-job-description-that-attracts-the-right-candidate

Talent Sourcing

When competition for top talent is fierce, as it is today, you need to broaden your methods of sourcing candidates. Here are some practices to consider:

- Expand internal talent mobility[3] (e.g., lateral job transfers, internal gig work) by drawing on a foundation of skills and aspirations as a basis for mobility and supporting retention.
- Embrace on-demand and gig platforms to increase labor-force flexibility (even for higher-wage workers), accelerate time-to-market, and enable innovation.
- Work to attract alumni with valuable institutional knowledge[4] back to your organization.
- Build an internal list of previously high-performing employees who might be candidates to re-engage for future roles.
- Tap into "hidden" populations, including retired,[5] neurodiverse,[6] and previously incarcerated workers.[7]
- Acquire companies with top talent – or enter into agreements to borrow and share talent with other companies.

Channel Strategy

Companies that integrate new and innovative channels into their talent strategy can better recruit critical, in-demand talent for years to come. Consider expanding your repertoire to include the following techniques:

- Deploy talent from Hire-Train-Deploy (HTD) partners who source high-potential candidates and equip them with the relevant skills for your needs.
- Use digital platforms to do more programmatic and personalized recruiting (including leveraging QR codes, text messaging).
- Partner with educational and community institutions, including job centers and community colleges, to offer tailored curriculum and term-time work experiences to build a talent pipeline with relevant skills.
- Embrace new ways of identifying talent on social-media platforms (such as layoff lists and LinkedIn posts).
- Develop and market a more effective referral program, particularly for in-demand roles.

---

3 https://hbr.org/2022/05/what-stops-employees-from-applying-for-internal-roles
4 https://hbr.org/2022/04/leave-the-door-open-for-employees-to-return-to-your-organization
5 https://hbr.org/2022/12/7-principles-to-attract-and-retain-older-frontline-workers
6 https://hbr.org/2022/02/is-your-company-inclusive-of-neurodivergent-employees
7 https://hbr.org/2022/10/how-employers-can-set-formerly-incarcerated-workers-up-for-success

Enhancing the Offer

Compensation and Benefits

Are you one of the many employers raising salaries to compete for talent? Half of the 800+ respondents in our survey reported increasing compensation for their employees, and nearly 75% of employers cite the talent shortage as the main driver[8] for salary budget increases. But there are other ways to strengthen your compensation and benefits package beyond increasing compensation. Try some of these practices to get started:

- Provide creative benefits, such as caregiver support programs,[9] childcare services, and wellness perks.
- Segment and develop tailored benefits for hard-to-fill talent populations.
- Provide incentives, such as higher bonuses during peak hours and step-ups on promotion, especially for lower-wage workers.
- Guarantee health care benefits and appropriate sick time for your full workforce.
- Reduce volatility by ensuring stable and predictable pay,[10] particularly for lower-wage workers.

Work Design

The COVID-19 pandemic has fundamentally changed how we think about work. Job flexibility has skyrocketed in importance since the pandemic, with some employees valuing flexibility[11] even more than a 10% pay raise. Rethinking work design can not only better attract and retain workers but also increase productivity and focus worker capacity on the highest-value tasks. Get started redesigning work with the following strategies:

- Break work into its components to assign responsibilities more clearly across a team or to freelance workers, and improve your approach to sourcing.
- Deploy talent more dynamically, by creating skills-based pools of talent that can be assigned to the most critical priorities on-demand.
- Use creative scheduling and shift redesign to allow lower-wage workers to move or switch shifts more flexibly while still providing adequate coverage.

---

8 https://fortune.com/2022/07/15/u-s-companies-raise-salary-budgets-amid-inflation-concerns/
9 https://hbr.org/2022/11/5-things-employers-get-wrong-about-caregivers-at-work
10 https://hbr.org/2022/03/give-service-workers-stable-schedules
11 https://twitter.com/I_Am_NickBloom/status/1478057506672832512

- Experiment with different flex models, including compressed work weeks, sharing jobs among multiple part-time employees, and/or scheduling split shifts to cover "rush hours."
- Redesign work by eliminating, re-assigning, or automating less-critical responsibilities.
- Embed technology that improves ease of work, including language assistance and tools to accommodate older workers.

Career Development

Providing opportunities for your employees to take on stretch assignments can help you not only develop but also retain your employees. According to the Pew Research Center, more than 60% of US employees cited a lack of career-advancement opportunities[12] as a leading reason for leaving their jobs. To expand your organization's portfolio of career-advancement opportunities, consider adding some of these innovative practices:

- Provide education benefits linked to individualized skill-development plans (for example, tuition reimbursement).
- Build targeted learning and development programs to support onboarding, upskilling, and reskilling across both hard and soft skills.
- Design mentorship and sponsorship programs, and peer-to-peer coaching systems.
- Upskill managers to be better people leaders and increase manager accountability for team development.

Culture

Companies need a compelling culture to maximize the engagement, productivity, and retention of their existing workforces. In recent years, company culture has become the most important driver of job satisfaction, with culture being 10× more predictive[13] of employee retention than compensation. Here are some innovative practices to help build a meaningful culture:

- Embed company purpose, strategy, and values in your operating and performance practices and feedback process, and train your leaders to become culture champions.

---

12 https://www.pewresearch.org/short-reads/2022/03/09/majority-of-workers-who-quit-a-job-in-2021-cite-low-pay-no-opportunities-for-advancement-feeling-disrespected/

13 https://www.shrm.org/executive-network/insights/shaping-culture-will-retain-employees#:~: text=Right%20now%2C%20company%20culture%20is,decides%20to%20leave%20their%20job.

- Set up robust onboarding programs[14] that build affiliation and mentorship into the process.
- Create opportunities and free up as much as 10% to 20% of capacity for passion projects.
- Boost affiliation by developing interest groups and communities of practice.
- Take pulse checks on employee sentiment to highlight opportunities for improvement in near real-time.
- Develop clear two-way communication channels for employee input and engagement.

***

The best talent strategy for your organization involves finding the right portfolio of practices that meet your needs and investing appropriately in their implementation, even during uncertain economic conditions. Many companies across industries have recognized how critical talent is to business success and have kickstarted their innovation journeys based on their target employee needs. For example, IBM removed degree requirements[15] from 50% of their US job postings to widen their talent pools, Walmart provides frontline associates with fully funded college tuition[16] and accelerated career paths after graduation, and some law firms have introduced concierge services to support aging family members.[17]

While you don't have to do everything on our list to have a successful talent strategy, you should identify where you can do more off to better compete for talent. Take stock of what your organization is already doing, then thoughtfully assess where there are gaps in your talent strategy and how our suggestions can be helpful. Keep in mind that you may need to tailor your talent strategies to different employee segments within your company. By experimenting with new innovations and putting the right feedback systems in place, you can develop a sustainable strategy that can help you create lasting talent advantage.

****

---

14 https://hbr.org/2022/04/onboarding-can-make-or-break-a-new-hires-experience
15 https://www.ibm.com/policy/education-skills/
16 https://corporate.walmart.com/news/2022/05/15/at-walmart-there-is-a-path-for-everyone
17 https://hrexecutive.com/companies-turn-to-eldercare-benefits-to-help-workers-during-covid-19/

How to Attract, Develop, and Retain AI Talent

Vinciane Beauchene, Julie Bedard, Julie Jefson, and Nithya Vaduganathan

The companies that capture the most value from AI follow the 10–20-70 rule: 10% of their AI effort goes to designing algorithms, 20% to building the underlying technologies, and 70% to supporting people and adapting business processes. To get the most from people and processes, companies need to address the following questions: (1) How do I attract, develop, and retain data and analytics talent to build sustainable AI capabilities? (2) How do I boost adoption of AI solutions at speed and at scale and drive real business transformation? (3) How do I rewire my organization to unlock the full benefits of AI at scale? This article, the start of a three-part series, focuses on the first question: how to attract, develop, and retain AI talent.

Artificial intelligence[18] is having a moment. The release of ChatGPT, AI-enabled Bing, and Google Bard has electrified public debate on the radical potential of AI. To be an industry leader in five years, companies need a clear and compelling AI talent strategy today, but many organizations are hitting a brick wall. Although demand for AI talent is at an all-time high, supply is extremely limited. With so few skilled professionals available, companies must find ways to stand out from the competition.

Incumbents beware: The approach to attracting, developing, and retaining AI talent is not business as usual. Companies must offer a unique and compelling value proposition to attract – and hold onto – these highly prized recruits. To build a first-rate AI workforce that will stick around for the long haul, companies must anticipate what mix of AI skills (rather than jobs) is needed, understand what AI workers want and how to attract them, invest in reskilling[19] and advancement opportunities, and keep AI talent fully engaged.

Common Mistakes to Avoid

AI and machine learning emerged as the most in-demand skills in 2022, and jobs for data scientists more than tripled over the past five years. Demand continues

---

18 https://www.bcg.com/capabilities/artificial-intelligence
19 https://www.bcg.com/capabilities/people-strategy/talent-development

---

Note: The authors thank the following experts for their contributions to this article: Romain Gailhac, Orsolya Kovács-Ondrejkovic, and Anne-Françoise Ruaud.

to outpace supply. Because AI employees have different job expectations than traditional workers do, recruiting and retention efforts need to be tailored to their unique needs.

Consider just a few common mistakes companies make when recruiting and hiring AI talent:

– Competing head-to-head with tech companies without highlighting non-tech-related differentiators that will entice AI hires
– Trying to recruit AI talent with the standard slow process led by generalist recruiters
– Paying premium prices for cutting-edge data scientists without considering the broader mix of skills needed
– Onboarding AI employees without creating a community and embedding them into the organization under AI-trained leaders
– Fiercely recruiting AI talent without providing advancement opportunities
– Overlooking reskilling opportunities within the organization

When companies make these kinds of mistakes, they not only struggle to hire the best and brightest but also face high levels of attrition. This is a serious problem in today's job market where as many as 40% of employees working in digital fields are actively job hunting, and nearly 75% expect to leave their current role[20] in the near future. The good news is that hiring AI talent doesn't have to turn into a costly bidding war. Companies must understand what motivates these highly sought-after employees to take a job – and what it takes for them to stick around.

Four Strategies to Recruit and Retain AI Talent

To build an AI advantage, companies need to excel in four areas: anticipate talent needs,[21] attract best-in-class candidates, develop talent quickly, and engage AI talent with an unmatched value proposition (see Figure 1.1).

Anticipate

Hiring the right talent to drive an AI transformation is not as simple as luring a strong team of data scientists and machine-learning specialists. An AI transforma-

---

20 https://www.bcg.com/publications/2021/what-digital-talent-expect-from-a-job
21 https://www.bcg.com/capabilities/people-strategy/overview

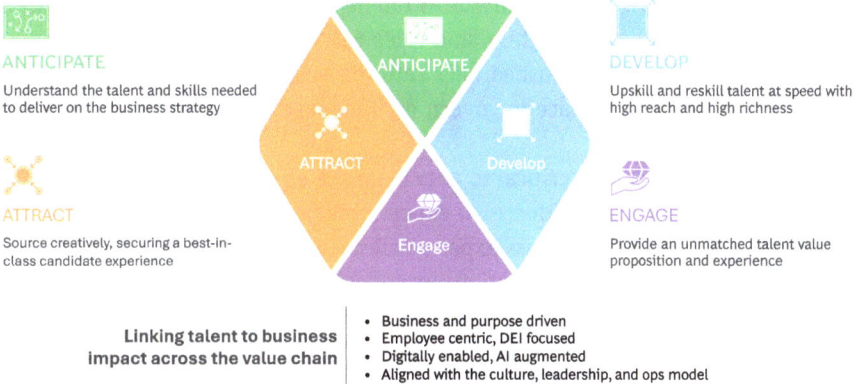

ANTICIPATE
Understand the talent and skills needed to deliver on the business strategy

ATTRACT
Source creatively, securing a best-in-class candidate experience

DEVELOP
Upskill and reskill talent at speed with high reach and high richness

ENGAGE
Provide an unmatched talent value proposition and experience

Linking talent to business impact across the value chain
- Business and purpose driven
- Employee centric, DEI focused
- Digitally enabled, AI augmented
- Aligned with the culture, leadership, and ops model

Source: BCG analysis
Note: DEI=diversity, equity, and inclusion.

Figure 1.1: Building a Talent and Skills Advantage Requires a Holistic Approach.

tion requires talent with a mix of skills, including people who can build the data infrastructure (data architects, solution architects, data engineers, and software engineers), employees who manage data governance (data governance analysts and data stewards), and those who engage with the business (product owners and domain experts).

Start by developing a taxonomy of the skills you need and then figure out how best to acquire those skills. This approach is particularly important in a tight job market where top talent is scarce. When building an AI team, companies tend to reflexively hire people to fill predefined jobs. But businesses often struggle to fill those roles because AI talent is so expensive and hard to find. By focusing on the skills they need, companies can assemble effective AI teams more quickly.

For example, a global pharma company wanted to recruit a team of four data scientists to build up its AI capabilities, but the competition was fierce. By thinking creatively about the skills the company needed, executives realized they could hire just one high-caliber data scientist, supported by three data analysts, which are much easier to source. By finding the right mix of skills, rather than filling predefined roles, the firm quickly assembled a strong team and hit the ground running.

Companies also need to decide how to organize for AI. Most begin their AI journey in an ad hoc fashion. IT owns the data architecture, systems, and analytics, and data capabilities are sprinkled throughout the business, but no standardized roles or "communities of practice" are in place for sharing AI knowledge. This type of IT-focused organization makes it difficult to share solutions across the business and fails to give AI workers a clear path for internal advancement.

As companies mature, the majority of AI talent will begin to work together in a centralized data and analytics hub, and roles will become standardized. Eventually, AI capabilities will be pushed back into the business while a small, centralized AI team remains in place to govern data management, develop capabilities, and codify best practices.

Last but not least, it is critical to anticipate the effect that incoming AI talent will have on the overall workforce. AI experts will become embedded in business processes, which means business experts will need to gain a working knowledge of data and analytics.[22] As AI solutions are deployed, other employees' roles will evolve over time, likely requiring them to acquire new skills or augment existing ones. In addition, processes will be redesigned and operating models will need to adjust.

Attract

In the fiercely competitive AI environment, companies must think proactively about how to attract talent. Here are some key concepts to bear in mind.

Understand what AI workers want. Our research shows that potential AI hires have different job expectations than traditional job seekers do, and companies should tailor their employee value proposition to meet these expectations. Two things, in particular, matter to AI employees: (1) working on exciting products, topics, and technologies, and (2) knowing the company has a clear strategy for advancement. People involved in the fast-growing, constantly evolving environment of AI want to work on cutting-edge projects; 44% of AI workers ranked this as a top need (compared with just 27% of non-AI talent). When asked about deal breakers, AI talent ranked "interesting job content" much higher than non-AI talent did. AI job candidates also want answers to some important questions: Does the company think about data strategically? Where will I be at this company five years down the road? Will I have advancement opportunities? To keep AI talent engaged, companies need to articulate a detailed data strategy that highlights clear advancement opportunities.

Seek out untapped talent. It's tempting to go after AI talent in the usual cities – San Francisco, Seattle, New York City, Bangalore, and London – but that guarantees you'll be competing with all the hottest tech companies. This is particularly problematic for nontech incumbents striving to get an AI transformation

---

22 https://www.bcg.com/capabilities/digital-technology-data/data-analytics

off the ground. By looking at secondary talent pools in other cities and countries, organizations can gain access to extraordinary talent at more affordable rates.

Many of these hidden markets offer companies an edge because job candidates may be seeking something unique, such as a position located in their home state or more flexible work.[23] In addition, our survey found that 68% of digital employees are willing to work remotely for a foreign employer. This opens up new options for hiring hard-to-find AI talent. Because visa limitations don't apply to remote work, businesses can explore sources of talent that previously were not attractive or feasible. Start by evaluating your competitive advantage in various regions in terms of compensation packages, attrition rates, size, and unique value proposition. BCG analysis shows that companies using a targeted location strategy save 7% to 10% in labor costs.

Create the right AI talent-sourcing strategy for your maturity. Customize your talent sourcing by making a clear-eyed assessment of your maturity. If you are new to AI, focus on recruiting an "anchor" hire; that is, a high-caliber AI expert who acts as a magnet to attract a broader network of AI specialists and establishes a strong starting strategy. As you scale up, elevate your approach to recruiting AI talent: leverage specialized AI recruiters, tailor hiring processes and compensation packages to meet AI talent needs, and ensure that leaders have complete transparency into recruiting outcomes. If you are fully mature and need to supplement existing data and analytics teams, build talent-sensing capabilities to understand where to find specialized AI talent and develop relationships with that talent in advance of your needs.

Tailor the recruiting process. The standard recruiting process does not work well when it comes to attracting AI talent. The process is too slow. By the time a hiring decision is made, the AI candidate may have taken another offer. In our survey, 66% of respondents said the number one way for an employer to stand out when recruiting AI talent is with a "smooth, timely recruitment process."

Digital and data experts also want to be interviewed by people who understand their value. Managers involved in hiring should be staff who are integral to the AI mission, not only because they're well equipped to assess candidates' AI skills and judge their talent, but because it sends a signal that the company is serious about data and analytics. When managers who have little digital knowledge or expertise interview AI candidates, it dampens the potential hires' enthusiasm for taking the job.

We recommend reviewing each recruiting step to expedite the process, particularly minimizing the time from final interview to offer, with the goal of fol-

---

23 https://www.bcg.com/capabilities/people-strategy/future-of-work

lowing up in hours or days, not weeks. A global industrial company began daily standups with specialty recruiters and hiring managers to coordinate quickly on the hiring process. They prepared offer letters in parallel with final interviews, and a small, dedicated group of digital and data experts interviewed AI talent to improve decision making and calibration across candidates.

Develop

Approximately 80% of AI talent leave companies because they either want a more interesting position or don't see opportunities for career advancement; however, BCG research shows that only 10% of new roles are filled by existing staff. A clear opportunity is at hand to support more internal mobility of talent. Reskilling internal employees offers a wealth of baked-in benefits. These workers are already committed to the organization, grounded in the business, and embedded in the company's ways of working – all characteristics that take a great deal of time and effort to cultivate in new hires.

There's another advantage to internal reskilling. The existing workforce can, in many cases, feel threatened by new AI hires, particularly if they are positioned as a separate group of young, highly compensated individuals poised to transform the organization. By offering reskilling opportunities, the business sends the message that anyone with the right skill sets, and a desire to learn, can play an integral role in the AI transformation. Not all jobs will lend themselves to reskilling; it's unlikely that companies will train from within for the position of data scientist, for example. But many less specialized positions, such as product owners, data stewards, and domain experts, can be recruited internally. These opportunities for upward mobility, in turn, strengthen job satisfaction and loyalty to the organization. According to research from LinkedIn, employees stay 41% longer at companies that regularly hire from within.

For AI talent recruited externally, companies need to articulate a clear career path. When organizations try to quickly spin up an AI team, they don't always take the time to develop a taxonomy that allows candidates to envision their progression within the organization. If young, ambitious AI analysts can be promoted to become senior AI analysts but are offered no other advancement opportunities, they will begin to look elsewhere just as they're achieving peak productivity. In-demand recruits, such as data scientists and data analysts, also expect to be promoted more frequently. The tech culture has instilled the expectation that digital talent will be promoted every 12 to 18 months (as opposed to every two to three years).

Engage

For organizations that are not viewed first and foremost as tech companies or for those with a long product development cycle (such as aerospace and defense, where security constraints exist), it can be difficult to keep AI talent engaged. These organizations may have no trouble attracting AI talent, but employees' enthusiasm can wane when they realize the development of next-generation hardware or products will take five or more years and they may not get to work in cutting-edge programming languages or platforms. In this case, it's important to sharpen your storytelling so that you aren't trying to compete with the best tech companies but instead can focus on your unique purpose and mission.

To become a purpose-driven organization, companies must answer two fundamental questions: What are our authentic and distinctive strengths? Why do we exist beyond what we make, do, or sell? Whether you're an up-and-coming renewable-energy company, a 100-year-old cosmetics business, or a global tech giant, it's essential to convey a strong narrative about what sets your company apart. Purpose-driven organizations energize people and keep them engaged.

The other key to keeping AI talent engaged is ensuring that they are seamlessly embedded within the organization as a whole. Onboarding should involve much more than a swift orientation. It should be a 6- to 12-month process that provides ample opportunities for new AI hires to work on meaningful, "quick hit" projects that have an immediate impact on the business. To make sure that top talent isn't bogged down with data management challenges (building the data platform, accessing data, cleaning data, and so forth), companies should adopt a two-speed approach. Allow a team of engineers to build digital capabilities[24] while AI specialists deliver high-impact AI initiatives that offer clear, compelling results for the business. The executive team should also include data and analytics initiatives in their annual goals so that AI teams aren't fighting for mindshare, business sponsorship, and budget allocations.

Case Study
By implementing many of these techniques simultaneously, a leading biopharma firm quickly ramped up its AI team. Here's what the company did:
– Reshaped job architecture and skills taxonomy to focus on hiring for skills that were most relevant in the market, defining roles for machine-learning engineers for the first time

---

24 https://www.bcg.com/capabilities/digital-technology-data/digital-transformation/overview

- Redefined its employee value proposition and created stronger communities of practice for AI talent, connecting AI practitioners across the R&D, commercial, and IT organizations
- Reframed the company's talent acquisition strategy to better communicate its value proposition, created a dedicated team of specialized AI recruiters, and changed hiring processes

In just six months, the company boosted the size of its AI drug discovery team by approximately 10%, increased its commercial analytics organization by about 25%, and dramatically reduced its attrition rate for data and analytics talent.

Talent scarcity is one of the main concerns for executives worldwide. To date, few companies have successfully scaled AI,[25] but this will change as organizations are ramping up very quickly. By embracing a smart approach to recruiting, retaining, and engaging AI talent, companies will gain a long-term competitive advantage in a field that is fundamentally redefining the future of business.

****

---

25 https://www.bcg.com/press/20october2020-study-finds-significant-financial-benefits-with-ai

The CEO Agenda for an Era of Innovation without Borders

Johann D. Harnoss, Anna Schwarz, Martin Reeves, and François Candelon

This article is part of a series that explores the innovative potential arising from the global movement of skilled workers.[26] It examines the implications for CEOs and policy makers.

David Bowie had a rare gift: the capacity to sense the future and bring it into the cultural fabric of the present. Visionary business leaders have achieved similar feats for society – from Henry Ford anticipating mass mobility, to Yvon Chouinard at Patagonia pushing for sustainability and climate action years ahead of others, to Elon Musk spearheading not just an e-mobility revolution but also the dream of humanity as an interplanetary species.

In the first article of this "Innovation Without Borders" series, we showed that people crossing borders are not only generating trillions of dollars of innovation and growth benefits for destination and origin countries but also spreading ideas, knowledge, capital, and even human rights. Yet migration remains a hotly debated topic and a source of political gridlock in many countries. As a result, firms, societies, and individuals are not fully capturing its promise:

- While the absolute number of globally mobile people now stands at about 200 million, the corresponding numbers for skilled people remain significantly lower at roughly 52 million.[27]
- In fact, migration rates for skilled people actually seem to be in decline: In 2000, 7.5% of all skilled talent had moved across borders. Today, the rate is close to 6.4% – this gap translates into 10 million skilled workers who stayed home.

We argue that there is now a window of opportunity to build bridges into opportunity for skilled global talent that would ignite innovative growth. It's not politicians but business leaders who hold the keys to make this happen. We lay out two reasons why forward-looking CEOs and aspiring founders should care, describe four strategies that they can pursue to drive firm-level advantage, and show what specific actions look like.

---

26 https://www.bcg.com/publications/2021/how-global-migration-drives-innovation
27 Evidently, skilled workers tend to have immediate positive effects on innovation and growth; unskilled workers do so as well, though more indirectly.

A Human Cause Meets Its Business Case

Close your eyes and fast-forward to 2050. In what world will our children and grandchildren live? With the benefit of hindsight, how might they look at the decisions we take today? Is there a chance they will call some of our actions morally questionable or even economically stupid?

We hope they will be gracious enough to say: "Your generation finally turned the corner on climate change, and you started addressing the persistent injustices of discrimination." Yet we can't help wondering if they'll continue: "But there were still massive differences between people. A bright-eyed, aspiring student from Lagos or Lahore simply did not have the same opportunities as you. How could you live in such an unfair world?"

Your grandchildren might have a point. Of all the economic differences between two randomly chosen human beings, 66% are due to one factor only: where they were born.[28] Righting this wrong by building bridges into opportunity for the world's most curious talents might soon be seen as a significant human achievement of the 21st century – a moral cause that also had a clear business case. The bridges to opportunity are already partly in operation but not yet scaled up to full potential. Globally remote teams, global freelance platforms, and global hiring are some of these bridges.

In our conversations with executives and startup founders, we sense a nascent excitement for the bigger cause and a clear awareness of the business case of "innovation without borders."

Why the Time Is Now

There are two basic reasons why now is the best time to act. First, talent is now truly universal. Just twenty years ago, global talent was relatively scarce (see Figure 1.2). The world had roughly 420 million skilled people and about 70 million recent college graduates (age group 25–29), but nearly 60% of them graduated from schools in the US, Europe, China, or Japan. Fast-forward to 2020: the world now counts roughly 840 million skilled people and about 140 million recent grads (twice as many as 20 years ago).[29] What's more, the ratio has flipped: now, young students from all other

28 Branko Milanovic, "Global Inequality of Opportunity: How Much of Our Income Is Determined by Where We Live?" *The Review of Economics and Statistics*, May 2015.
29 Wittgenstein Centre Human Capital Data Explorer

Distribution of university and trade school graduates (age cohort 25-29), %

USA, Canada, EU, China, Japan	59	51	56	62	63	66
Rest of world	41	49	44	38	37	34

Number of skilled adults, globally (age cohort 25-29), in millions

2000	2010	2020	2030	2040	2050
70	110	140	160	210	230

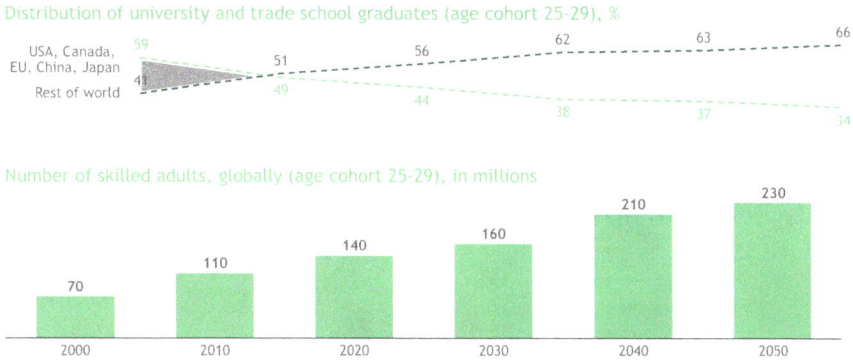

Sources: Wittgenstein Centre for Demography and Global Human Capital (2018), Medium Scenario (SSP2); BCG analysis.
Note: Graph shows post-secondary education (includes anyone with at least one year of tertiary education), including bachelor's, master's, and doctoral degrees.

Figure 1.2: A Seismic Shift: Talent Is Now Truly Universal.

countries are in a clear majority, and on path to represent 66% of all college graduates in 2050.

Second, it's easier than ever for firms to work with global talent. The COVID-19 crisis led to a surge of startups that support firms in managing globally distributed teams. Meanwhile, counterintuitively, it's never been easier for firms to hire and relocate qualified workers from abroad. We spoke to legal relocation experts, HR managers, and field practitioners across the world. They showed us that in 11 out of the 12 countries we studied, the legal and administrative hurdles to global movement are low or very manageable. Two notable exceptions: China and the US (see Figure 1.3).

Germany emerged as the country most open to skilled foreign talent – ahead of even the well-established mobility destinations Australia and Canada. Even Japan, a country not traditionally known as a global talent hotspot, has opened the gates. In the past, firms often faced a complex visa and work regulation landscape that was hard and costly to navigate. Today, countries designated as "easy" or "medium" tend to have an ample supply of work visas, which are given out in a (mostly) predictable fashion and at low or manageable cost. And the process typically doesn't add substantial waiting time compared with the hiring of a qualified local candidate. Meanwhile, on the labor demand side, BCG research shows that people's desire to pass through these gates remains strong; about 50% of skilled talent say they would consider relocation if offered the chance.

How difficult is it today for a college graduate to relocate for work?

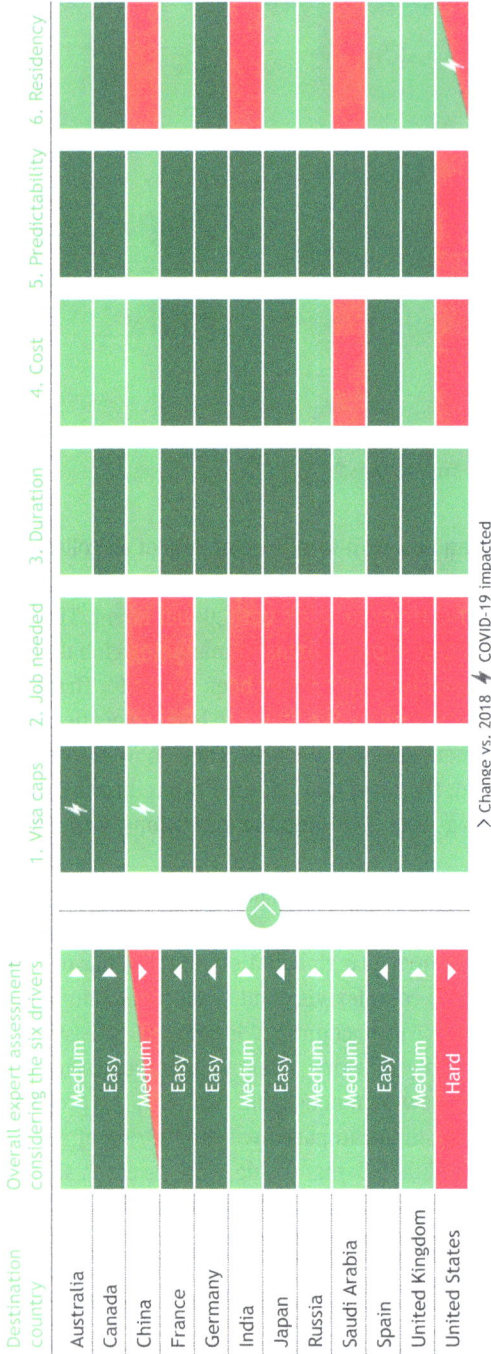

Destination country	Overall expert assessment considering the six drivers	1. Visa caps	2. Job needed	3. Duration	4. Cost	5. Predictability	6. Residency
Australia	Medium ▲						
Canada	Easy ▲						
China	Medium ▶						
France	Easy ◀						
Germany	Easy ◀						
India	Medium ▲						
Japan	Easy ◀						
Russia	Medium ▲						
Saudi Arabia	Medium ▲						
Spain	Easy ◀						
United Kingdom	Medium ▲						
United States	Hard ▶						

〉 Change vs. 2018   ⚡ COVID-19 impacted

Sources: Global expert interviews; Localyze; Silk Relo; BCG analysis

Note: Assessment assumes a worker with a bachelor's degree and a minimum salary of $60,000 gross/year. Easy = facilities relocation. Hard = restricts relocation relative to other countries. As of August 2021; COVID-19 restrictions in many destination countries impose additional processing delays and no-travel restrictions for people from some origin countries.

Figure 1.3: The World is More Open to Immigration Than We Might Think.

Four Plays for the CEO Agenda

Talent is now more globally spread, and political hurdles to global mobility are lower than ever. What then can leaders in business do to embrace this cause and gain strategic advantage while doing so? To answer this question, we spoke to corporate executives, founders of unicorn startups, and investors in industries ranging from technology and software to FMCG, logistics, travel and tourism, and media and entertainment. In these conversations, a picture of four complementary strategic approaches, or "plays," took shape (see Figure 1.4).

Talent play	Ecosystem play	Innovation play	Purpose play
Tap into deep global talent pools to hire and onboard new talent	Build a global talent pipeline for your company and your ecosystem	Assemble diverse teams that are capable of imagining and shaping the future	Seek strategic differentiation by embracing a unique purpose

Source: BCG analysis.

Figure 1.4: Four Plays Shape the CEO Agenda.

– The **"talent play"** is a typical starting point. This play views foreign-born workers mainly as a valuable resource, as scarce talent to fill open vacancies in hard-to-fill roles or to flexibly cover short-term skill needs. Its strategic value lies in superior access to qualified talent. This play is most relevant for companies facing talent access as a barrier to future growth, which holds especially for asset-light software and people-intensive businesses, fast-growing startups, and heavy industry players facing significant digital transformation[30] challenges.

– The **"ecosystem play"** adds an important leg to the talent play for companies facing restrictions on legal immigration of skilled talent (a factor in China and the US, for example) or for those having difficulty attracting talent, often those with operations outside the main metropolitan areas. Companies executing this play globalize their teams by using global hubs and remote setups, and by inves-

---

30 https://www.bcg.com/capabilities/digital-technology-data/digital-transformation/overview

ting in their immediate local ecosystem. The ecosystem play is especially prevalent in asset-heavy industries like automotive,[31] chemicals, and manufacturing.[32]

- The **"innovation play"** is a natural extension of the talent play. Strategic value in this play comes from seeing skilled foreign talent not merely as a resource but as a catalyst to drive growth via culturally diverse teams.[33] It's most relevant for firms facing complex product or business model innovation[34] challenges, and firms that are valued by public markets or venture capitalists primarily on the basis of their future growth potential.

- Finally, we discovered the **"purpose play,"** which puts the cause of global equality of opportunity at the center of the company's declared purpose, much like Patagonia did with environmental protection or Tesla with sustainability. Not surprisingly, few executives see it as currently relevant for their business, showing that in comparison with other topics of global scope, promoting skilled migration is not yet a mainstream movement. But this is precisely why the purpose play can yield first-mover advantage.

Let's now dive into each play and explore what leading firms are already doing.

The Talent Play

Talent plays create value for companies under two conditions: if companies avoid the "revolving door" problem (attraction but low retention), and if they manage to scout global markets for overlooked talent.

1. **Switch to English-first.** Change management practices to allow for hiring of English-only talent, even if only initially in a few teams. Douglas, a leading European beauty retailer, for example, switched its default language in its tech teams to English and thus opened itself to global talent. Yet this easy-looking switch is in practice often hard to make. Changing a company's language means changing its culture, and what is a gain for newcomers can be perceived by others as a loss.

2. **Globalize your employer brand.** Build a global employer brand. Use existing talent and diaspora networks in your own recruiting. Firms like Delivery

---

31 https://www.bcg.com/industries/automotive/overview

32 https://www.bcg.com/capabilities/manufacturing/overview

33 Such teams tend to outperform homogenous teams on complex tasks because they can draw on a broader collective experience and thus develop novel solutions more easily. (Hong and Page, PNAS, November 2004.)

34 https://www.bcg.com/capabilities/innovation-strategy-delivery/business-model-innovation

Hero and Zalando motivate employees to recommend their peers from their places of origin and encourage them to apply.

3. **Create new depth.** Build bridges for global (junior) talent with coaching, extended training and vocational programs, and starter jobs. The Berlin-based music-streaming platform Soundcloud, for example, has established the "DeveloperBridge" trainee program, an effort to bring in more junior talent from other countries.

4. **Globalize hiring.** Use global sourcing teams to scout for talent in specific places around the world, and add referral programs that are tailored to hiring talent from countries other than that of the firm's headquarters. The German HR tech unicorn Personio, for example, deployed special temporary recruiting teams to Brazil after realizing it could hire top-notch engineers from various Brazilian cities.

5. **Hire for attitude.** Hire not on the basis of degree credentials but on attitude. Rely on your own subject matter and personality tests to screen applicants – this avoids rejection of good candidates simply because they do not fit the established domestic hiring expectations. Examples abound in tech firms. One outstanding illustration is Red Bull's "Wingfinder," a personality self-assessment test that offers personalized improvement paths for prospective job applicants.

6. **Leverage global platforms as a screening device.** Virtualize migration by working with global digital talent platforms, leveraging both their cost advantages abroad and their value as a talent hiring screening device. Collaborate remotely and, if conditions are right, bring the best freelancers in-house.

7. **Internationalize onboarding.** Add financial or in-kind relocation support to your onboarding package to ensure a smooth transition for global talent, and be ready to run remote onboarding sessions. These practices are already the standard in the startup world but are now also being adopted at scale by others.

The Ecosystem Play

Firms use the ecosystem play either to circumvent hard legal restrictions to the hiring of skilled talent from abroad or to attract skilled global talent to their region by making targeted investments in the broader ecosystem, often together with other players. It turns out there are often some very concrete opportunities for large firms, startups, and NGOs to work together de-bottleneck the talent migration journey and thus improve their own base of competition vis-à-vis global competitors located elsewhere.

1. **Set up your own global network.** Internalize the global migrant networks by moving product or R&D hubs to new locations that improve access to global talent. Those locations could be centers of technology (for example, Toronto, Berlin, London, Tokyo). Vodafone, for example, opened an IT and service hub in Cairo many years ago to hire Egyptian talent, because immigration to Europe sometimes proved a lengthier and more costly process.

2. **Go remote.** Recognize that, in some fields, speed beats in-person setups. Putting in place mechanisms that support remote full-time employment globally can help you quickly staff some of your core teams with global talent. In typical origin countries, both cost advantages abroad and a captive talent hunting ground (for attracting talent who are not yet ready to migrate in a given location) can be found. Firms such as the Germany-based logistics scaleup Forto often start onboarding talent remotely and then later transfer them into larger hubs to work in hybrid setups.

3. **Join hands with the public sector.** Work with local governments and private partners to set up public-private partnerships (PPPs) that significantly accelerate key bureaucratic processes. In Berlin, firms collectively fund a PPP entity called BerlinPartner, which facilitates and speeds up work visa, work regulation, and other key administrative processes for Berlin-based businesses. This model has recently been replicated in the Netherlands, Sweden, Austria, and elsewhere, but it deserves much wider adoption.

4. **Drive ecosystem attractiveness.** Especially in cities that are not among the top three talent hubs in their country, ecosystem activation strategies to create a more attractive environment for global talent are key. These strategies not only benefit global talent but also create a more vibrant community for all talent, along with local innovation spillovers that benefit everyone. One way to increase local ecosystem attractiveness is by hosting industry-specific meetups for a diverse set of practitioners to foster cross-company knowledge exchange. Another way is by committing your own talent and resources with that of others, as BCG does via the Joblinge Program, initiated with BMW's Eberhard von Kuenheim Foundation to address the integration challenges of disadvantaged youth from all backgrounds in Germany.

5. **Be open source.** Spread what works. A visa regulation and support ecosystem exists; use it. Look to firms like Localyze, which proactively supports visa and relocation processes for skilled talent from abroad, and share your learnings in an open source manner with other companies.

6. **Build for circularity.** Close the loop and find partners in origin countries to support knowledge transfer. In the European tech scene, we see some early innovative models in which certain agency tasks are delegated to partners in the same time zone (in Rwanda for example).

The Innovation Play

The innovation play is a strategy for companies with culturally and cognitively diverse workforces to launch new products, services, and business models to the market. Based on BCG's innovation research,[35] firms that succeed in making diversity work – those that maximize the variety of ideas and then select the best for scale-up – are significantly more likely to outperform their peers.

1. **Mix and match diverse teams.** Create teams that go beyond compositional diversity and show genuine functional diversity by having staffing mechanisms that take into account metrics of such diversity. GetYourGuide, a global travel and tourism player, ensured that the foreign-born talent it recruited was spread through the organization, avoiding monocultural silos of any particular nationality or origin, which can often work effectively but lose their creative edge.

2. **Circulate innovators globally.** Set up internal migration networks ("mobility programs") to attract daring, unconventional problem solvers from a variety of geographic locations. BCG's think tank, the BCG Henderson Institute, for example, offers secondments for BCG employees to physically relocate to one of its innovation hubs and explore a new research topic. Programs like this should be framed as an innovation rotation – a valuable career step toward leadership that is supported by top management.

3. **Break organizational boundaries.** Set up circular externship programs with smaller, faster growing organizations. Earlier this year, BCG encouraged employees to join a rapidly growing pharmaceuticals company producing COVID-19 vaccines. BCG regularly offers its employees growth opportunities like this because it believes in the innovative exchange that results from such deployments.

4. **Foster divergence.** Shape a culture that respects the individual and values new ideas irrespective of place in hierarchy, for example, by having regular exchange forums to pressure test ideas in a trusted environment. Stripe, a global financial services firm, forms internal interest groups based on origin. These groups have a dual purpose; first, they provide a second "home" to foreign talent at Stripe, which helps build the employer brand, and second, they play an active role in customizing products and go-to-market strategy for global markets.

5. **Remain mission-first.** Train innovation product managers to create alignment in multicultural, multifunctional teams and to guide their teams toward maximal outcomes, not maximal output. Tech companies often pride themselves in creating a culture that celebrates the focus and goal-mindedness of "missionaries" in service of their purpose, often a customer need, over "mercenaries," managers managing perception first, outcomes second.

---

35 https://www.bcg.com/publications/2021/most-innovative-companies-overview

6. **Guide via a pragmatic decision-making process.** Guide diverse innovation teams toward maximized outcomes or fast failure, by subjecting them to a lean decision process that ensures the best projects survive. While nearly all companies have such staggered funding logic processes, they often fail to produce desired outcomes because teams are either not empowered or not incentivized to recommend a course correction or a project shutdown.

The Purpose Play

Companies that follow a purpose play strategically differentiate from competitors by credibly embracing the cause of global equality of opportunity. Doing so takes foresight, conviction, and courage.

Such purpose-led companies are not rare in other causes, for example, in the fight to combat climate change. Patagonia is a globally celebrated brand that spearheads corporate environmental activism, but it had the foresight back when climate change was just a niche topic.

Founded in 1973, Patagonia had sustainability sewn into its cultural fabric from the onset, and it formed dedicated climate change charity efforts early on. The company never stopped at changes that merely advanced its own strategic position. For example, it imposed a 1% planet tax on its annual revenue and rallied like-minded companies to do the same. With the proceeds, the companies fund a platform that connects grassroots movements, activists, and environmental protection experts. Patagonia became the single most credible brand in sustainable clothing.

The cause of global equality of opportunity is still a strategic white spot, which makes it a strategic opportunity up for grabs. As of today, we see only a few companies embracing this play:

– **Chobani,** the dairy produce manufacturer founded by a Turkish-born immigrant to the US, is an example thanks to its embrace of hiring refugees as workers. The company currently employs 300 refugees (15% of the total workforce) across all sites and uses its marketing muscle and voice to celebrate the positive impacts of refugee workers on society at large.

– **Airbnb** (the US-based platform for homestays and vacation rentals) famously commits to "create a world where anyone can belong anywhere." Airbnb is not only a company thinking and acting globally; it also believes in diversity as a fundamental source of strength and builds its business operation to reflect that belief. The company installed a permanent team of product managers, designers, engineers, and others whose sole purpose is to root out bias and advance belonging and inclusion, thereby creating a culture of boundless innovation. With its foundation, Airbnb.org, the company pioneers activism concerning refugees and displaced communities. It recently offered homes to 20,000 Afghan refugees when the Taliban surged back to power.

When is a good time to credibly embrace such a purpose? The founders of firms like Patagonia, Chobani, and Airbnb embraced a wide societal mission for their firms from day one, and, not coincidentally, they communicated it loudly to differentiate themselves from competitors. Will these early differentiation advantages last forever? The jury is still out, but more than ever, purpose-first companies succeed in achieving category leadership and as a result often see substantial valuation premiums.

Leading into What's Next

"Tomorrow belongs to those who can hear it coming," as David Bowie famously put it when releasing his iconic hit "Heroes." Could a world of global opportunity, facilitated by firm-led migration, be a "tomorrow" discovered by those who are among the first to see it coming? We lay out a pragmatic agenda that helps CEOs and aspiring founders identify their most suitable strategic play and then choose from a list of concrete actions – all with the objective of bringing forward the cause while securing firm-level strategic advantage.

We argue that the best time to get started is now. Younger voters, employees, and consumers increasingly expect CEOs to act on global mobility and opportunity. The majority of populations polled (not just in North America and Europe but also across the globe in China, Japan, Saudi Arabia, Brazil, and South Africa) demand corporate initiative on this very topic.[36]

What starts with better company performance could then trigger a broader change that leads to more widespread innovation, growth, and human happiness.

✶✶✶✶✶✶✶✶✶✶✶✶✶✶✶✶✶✶✶✶✶

---

36 2021 Edelman Trust Barometer: Spring Update.

Building a Globally Diverse Team Is Actually Getting Easier

Johann Harnoss, Anna Schwarz, and Martin Reeves

If you follow only the global headlines, you'll get the impression that the outlook for global talent mobility is bleak. However, a new analysis finds that, in fact, it's rarely been easier for skilled talent to cross borders. BCG researchers analyzed the relative ease of global relocation for skilled talent, comparing the world's 10 most popular destination countries as well as China and Japan. They found that with two exceptions (the US and China), many countries have now put the legal framework in place to hire and relocate global talent at a cost and speed that is broadly comparable with hiring domestically, and they offer five tactics for corporate leaders looking to build globally diverse teams.

Open your favorite news site, and you'll soon immerse yourself in a bleak reality of global migration, spanning from the US-Mexican border, to China sending home expats, to urgent labor shortages in post-Brexit UK. These struggles are real. But they are not the entire story.

From a global perspective, it has in fact rarely been easier for skilled talent to cross borders. By and large, we see more and more firms build globally diverse teams, as research[37] has shown[38] these teams tend to drive firm-level and ultimately also country-level innovation.[39] Germany is now considering a points-based visa system[40] to attract skilled talent. France has introduced a new visa for entrepreneurs.[41] Although it's not widely known, Japan offers a visa category[42] aimed mainly but not exclusively at tech talent. Even in post-Brexit UK, a points-based skilled worker visa[43] remains a core pillar of the country's talent strategy. Australia's COVID-19 restrictions today make mobility challenging, but this is expected to be a transitory phenomenon.

37 https://www.pnas.org/doi/10.1073/pnas.0403723101
38 https://link.springer.com/article/10.1007/s10887-016-9127-6
39 https://www.bcg.com/publications/2021/how-global-migration-drives-innovation
40 https://www.telegraph.co.uk/world-news/2021/10/16/german-coalition-parties-agree-british-style-points-based-immigration/
41 https://www.bloomberg.com/news/articles/2021-11-03/macron-s-startup-nation-wants-to-make-london-worry-in-long-run?sref=gKSeqgQQ
42 https://www.tokyodev.com/articles/japanese-engineering-visa-options#hsfp
43 https://www.bbc.com/news/uk-48785695

As part of our research on "Innovation Without Borders,"[44] we analyzed the relative ease of global relocation for skilled talent, comparing the world's 10 most popular destination countries as well as China and Japan. Many countries have now put the legal framework in place to hire and relocate global talent at a cost and speed that is broadly comparable with hiring domestically. The world is now "flat" for global talent (Figure 1.5):

Below the surface, the picture varies considerably:

– **The US and China are the exception, not the rule.** Unlike other countries, the US has hard caps in place for its highly skilled H1B visa program, and it struggles with administrative bottlenecks around other visa and permanent residency cards. Meanwhile, in addition to stringent COVID-19 quarantine laws, China is introducing new tax laws in January 2022 aimed at expat talent, making it harder to deduct housing rent and schooling expenses from personal taxable income.

– **Western countries are surging ahead.** France, Germany, and Spain are now among the most open to skilled talent, on par with Canada which historically has been seen as most welcoming thanks to its straightforward points-based visa system.

– **The race for skilled talent is now global.** Even India and Japan, countries not traditionally known for their openness are actively trying to attract foreign talent and make it easier for their firms to hire globally.

Why now?

Access to talent has become the number one growth constraint for firms accelerating out of the COVID-19 crisis. Besides this pull factor, important push factors remain in place: There is now more global talent, talent remains willing to move, and remote work is so far not slowing down global mobility.

– **The talent pool is growing.** In the next 10 years, more than 260 million university graduates[45] will hit global labor markets. This growth is equivalent to the total stock of talent as recently as 1990 – and nearly all this growth comes from outside the traditional powerhouses: North America, Europe, China, and Japan.

---

44 https://www.bcg.com/publications/2021/how-global-migration-drives-innovation
45 https://dataexplorer.wittgensteincentre.org/wcde-v2/

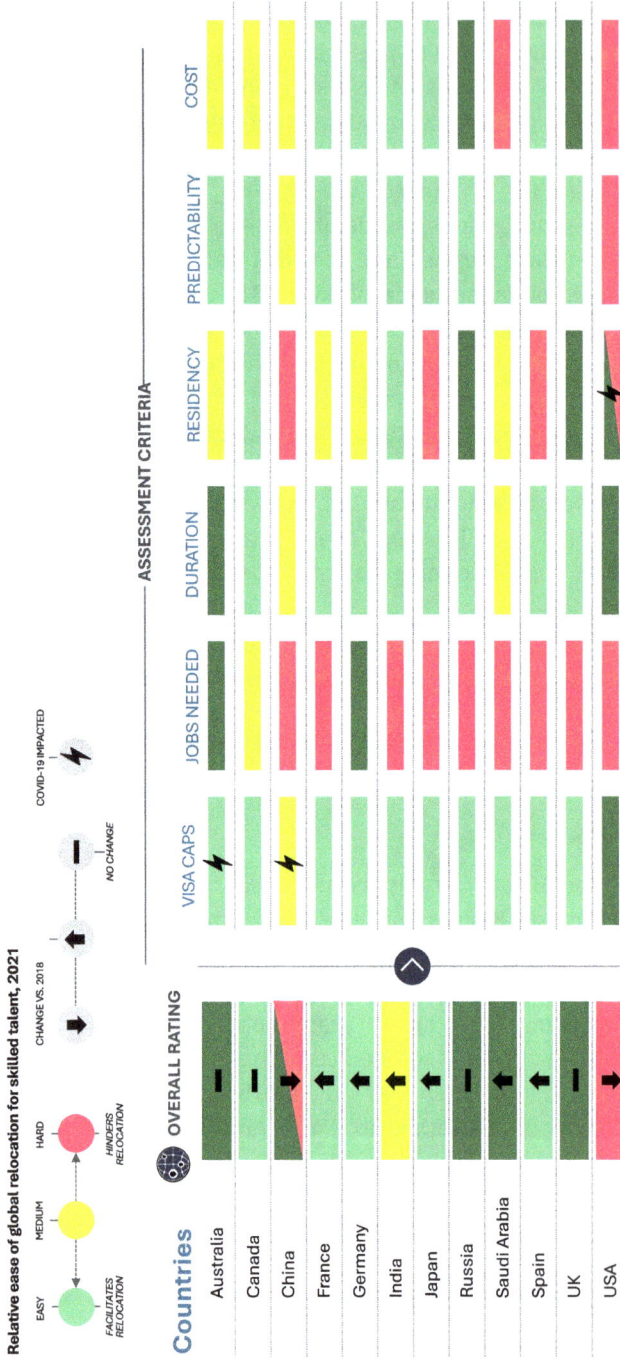

Source: Boston Consulting Group

Note: As firms move to build more globally diverse teams, it's rarely been easier for skilled talent to cross borders. BCG analyzed the 10 most popular destination countries, as well as China and Japan, and found that most countries have the legal framework and administrative processes in place to hire and relocate talent at a cost and speed that's comparable to hiring domestically. The two exceptions? The United States and China.

Figure 1.5: The World is Becoming Increasingly "Flat" for Skilled Talent.

-   **Many are willing to relocate.** While it's down from a peak of 64% in 2014, 50% of global talents surveyed in 2021 remain willing to move[46] to seek better job opportunities elsewhere. Many also seek global mobility as a lifestyle choice.
-   **Remote work can kickstart a relationship.** Startup CEOs and HR executives tell us that remote lowers the barrier to hiring globally. Starting remotely allows both sides to "try before buy," making it less risky to hire from abroad.

As a result, we would not be surprised to see the 2020s be a decade of more talent moving globally particularly to European and Asian countries (outside of China). The data gives some early hints of that possibility: In 2019, annual inflows hit new highs in 20 out of 25 OECD countries[47] – but not in the US. During COVID-19, work-visa-based migration certainly dropped in many countries, but it also tended to be more stable than any other visa category and, at least in Europe, has strongly rebounded since, approaching prepandemic levels.

Business Leaders Face Hard and Soft Constraints

As part of our forthcoming research, we recently ran a survey of 850 senior executives and found a large gap between awareness and action however. A whopping 95% say they intend to build teams that are more globally diverse. But only 2% already see the full results.

The front runners use the diversity of their global teams as a catalyst for innovation. This translates into performance: They are more than twice as likely to be innovative and fast growing than their more homogenous peers. Take, for example, Delivery Hero, a global "decacorn" quick commerce player. Founded in 2009, the firm is now hiring globally not just in tech but across all functions, much like many startups on their journey toward unicorn status.

Meanwhile, late comers face a mix of hard and soft constraints. Hard constraints hit, in particular, smaller firms in the US or China, who cannot circumvent hard limits on foreign hiring (e.g., via global intercompany transfers).

Soft constrains are often self-imposed: Many globally active firms outside the Anglo-Saxon world don't have a "one language" policy, putting big language and cultural barriers in front of foreign talent that is often fluent in English, but not

---

46 https://www.bcg.com/publications/2021/virtual-mobility-in-the-global-workforce
47 https://www.oecd-ilibrary.org/sites/29f23e9d-en/index.html?itemId=/content/publication/29f23e9d-en

other languages. Rakuten, the Japanese tech player famously shattered this soft barrier when Founder and CEO Hiroshi Mikitani launched his full scale "English-nization"[48] requiring all teams to speak English in 2010.

Building a Globally Diverse Team

There are five tactics we've seen corporate leaders adopt to build globally diverse teams that drive innovation. The first two are aimed at firms facing hard constraints, the latter three are for those facing soft constraints or no material constraints at all.

1. **Diversify geographically.**
   If you can't legally bring foreign talent to you, open hubs abroad. Wayfair, an online furniture retailer, understood that to hire all the developers and data scientists it needed, it would have to move beyond their Boston headquarters. As a result, it first built an engineering hub in Berlin. Then, in a move designed to tap not just into the local tech scene but also the wider global talent community, it opened a Toronto hub.

2. **Team up.**
   Countries that make skilled work visas relatively easy to get can still make the administrative process to get there painfully slow. Public-private partnerships can help solve this.

   Germany offers a good example. Even though the country is very open to skilled talent, its bureaucracy does not always reflect this new welcoming attitude, or German *Willkommenskultur*. To drive this culture change, Berlin-based firms joined forces and cofounded BerlinPartner, a public-private partnership. The team quickly realized that a "business fast lane" for international hires was needed the most. Today, a small, dedicated team at BerlinPartner works shoulder-to-shoulder with local government secondees to speed up and de-risk global hiring for employers and to help send a welcoming message to new Berliners.

3. **Become global first.**
   Switching a firm's main language to English as the global lingua franca is a simple operative act but can be a massive culture shock for teams used to running smoothly in their native language. To soften the blow, E.ON, a European energy networks operator switched all group-level communication to English nearly a decade ago, but it gives operating units the flexibility to run in their respective domestic languages. In practice, this choice leaves room

---

48 https://rakuten.today/sports-entertainment/tsedal-neeley-englishnization-story.html

for people to communicate in their native language but ensures seamless communication as all key documents are provided only in English.

4. **Try before buy.**

Firms of all sizes now use global freelance or employer-of-record structures to onboard people remotely before physical relocation. Germany-based logistics startup Forto begins onboarding talent remotely and then decides to later transfer them into larger hubs to work in hybrid setups. What has started as a quick fix during the heydays of COVID-19 has now become a purposeful strategy to screen global talent.

5. **Value all talent.**

Companies that are not attractive for domestic talent often end up not sustainably attracting foreign talent either. Firms must thus aim to improve the employer value for all employees, for example, by optimizing the full talent journey from branding, to fast recruiting, to personal onboarding support, to mentorship for new joiners. Douglas, the European market leader in beauty retail, credits its recent success in scaling its digital beauty platform in part to its ability to attract skilled digital talent both from Germany, where it's headquartered, and from outside Europe. To this end, the company recently introduced a smooth, remote hiring process for digital talent and has also added targeted relocation packages that not only help new recruits with housing support, but ultimately also ensure better retention of its globalizing workforce.

If you follow only the global headlines, you'll get the impression that the outlook for global talent mobility is bleak. Dive deeper, and you will see an exciting opportunity to address urgent talent shortages and drive innovation. Now is the time to grasp this exciting possibility and deliver on it – while others are still sleeping.

✶✶✶✶✶✶✶✶✶✶✶✶✶✶✶✶✶✶✶✶✶✶

What Outperformers Do Differently to Tap Internal Talent

Nithya Vaduganathan, Ben Zweig, Colleen McDonald, and Lisa Simon

In a tight labor market, companies are in trouble when career growth opportunities within the organization are misaligned with the needs of employees.

According to Pew Research Center data, more than 60% of US employees who quit their jobs in the past year cited a lack of career advancement opportunities[49] as a leading reason for leaving, and a recent study by researchers at the MIT Sloan School of Management, New York University's Stern School of Business, and Revelio Labs found that lateral career opportunities[50] are more than twice as important as compensation in predicting employee retention. Additionally, lateral moves and promotions allow employees to experience professional growth and develop new skills. Yet our research finds that only 10% of job opportunities today are filled with internal lateral hires.

While often overlooked as a lever for talent, offering employees lateral moves can be an untapped gold mine for companies. By adopting leading practices for internal mobility, companies can better deploy existing worker capacity and benefit from more successful hires who hit the ground running in new roles with greater institutional knowledge, higher levels of engagement and retention, and even improved gender equity. At the same time, employees benefit from meaningful skill and career development opportunities that better align with their goals, making this a win-win for employers and employees alike.

In our research, we have identified companies that are leading the way as *talent mobility outperformers*. These organizations have higher internal lateral mobility rates and higher employee satisfaction. In this article, we explore four practical insights based on best practices of outperformers, offering ways for companies that are currently underutilizing internal talent to learn from those at the leading edge of this trend.

---

49 https://www.pewresearch.org/short-reads/2022/03/09/majority-of-workers-who-quit-a-job-in-2021-cite-low-pay-no-opportunities-for-advancement-feeling-disrespected/
50 https://sloanreview.mit.edu/article/toxic-culture-is-driving-the-great-resignation/

What Talent Mobility Outperformers Do Differently

We identified internal and external hires at the 750 largest US public and private companies by analyzing the employment histories described in their professional online resumes (See "Identifying Internal Lateral Mobility Outperformers", Figure 1.6). We define an internal lateral career move as a new position of an employee within the same company, where the occupation changes but the level of seniority remains the same. We found that the median lateral mobility rate for large US companies is 8%, and only about a quarter of companies in the data set boasted rates above 15%.

We also found that certain industries, growth stages, and occupations (including business process specialists, brand managers, and strategists) are more conducive than others for employees to make lateral moves. Perhaps more surprising is the fact that these variables explain only about a quarter of the variation in companies' internal lateral mobility rates. Other factors, such as company talent practices, play a more significant role.

In the following section, we look at four talent practices that are setting talent mobility outperformers apart.

Put More Power in the Hands of Employees

Talent hoarding is one of the greatest barriers to talent mobility. Only 20% of employees feel supported by teams to make an internal move.[51] And many employees – especially women – leave companies without even exploring internal options. Talent mobility outperformers overcome this tension in part by giving employees the ability to browse and apply for opportunities directly on talent marketplaces[52] without first notifying their line managers.

While conversations with managers are often encouraged, most don't require approval from line managers for job changes or project opportunities. Asaf Jackoby, vice president of global HR at Amdocs, explains that resistance to change can come at a cost for the organization. "While it's only human nature to want to hang on to your talent," says Jackoby, "managers simply don't have the opportunity to limit mobility for their teams."

For companies like Amdocs and HSBC, the shift from *organization-led* mobility, where managers must initiate and approve mobility opportunities, to *employee-led* mobility is intentional, designed to give employees more agency while reducing the friction associated with finding opportunities internally.

---

51 https://hbr.org/2022/05/what-stops-employees-from-applying-for-internal-roles
52 https://sloanreview.mit.edu/article/create-a-crisis-growth-plan-start-with-opportunity-marketplaces/

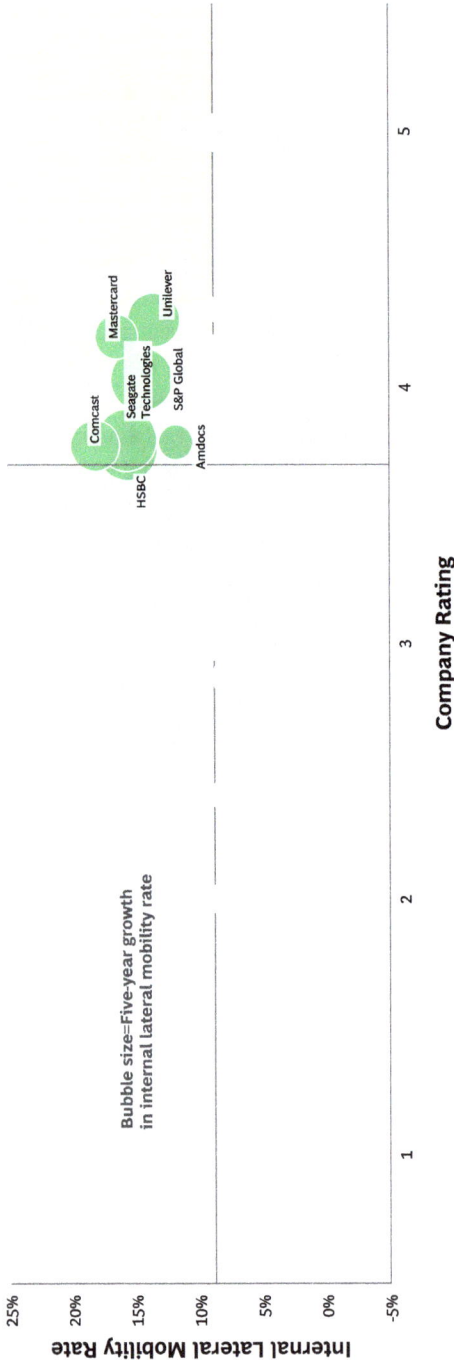

Bubble size=Five-year growth
in internal lateral mobility rate

Company Rating

Internal Lateral Mobility Rate

Note: This chart uses data from 2021 to show the relationship between the lateral mobility rate and employee satisfaction ratings from more than 400 large US public and private companies. Those in the top right quadrant fall into the outperformer category, scoring higher on both internal mobility rate and employee satisfaction.

Figure 1.6: Identifying Internal Lateral Mobility Outperformers.

Of course, designing mobility processes to empower employees is only part of the equation. Change management is still critical. No matter how well companies design their internal talent systems, a layer of skeptical managers telling their teams that staying put is the surest path to advancement is sure to slow adoption. At Mastercard, chief talent and organizational effectiveness officer Lucrecia Borgonovo emphasizes the importance of showing leaders the benefits of tapping into talent in other parts of the organization. Amdocs monitors mobility metrics at all levels of the organization, reviewing which businesses are talent exporters and which are talent importers on a monthly basis, helping to surface insights for leaders and hold them accountable for internal mobility goals.

Expand the Mobility Option Menu

While historically many internal mobility programs have focused on permanent job transfers, a growing number of companies are embracing more varied models for lateral mobility – especially through project or internal gig work, in which employees contribute to a project while remaining in their jobs. In fact, most companies that are outperforming in terms of internal lateral mobility based on job changes are also implementing some form of project matching.

Fidelity International has launched a pilot career vitality program focused on growing internal talent. Internal project work and job-shadowing opportunities that offer a promising path to permanent internal transfers are at the core of the program. "We recently had an employee who undertook job shadowing and project work in our asset management team," Fidelity International's global head of talent, Carmel Mitchell, explained. "When that team had a job opening, this individual applied and transferred into the department. They would have never applied had they not gained experience through project participation."

At Seagate Technology, an employee from marketing helped the talent acquisition team with a project so successfully that they then transferred into a full-time employer branding role. And an engineer who took part in a six-month innovation project became an innovation lead in addition to their day-to-day responsibilities.

Projects offer employees the opportunity to explore a passion and develop new skills while unlocking additional worker capacity and innovation for their employers. "It's easy for people to think that internal mobility is all about moving from one role to another," says Hamish Nisbet, global head of resourcing for HSBC. "But if you think about it from a future-of-work lens, internal mobility might also be about stretching into other areas while remaining in your job role or unit."

Take Advantage of Recent Innovation

Third-party solutions that help companies tap into internal talent have blossomed in recent years. In 2021 alone, $12 billion was invested in the HR technology[53] space. Where companies used to create their own custom technologies for internal mobility, platform developers like Gloat, Fuel50, and Eightfold AI now offer internal talent marketplaces powered by artificial intelligence. Human capital management providers like Workday have introduced talent marketplaces of their own.

Third-party offerings can accelerate a company's internal mobility journey and create a virtuous cycle of adoption and learning (from data collected through the marketplaces) while avoiding common traps that come with developing and maintaining custom internal platforms (such as maintaining a growing list of APIs). Most outperformers use third-party solutions for their talent marketplaces, and many of those that have built their own are exploring options to partner.

These partnerships also reflect a philosophy of looking outward to fuel internal talent innovation. Unilever's vice president of global learning and future of work, Paddy Hull, reflects that companies at the leading edge look at "the trends and beyond the walls of their own organizations." Unilever is a prime example. In 2018, Unilever went on a digital safari to visit future of work startups in five cities around the world. It was then that they met Gloat, with whom they would partner to launch Unilever's Flex experiences program, which uses AI to help employees match with open career opportunities.

Integrate Mobility with Other Talent Practices

In order to build a successful talent program around internal mobility, leaders need to think about bringing these practices into day-to-day routines – such as onboarding, learning and development planning, and performance management. A focused approach to talent mobility can also help companies to integrate talent processes that have historically been disconnected.

Take the example of Comcast, which reimagined quarterly reviews, rebranding them as quarterly connections to allow for conversations about next steps and potential job changes in addition to in-role performance. At Unilever, purpose workshops where employees can develop future-fit skill plans create opportunities for talent mobility to support employees' development goals. And S&P Global has a dedicated internal career development coaching team that provides

---

53 https://www.bcg.com/publications/2022/billion-dollar-opportunity-in-hr-technology

confidential support to employees at all levels of the organization as they navigate their career paths.

Companies are also tightening the links between talent mobility and talent development. Seagate Technology, which requires that jobs be posted internally before being posted externally, has set an 80% skills match threshold for job transfers. The company started an upskilling program to help employees bridge the gap from 80% to 100% and ensure that employees are successful as they transition to new roles. Using data from the talent marketplace allows Seagate to identify skills gaps in the organization and tailor learning and development programs to help close them.

Tapping internal talent in the workforce is a meaningful opportunity for companies facing growing skills gaps, hiring pressures, and retention risks – especially in an economic downturn. As more organizations follow the lead of outperformers to invest in internal lateral mobility, companies that overlook this strategy risk becoming less competitive for talent in a market in which career opportunity matters more than ever.

Chapter 2
Shaping Winning Talent

Your Strategy Is Only as Good as Your Skills

Sagar Goel and Orsolya Kovács-Ondrejkovic

Corporate leaders frequently proclaim, "Our people are our greatest asset." But when it comes to ensuring that this asset is fully prepared and capable, it's clear that improving workers' skills isn't a top priority.

Even though leading companies spend up to 1.5% of their annual budgets on learning and skill building – comparable to what many firms spend on transformation programs or IT – their leaders do not discuss skill building in the same way they do other goals. Our research shows that few companies tie skill building to strategy or report on how they manage skills in the same way they do for other important assets.

This lack of prioritization threatens to become an existential problem at both the individual-company and macroeconomic level. The World Economic Forum has estimated that 50% of the global population needs new skills to meet shifts in demand driven by new technologies. By 2030, this figure may grow to as high as 90%. Failing to meet the demand for new skills could cost as much as $15 trillion in lost GDP. Governments have a huge role to play in closing the projected gaps, but business has an essential job to do as well – and it is in companies' self-interest to step up.

The State of Skill Building Today

To assess the state of skill building, we examined the annual reports and environmental, social, and governance[1] (ESG) reports of 88 leading firms chosen from *Fortune*'s rankings of the 50 largest US firms and the 50 "best places to work." We analyzed how these firms describe their skill-building efforts and the KPIs they report. We combined this data with our own experience working closely with C-level

---

[1] https://www.bcg.com/capabilities/climate-change-sustainability/overview

Note: The authors wish to thank Laura W. Geller, Executive Editor at the BCG Henderson Institute.

https://doi.org/10.1515/9783111369921-003

leaders around the world on learning and skill building.[2] Our findings suggest that companies need to devote far more attention to fostering skill building, tracking its outcomes, and elevating its role and profile in the organization (see Figure 2.1).

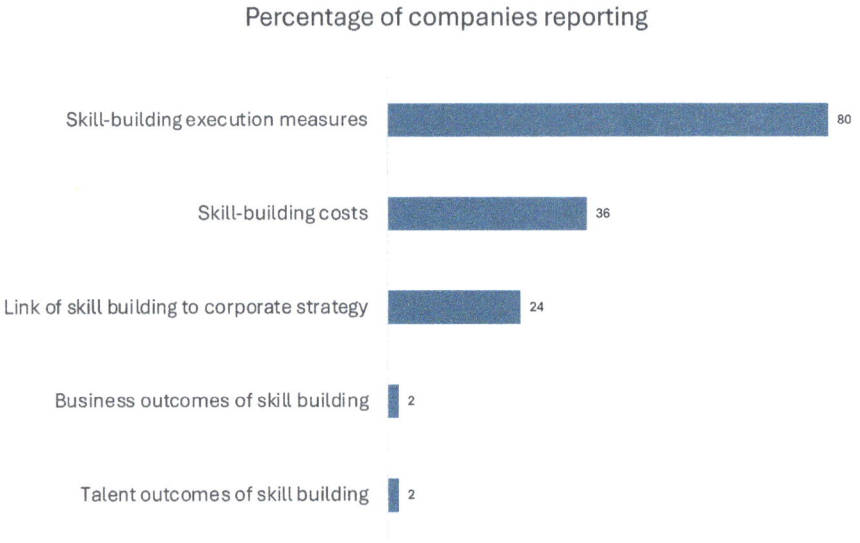

Percentage of companies reporting

Skill-building execution measures	80
Skill-building costs	36
Link of skill building to corporate strategy	24
Business outcomes of skill building	2
Talent outcomes of skill building	2

Sources: Annual reports and ESG reports of 88 companies, drawn from the 50 largest firms in *Fortune*'s rankings and *Fortune*'s 50 "best places to work"; BCG analysis.

Figure 2.1: What Leading Employers Report About Skill Building.

Skill building is not on top of mind. Of the company reports we analyzed, 20% do not include any mention of learning or skill building, and in many others, the topic is only touched on in a generic paragraph on HR or social responsibility. The consideration paid to skills today compares with the attention given to diversity, equity, and inclusion[3] (DEI) about 15 years ago. Now, it's not uncommon for a company to devote three to five pages to DEI, including details on measurement and commitments, and individual employee stories.

In our experience, senior leaders do not put much internal emphasis on skill building either. In a 2020 BCG study[4] of the learning capabilities of 120 large global companies, only 15% said they granted corporate learning the high priority it deserves.

---

2 https://www.bcg.com/capabilities/people-strategy/learning-programs

3 https://www.bcg.com/capabilities/diversity-inclusion/overview

4 https://www.bcg.com/publications/2020/turn-your-company-into-a-learning-powerhouse

Skills are not linked to corporate strategy. The same BCG study shows that less than 15% of leaders believe that learning constitutes a core part of their company's overall business strategy.[5] For most organizations today, skill building is viewed as an HR initiative instead of being tightly integrated with corporate strategy.[6] Only 24% of corporate reports put skill-building efforts in the context of corporate strategy, and those that do describe these efforts in simple, qualitative ways, typically discussing strategic priorities and referencing skill building in this context. Only a handful of companies indicate that they have a structured process for forecasting skill gaps based on corporate business needs.

Companies' reporting on skill-building outcomes is limited. Companies talk about the process they follow to build workers' skills, but few disclose the results they achieve. Four out of five companies report on process metrics related to training, such as hours of training delivered or number of people who attended courses. But these numbers tell us very little about what was actually achieved. Here's a typical (sanitized) example from our research: "In 2021, we rolled out 56 new programs. . . . [We] issued more than 24,800 certifications and provided almost 350,000 hours of training." Meanwhile, only 4% of companies report on the outcomes of their skill-building programs in terms of business outcomes (such as improved productivity or application of a new tool at work) or talent outcomes (such as higher employee engagement or the employability of participants).

Skill building is typically described as an expense. Despite the clear importance of skill building and the significant budgets devoted to it, most leaders view it simply as an expense, not unlike equipment maintenance. Only 36% of companies report on the financial resources they dedicate to skill building, and those that do mostly position it as a cost and rarely as an investment, or more specifically, an investment in future capabilities. The spending is significant: companies in our analysis allocated between 0.5% and 1.5% of their annual budget to skill building, an average of $150 million per year and often much more. Learning and development budgets of $300 million or even $400 million are not uncommon. But as long as these budgets are considered costs, this spending is likely to have a lower priority than other investments. As the chief human resources officer of a global industrial goods firm told us, "When there is a pressure on costs, the first thing to be cut is the learning and development budget. How do we expect the business to sustain results when the core resources – that is, the people – don't have the capabilities to deliver?"

---

5 https://www.bcg.com/capabilities/corporate-finance-strategy/business-strategy
6 https://www.bcg.com/capabilities/corporate-finance-strategy/corporate-strategy

Upgrading Skill Building

Companies need to step up their efforts in skill building, which starts with re-framing it as a strategic priority. As the former chief human resources officer of a large automotive company put it, "Investors, regulators, and employees are interested in what a company does to future-proof the skills of the workforce. Since COVID, people topics are taken much more seriously, and it is only a matter of time until the skills topic is elevated to the strategic importance that it deserves."

Our research and client experience suggest five practical strategies to elevate the importance of skill building in the organization.

Start with strong strategic intent. All companies need a plan to develop the skills required to deliver on their business strategy. They should also take steps to reassure investors and other stakeholders that they have such a plan. This doesn't need to take the form of a complicated workforce plan; it can start with a sharp articulation from the C-suite of how skill-building efforts tie to key strategic business priorities. For example, the German insurer Allianz states in its 2021 sustainability report that "Digitalization and automation will change the composition of the future workforce with some job profiles no longer existing, new profiles and capabilities emerging, and considerable changes in existing profiles and skills. This will require major upskilling and reskilling[7] initiatives to prepare the workforce for the future. Our main focus will be on developing digital, data and agile[8] working skills. Skills like IT security,[9] communications and HR will also be essential." Allianz also reports what this ambition means in quantitative terms: "3,155 FTEs recruited and reskilled in strategically relevant talent segments in Allianz operating entities in 2021 (2021 plan: 2,177)."

Account for the will behind skill. Companies should position skill building as they do other investments. The World Economic Forum recommends "treating investment in human capital in the same way we do investment in natural resources, particularly oil. . . . [T]he investment in the workforce could be capitalized and recognized on the balance sheet." As our analysis shows, this is not a common practice today. Reclassifying balance-sheet categories may be difficult, but employers can clearly dedicate a budget to strategic skill building and measure how it is spent. Doing so will send a strong signal to the workforce that the company is invested in them. For example, Bosch has announced it will spend €2 billion on reskilling work-

---

7 https://www.bcg.com/capabilities/people-strategy/talent-development
8 https://www.bcg.com/capabilities/digital-technology-data/overview
9 https://www.bcg.com/capabilities/digital-technology-data/cybersecurity-digital-risk-management

ers as the auto industry shifts to electric vehicles. Amazon plans to spend $1.2 billion to give 300,000 employees access to education and training programs.

Focus on outcomes over process. Public disclosure can be a powerful motivator, but only if the focus is on the right metrics. By shifting the reported results from "number of employees trained" to "business and talent outcomes achieved," companies can drive higher-order impact and keep the organization focused on skill-building investments. Business outcomes can be measured on multiple levels, such as looking at the application of learning at work (Did workers use the new technology? Did they exhibit new competencies?) or by looking at metrics of achievement (faster or cheaper production or greater sales). The assessment of outcomes should also focus on how learning improves the skills, capabilities, engagement, and employability of participants.

Take the example of AT&T, whose March 2022 *ESG Summary* reports on the impact of the company's new Real Time Training program: "We identify who needs training and when, as well as which training solution is most likely to drive the greatest performance improvement for an employee's respective KPIs. In 2021, approximately 1,950 employees received real time tutorial recommendations, resulting in [about] 4.3K incremental new customers [and about] $4.5M in incremental annual revenue."

In addition to tracking business results, AT&T also monitors the impact of training on participating talent. According to the company's March 2022 *ESG Summary*, "Our metrics show that those who take part in our training and development initiatives are:
– more likely to receive a higher performance rating at the end of the year
– more likely to receive a higher key contributor award at the end of the year
– more likely to move laterally
– less likely to leave the company"

Many companies shy away from trying to quantify outcomes because the exercise can be difficult, but as the experience of one large North American retailer shows, it does not have to be a complex problem-solving exercise. The company ran a pilot using a test and a control group to demonstrate a clear business case for its frontline leadership-development program before scaling the program across the organization. The pilot showed a sales increase of 150 basis points for the test-group stores over the control group. Other companies use existing or easy-to-capture data, such as information from learning-management systems or self-reported training results. When no data is available on outcomes, companies can at least tell success stories or showcase case studies on the impact of skill building.

Inspire commitment, not compliance. Measurement is critical, but numbers alone won't drive new behaviors. Senior business leaders, not just HR, need to highlight the importance and urgency of skill development for every individual – including themselves. Leaders can encourage buy-in with stories of their own skill-building journeys. For example, one professional services firm began implementing its strategic "upskilling" program by asking senior leaders to participate in training programs and then share their experience with their teams. Corporate communications vehicles can showcase examples of "skills heroes" who make successful career pivots or create real business value by building new skills in such areas as data analytics[10] or agile ways of working.[11]

Put skill building on the everyday agenda. Leaders don't need to wait for investor days or quarterly strategy reviews to emphasize the importance of skill building. They can instill a life-long learning culture in their organizations through simple, regular reinforcements. For example, they can make it a practice to ask, "What would we like to learn as a team and individually?" at the beginning of new assignments and encourage team members to identify new skills acquired during weekly team meetings.

✳✳✳

Companies can count on two developments: the importance of a skilled and capable workforce will only increase, and the half-life of critical skills, particularly those related to advanced technology, will continue to shorten. The successful companies of the future will not only invest in human capital but also put the same level of effort and attention into tracking and reporting on skill building that they devote to investing in financial or tangible assets.

✳✳✳✳✳✳✳✳✳✳✳✳✳✳✳✳✳✳✳✳✳✳✳✳✳✳✳✳✳✳✳✳✳✳✳✳✳✳✳

---

10 https://www.bcg.com/capabilities/digital-technology-data/data-analytics
11 https://www.bcg.com/capabilities/digital-technology-data/agile#agile-ways-of-working

6 Strategies to Upskill Your Workforce

Sagar Goel, J. Puckett, Pablo Claver, and Orsolya Kovács-Ondrejkovic

The World Economic Forum estimates that more than half of all employees around the world need to upskill or reskill by 2025 to embrace the changing nature of jobs. So many organizations in these situations are turning toward reskilling to build the talent they cannot acquire or productively deploy. As companies reimagine how they bring learning to a scale of thousands of people and at speed, the authors share six practical insights based on BCG's extensive experience supporting more than 100 global clients.

Imagine this scenario: You are behind your competitors in digital transformation and are even more worried about startups with massive funding that may leapfrog you. You are trying to make progress, but cannot hire enough data scientists, agile coaches, engineers, product owners, cyber experts, or design thinkers. They are going to fun, young organizations, not the old-school companies with siloes, command-and-control leaders, and matrix structures that grind decision making to a halt.

At the same time, many of your current workers are in roles that are slowly becoming obsolete due to automation. What's more, you have too many unproductive middle managers, and your digitally unskilled frontline workers are not prepared for the changing world ahead.

Does this ring familiar? These are the challenges we're hearing from many of our clients, and they're representative of the crossroads we're at in the global skills crisis. The World Economic Forum estimates[12] that more than half of all employees around the world need to upskill or reskill by 2025 to embrace the changing nature of jobs. Many organizations in these situations are turning toward reskilling to build the talent they cannot acquire or productively deploy. And yet a 2020 global BCG study[13] showed that "talent and skills" was the second-most underinvested area in corporate transformation efforts.

As companies reimagine how they bring learning to a scale of thousands of people and at speed, we share six practical insights based on BCG's extensive ex-

---

12 https://www.weforum.org/agenda/2021/01/calling-global-upskilling-movement/
13 https://www.bcg.com/publications/2020/leadership-agile-blindspot

perience supporting more than 100 clients globally, touching hundreds of thousands of learners in the past four years.

1 Treat Skilling as a Business Investment, not an Expense

The majority of skilling efforts fail because they are set up to optimize for learning and development (L&D) costs instead of driving real business impact. Globally, more than $300 billion is spent on corporate education each year, according to an estimate from Allied Market Research.[14] From our experience working with clients, the majority of corporate education initiatives demonstrate limited measurable impact.

Leaders should treat skilling as a business investment – an asset that will help produce profits over several years, with clearly defined business, people, and learning KPIs as a starting point for the program design.

For example, an Asian real estate firm undertaking a leadership development program designed it by first defining the end business objectives: 50% faster time to new market entry and a two-fold increase in target achievement for land acquisition through faster decision making.

This completely changed the design of its L&D intervention. In the past, the company would have run a series of facilitated workshops on leadership and decision-making skills. Instead, participants went through a hands-on learning intervention, where they were shadowed and coached on how to run their monthly business review meetings differently to achieve their business objectives. The result was a steep jump in their market position and a successful initiative to cascade down to their mid-level management.

2 Serve "Salads" for Healthy Skilling

Too often today's skilling programs are offered to employees as a menu of "main course" options to choose from – for example, functional, digital, leadership, business, or soft skills. Our experience shows that high-impact reskilling is better achieved through creating appetizing "salads" that blend all these different skills in a specific context.

We worked with the government in Singapore on a large-scale workforce reskilling program to help mid-career professionals move from traditional jobs to

---

14 https://www.alliedmarketresearch.com/press-release/corporate-training-market.html

data and digital roles. The program needed to address a wide range of skills, from hard skills like problem-solving, insight generation, and analytics, to soft skills like stakeholder engagement and communication.

Instead of creating a module for each of these topics, the program focused on projects where all these skills needed to be applied in tandem. The result was a rapid learning curve over six months, where more than 65% of learners pivoted to new data and digital roles within just a few months of program completion.

3 Bring the Joy back to Learning

Too much corporate learning is spent in hours of e-modules or Zoom workshops. Learning experience designers need to reimagine how, when, and where learning happens with a leading question in mind: How do we bring the joy and curiosity of learning that children experience to adult learners?

Instead of just sharing case studies on customer centricity, a leading mobile phone player in China brought real customers into their learning workshops, which led to several myths being busted and new insights being generated for the business. A major consumer goods player in India built communication skills for their mid-level managers by having them shoot and analyze selfie videos. This led participants to a heightened sense of self-awareness about how they communicate, as compared to the traditional approach of receiving feedback from a facilitator. A global public sector organization leveraged improv to get middle managers to immerse themselves in and understand the agile way of working by first playing typical work scenarios in "command-and-control" mode and then replaying the same scenarios in "autonomy-and-alignment" mode.

4 Power up with Data

Learning design and delivery is both a science and an art. Data can be used to inform decision making in every step of the learning journey.

For instance, AI tools can look at an employee's job experience and career trajectory in order to analyze their skills gap and personalize their learning experience. These tools can also identify pathways for groups of employees whose jobs will be significantly disrupted to transition them to in-demand roles. Another approach is to run A/B tests on different formats of the program or modes of learning for different cohorts and let data make the decisions as the programs scale. Finally, measuring outcomes with both leading and lagging indicators over time can allow for continuous improvement of skilling initiatives.

5 Assemble Your Own Skilling Stack

Reskilling at scale for thousands of employees requires significant investment in creating an end-to-end skilling stack – including assessments, skills inventory, content curation, learning technology and analytics, training, delivery, learning experience management, credentialing, and career transition support.

Instead of "building" this infrastructure from the ground up, companies can now move at speed by "buying" or "renting" through partnerships to assemble their own skilling stack. Critics of this approach cite the lack of customization to the organization's context. But your L&D team can distinguish between core commodity skills that are universal and can be sourced externally (for example, learning a new programming language) and where the value for customization can be high (for example, an internal expert sharing which data analytics use cases are most critical in your organization).

6 Empower Employees to Learn

Skilling is often discussed as something that "needs to be done *to* the workers," but research shows that workers know change is coming and are ready to act upon it. Data from BCG's Decoding Global Talent report[15] shows that 68% of workers globally are ready to retrain to new careers to stay competitive. If we believe people can be responsible for their own reskilling, interventions that allow them to decide what skills they need and pick from various options are best. Employers should empower their employees with the right tools, flexible resources, and supportive context to own their personal reskilling journeys.

For example, BCG empowers its expert consultants to stay relevant and up to date by designing their own learning intervention with an annual budget allocated. This has led to many creative learning paths – for example, collaborations on public-sector initiatives, codesigning with startups, immersion trips to completely different business environments, and more.

By reimagining the traditional approaches to skilling, business and HR leaders can take timely action to prepare their workforces to be today- and future-ready. Organizations have a choice: Create a skilling competitive advantage or else run the imminent risk of falling behind.

✳✳✳✳✳✳✳✳✳✳✳✳✳✳✳✳✳✳✳✳✳✳✳✳✳✳✳✳✳✳✳✳✳✳✳✳✳✳✳

---

15 https://www.bcg.com/publications/2021/decoding-global-trends-reskilling-career-paths

Reskilling in the Age of AI

Jorge Tamayo, Leila Doumi, Sagar Goel, Orsolya Kovács-Ondrejkovic, and
Raffaella Sadun

In the coming decades, as the pace of technological change continues to increase, millions of workers may need to be not just upskilled but reskilled – a profoundly complex societal challenge that will sometimes require workers to both acquire new skills and change occupations entirely. Companies have a critical role to play in addressing this challenge, but to date few have taken it seriously. To learn more about what their role will entail, the authors – members of a collaboration between the Digital Data Design Institute at Harvard's Digital Reskilling Lab and Boston Consulting Group's Henderson Institute – interviewed leaders at some 40 organizations around the world that are investing in large-scale reskilling programs. In synthesizing what they learned, they became aware of five paradigm shifts that are emerging in reskilling: (1) Reskilling is a strategic imperative. (2) It is the responsibility of every leader and manager. (3) It is a change-management initiative. (4) Employees want to reskill – when it makes sense. (5) It takes a village. The authors argue that companies will need to understand and embrace these shifts if they hope to succeed in adapting dynamically to the rapidly evolving new era of automation and AI.

Back in 2019 the Organisation for Economic Co-operation and Development made a bold forecast. Within 15 to 20 years, it predicted, new automation technologies were likely to eliminate 14% of the world's jobs and radically transform another 32%. Those were sobering numbers, involving more than 1 billion people globally – and they didn't even factor in ChatGPT and the new wave of generative AI that has recently taken the market by storm.

Today advances in technology are changing the demand for skills at an accelerated pace. New technologies can not only handle a growing number of repetitive and manual tasks but also perform increasingly sophisticated kinds of knowledge-based work – such as research, coding, and writing – that have long been considered safe from disruption. The average half-life of skills is now less than five years, and in some tech fields it's as low as two and a half years. Not all knowledge workers will lose their jobs in the years ahead, of course, but as they carry out their daily tasks, many of them may well discover that AI and other new technologies have so significantly altered the nature of what they do that in effect they're working in completely new fields.

To cope with these disruptions, a number of organizations are already investing heavily in upskilling their workforces. One recent BCG study[16] suggests that such investments represent as much as 1.5% of those organizations' total budgets. But upskilling alone won't be enough. If the OECD estimates are correct, in the coming decades millions of workers may need to be entirely reskilled – a fundamental and profoundly complex societal challenge that will require workers not only to acquire new skills but to use them to change occupations.

Companies have a critical role to play in addressing this challenge, and it's in their best interests to get going on it in a serious way right now. Among those that have embraced the reskilling challenge, only a handful have done so effectively, and even *their* efforts have often been subscale and of limited impact, which leads to a question: Now that the need for a reskilling revolution is apparent, what must companies do to make it happen?

In our work at the Digital Data Design Institute at Harvard's Digital Reskilling Lab and the BCG Henderson Institute we have been studying this question in depth, and as part of that effort we interviewed leaders at almost 40 organizations around the world that are investing in large-scale reskilling programs. During those interviews, we discussed common challenges, heard stories of early success, and discovered that many of those companies are thinking in important new ways about why, when, and how to reskill. In synthesizing what we've learned, we've become aware of five paradigm shifts that are emerging in reskilling – shifts that companies will need to understand and embrace if they hope to succeed in adapting dynamically to the rapidly evolving era of automation and AI.

In this article we'll explore those shifts. We'll show how some companies are implementing them, and we'll review the unexpected challenges they've encountered and the promising wins they've achieved.

1 Reskilling Is a Strategic Imperative

During times of disruption, when many jobs are threatened, companies have often turned to reskilling to soften the blow of layoffs, assuage feelings of guilt about social responsibility, and create a positive PR narrative. But most of the companies we spoke with have moved beyond that narrow approach and now recognize reskilling as a strategic imperative. That shift reflects profound changes

---

16 https://www.bcg.com/publications/2023/your-strategy-is-only-as-good-as-your-skills

in the labor market, which is increasingly constrained by the aging of the working population, the emergence of new occupations, and an increasing need for employees to develop skills that are company-specific. Against this backdrop effective reskilling initiatives are critical, because they allow companies to build competitive advantage quickly by developing talent that is not readily available in the market and filling skills gaps that are instrumental to achieving their strategic objectives – before and better than their competitors do.

In recent years several major companies have embraced this approach. Infosys, for example, has reskilled more than 2,000 cybersecurity experts with various adjacent competencies and capability levels. Vodafone aims to draw from internal talent to fill 40% of its software developer needs. And Amazon, through its Machine Learning University, has enabled thousands of employees who initially had little experience in machine learning to become experts in the field.

Some companies now consider reskilling a core part of their employee value proposition and a strategic means of balancing workforce supply and demand. At those companies, employees are encouraged to reskill for roles that appeal to them. Mahindra & Mahindra, Wipro, and Ericsson have policies, tools, and IT platforms that promote reskilling resources and available jobs – as does McDonald's, where restaurant employees have access to an app called Archways to Opportunity that maps skills learned on the job to career paths within the company and in other industries.

Finally, some companies are using reskilling to tap into broader talent pools and attract candidates who wouldn't otherwise be considered for open positions. ICICI Bank – headquartered in Mumbai and employing more than 130,000 people – runs an intense, academy-like reskilling program that prepares graduates, often from diverse backgrounds, for frontline managerial jobs. The program reskills some 2,500 to 4,000 employees each year. CVS used a similar approach during the COVID-19 pandemic to hire, train, and onboard people (some of them laid-off hospitality workers) to create capacity for its critical vaccine and testing services.

2 Reskilling Is the Responsibility of Every Leader and Manager

Traditionally, reskilling is considered part of the overall corporate-learning function. When that's the case, responsibility for the design and implementation of the program is often siloed within HR, and its failure or success is measured very narrowly – in terms of the number of trainings delivered, the cost per learner, and similar training-specific metrics. According to a recent BCG report, only 24% of polled companies make a clear connection between corporate strategy and reskilling efforts. Reskilling investments need a profound commitment from HR leaders, of course, but unless the rest of the organization understands the strategic relevance of those investments, it's very hard to obtain the relentless and distributed effort that such initiatives require to succeed.

At most of the organizations where we interviewed, reskilling initiatives are visibly championed by senior leaders, often CEOs and chief operating officers. They work hard to articulate for the rest of the company the connection between reskilling and strategy and to ensure that leadership and management teams understand their shared responsibility for implementing these programs. For example, as part of its ongoing digital transformation, Ericsson has developed a multiyear strategy devoted to upskilling and reskilling. The effort involves systematically defining critical skills connected to strategy, which correspond to a variety of accelerator programs, skill journeys, and skill-shifting targets – most of them dedicated to transforming telecommunications experts into AI and data-science experts. The company considers this a high-priority, high-investment project and has made it part of the objectives and key results that executives review quarterly. In just three years Ericsson has upskilled more than 15,000 employees in AI and automation.

Similarly, the executive team at CVS has made training and reskilling an integral part of the company's business strategies. Each individual business leader is now responsible for designing and delivering workforce-reskilling plans to help the company reach its goals, and the ability to do so is factored into performance assessments. Amazon, too, has famously committed to reskilling as a core strategic objective and now mentions it prominently in its leadership manifesto for managers. The visibility of this commitment contributes to Amazon's ability to achieve scale in reskilling programs.

3 Reskilling Is a Change-Management Initiative

To design and implement ambitious reskilling programs, companies must do a lot more than just train employees: They must create an organizational context conducive to success. To do that they need to ensure the right mindset and behaviors among employees and managers alike. From this perspective, reskilling is akin to a change-management initiative, because it requires a focus on many different tasks simultaneously.

Let's consider several of the most important.

Understanding supply and demand. To create a successful reskilling program, companies need a sophisticated understanding of supply (skills available internally and externally) and demand (skills needed to beat the competition). A useful way to develop this understanding is with a "skill taxonomy" – a detailed description of the capabilities needed for each occupation at a company. Employers used to put a lot of effort into creating such taxonomies from scratch, but many leading companies now rely on external providers for the bulk of the work. HSBC, for example, has adopted the taxonomy published by the World Economic Forum and customized it slightly to add skills specific to parts of its business. Similarly, SAP, which used to maintain an in-house taxonomy of 7,000 skills, has recently started working with Lightcast, which keeps a continually updated skill database. But developing a skill taxonomy is only the first step. Next comes the difficult job of deciding which skills get mapped to which jobs. Managers from different divisions may disagree about this. Such disagreement is often symptomatic of a deeper misalignment, and companies will need to resolve that before they undertake any major reskilling initiative.

Leaders must also determine what skills they will need in the future – a dynamic process that's critical for strategic reskilling programs. To do that well, they should focus on figuring out what skills the current strategy demands. Here they'll need to develop a rigorous strategic workforce-planning methodology. The European insurance company Allianz has done interesting work on this front: It regularly translates forecasted business growth into talent demand, focusing on the number of people needed in various jobs and the skills they'll require. The model, which is updated as part of the annual planning process, involves economic scenario planning and takes into account the possible effects of digitalization on the workforce.

Recruiting and evaluating. Traditionally, candidates are recruited for training opportunities or internal roles on the basis of their degrees or relevant work experience, but that obviously doesn't work for reskilled workers. A well-developed skill taxonomy can help here, by allowing organizations to think about enrollment policies in light of skill adjacencies, which can facilitate the transition from one skill set to another. Novartis has implemented an AI-powered internal talent marketplace that predicts, matches, and offers roles and projects related to employees' skills and goals. In our research we've also found that if reskilling programs are to succeed, companies must develop a clear set of enrollment criteria for employees, not all of whom will have the right combination of motivation and personality traits to be a good fit for reskilling.

Shaping the mindset of middle managers. Middle managers are often resistant to the idea of reskilling, for two main reasons: They worry (1) that their reports won't be able to keep up with their regular responsibilities while being reskilled, and (2) that once their reports *are* reskilled, they'll move to other parts of the organization. In both cases this can lead to "talent hoarding," in which managers try to hold on to their favorite reports by denying them the ability to participate in reskilling. Several of the companies we spoke with have addressed this problem by making talent development an explicit managerial responsibility.

Wipro evaluates managers according to their teams' participation in training offers, and Amazon promotes leaders on the basis of a performance assessment that includes the question "How have you developed your team?" Middle managers may also resist the idea of hiring reskilled employees, believing that they're not as desirable as traditionally skilled workers. This problem can be addressed by involving managers in the design and delivery of reskilling programs and by providing sensitivity and unconscious-bias training. No matter what form the resistance takes, senior leaders' role modeling in support of reskilling is vital to overcoming it.

Building skills in the flow of work. It can be costly and logistically challenging to take employees away from their day jobs to participate in training. And adults tend not to like or learn well in classroom-style situations. In a 2021 BCG survey[17] 65% of the 209,000 participating workers said they prefer to learn on the job. As a result, the best approach for reskilling is to do as much training as possible by means of shadowing assignments, internal apprenticeships, and trial periods. The reskilling program at ICICI Bank, for example, consists of a four-month vocational residency, during which employees take part in simulation-style trainings for the managerial role they hope to get, and an eight-month deployment in the field that involves a structured internship in a bank branch and closely shadowing a current manager.

Noma Bar

Matching and integrating reskilled employees. Employees need to be matched with new jobs. Our interview data shows that if destination roles are clearly described in advance, employees become more interested in reskilling because new career trajectories become apparent to them, and the reskilling itself becomes more effective because it's more position-specific. Once in their new jobs, reskilled employees need several kinds of support to integrate successfully: help with learning new work norms and culture, building networks, and developing soft skills. Here coaching and mentoring can be particularly effective tools. Amazon has demonstrated leadership in this area: It runs a variety of mentoring programs for reskilled employees, among them a buddy system, part of its Grow Our Own Talent program, that connects previous and current program participants. The company also provides career coaching for employees who are making particularly difficult transitions, such as from warehouse worker to software developer.

---

17 https://www.bcg.com/publications/2021/decoding-global-trends-reskilling-career-paths

4 Employees Want to Reskill – When It Makes Sense

Many of the companies we spoke with mentioned that one of their biggest challenges was simply persuading employees to embark on reskilling programs. That's understandable: Reskilling requires a lot of effort and can set a major life change in motion, and the outcome isn't guaranteed. The OECD reports[18] that only a very small fraction of workers typically take part in standard training programs, and those who do are often the ones who need them the least.

But workers may be more willing to engage in reskilling than prior data suggests. BCG data shows,[19] for example, that 68% of workers are aware of coming disruptions in their fields and are willing to reskill to remain competitively employed. The key to success in this domain, our interviews suggest, is to treat workers respectfully and make the benefits of their participation in reskilling initiatives clear. As one of our interviewees explains, "The secret to scaling up reskilling programs is to design a product your employees actually like."

So how can organizations do that? We have several suggestions.

Treat employees as partners. Because reskilling programs are often associated with organizational disruption and job loss – or at least job change – leaders often avoid talking openly about the rationale for the programs and the opportunities they present. But employees are more likely to participate if they understand why the programs are being implemented and have had a role in creating them. Aware of this, several of the companies we spoke with made a point of being honest and clear about why they were creating reskilling programs and involving workers early. One large auto manufacturer, for example, told its diesel engineers that because of changes in the automobile industry, it had less and less need for their skills; it presented its program as a way of ensuring that they would have new jobs and job security in the years ahead. The companies also told us that in designing and implementing reskilling programs, it's critical to align with worker councils and unions early on and to involve them in advocating for the programs.

Design programs from the employee point of view. Reskilling programs require participants to make a major investment of time. So it's important to try to reduce the risk, cost, and effort involved and to provide (almost) guaranteed outcomes. Amazon allows employees in its Career Choice program to pursue everything from bachelor's degrees to certificates – and covers all costs in advance.

---

18 https://www.oecd-ilibrary.org/employment/training-in-enterprises_7d63d210-en

19 https://web-assets.bcg.com/93/b6/11ba136841189e51cc50486f1340/bcg-decoding-global-reskilling-and-career-paths-apr-2021.pdf

That has proved to be a key factor in scaling up the program, which has already had more than 130,000 participants. CVS, for its part, uses an effective "train in place" model for new employees.

Dedicate adequate time and attention to the task. Because reskilling involves occupational change, it usually requires intensive learning, which is possible only if employees have the time and mental space they need to succeed. To that end, four times a year Vodafone dedicates days during which employees may devote themselves entirely to learning and personal development. Bosch goes even further: To help traditional engineers at the company earn degrees and get training in emerging fields, its Mission to Move program covers the cost of tuition and time spent learning for as much as two days a week for a whole year. It even gives participants days off before exams to prepare.

Noma Bar

Naturally, providing employees the time and space for skilling can be harder in industries where most workers are hourly or shift-based. Iberdrola, a renewable energy company, faced this challenge as it digitized. Because it was embracing new technologies, the company realized it would need to reskill 3,300 employees in various hourly roles. Its leaders got the job done by working closely with frontline managers to ensure that operations weren't disrupted by workers' taking time off for training. The company considered all training hours to be work hours and paid employees for them accordingly.

5 Reskilling Takes a Village

Companies have tended to think of reskilling as an organization-level challenge, believing that they have to do the job by and for themselves. But many of the companies where we interviewed have recognized that reskilling takes place in an ecosystem in which a number of actors have roles to play. Governments can incentivize reskilling investments by means of funds, policies, and public programs; industry can team up with academia to develop new skill-building techniques; and NGOs can play a role in connecting corporate talent needs with disadvantaged and marginalized talent groups. Coalitions of companies may be more effective at the reskilling challenge than single organizations are.

When designing reskilling programs for the rapidly evolving era of AI and automation, companies need to harness the potential of this wider ecosystem. We've identified several ways in which they can do so.

Consider industry partnerships. Instead of thinking of themselves as competitors for a limited talent pool, companies can team up to conduct joint training efforts, which may significantly attenuate some of the challenges outlined above. For example, industry-wide skill taxonomies would provide a useful infrastructure and could in some cases help companies pool the knowledge and resources needed to invest in certain types of capabilities, such as cutting-edge AI skills, which are so new that individual organizations may not yet have the knowledge or the capacity to develop solutions on their own. Industry coalitions could also reassure participants that their investments in learning might open up broader future opportunities.

The Technology in Finance Immersion Programme, offered by the Institute of Banking and Finance Singapore, a nonprofit industry association, is a case in point. The program aims to build up an industry pipeline of capabilities in key technology areas, with participation from all major banks, insurance players, and asset managers in the country, to meet the talent needs of the financial services sector. Similarly, within the European Union a variety of stakeholders have formed the Automotive Skills Alliance, which is dedicated to the "re-skilling and up-skilling of workers in the automotive sector."

Partner with nonprofits to reach diverse talent. Many reskilling nonprofits work with populations that are underrepresented in the workforce. By teaming up with these nonprofits, companies can significantly expand access to talent and employment opportunities in ways that benefit both parties, often at low cost. Some of the ongoing reskilling efforts we learned of in our research involve corporate partnerships with such innovative entities as OneTen (which helps Black workers in the US), Year Up (which helps disadvantaged youths in the US), Joblinge (which helps disadvantaged youths in Germany), and RISE 2.0 (a BCG program that helps workers in Singapore without a digital background move into digital roles). Year Up stands out among these initiatives for its careful use of statistical techniques to study the impact of its training on participants. Since 2011 the program has placed more than 40,000 young people in corporate roles and internships that would have been inaccessible to them without the reskilling support and network it provided. The program has an 80% placement rate at more than 250 participating companies.

Partner with local colleges and training providers. Companies have a lot to gain by teaming up with educational institutions in their reskilling efforts. Examples of such partnerships include the UK-government-funded Institutes of Technology, which bring together colleges and major employers to provide practical technical training for workers without tech backgrounds, in ways that allow companies to quickly react to new technologies and meet rapidly evolving skills needs; and BMW's collaboration with the German Federal Employment Agency and the Association of German Chambers of Industry and Commerce, which supports the transition to electric vehicles with reskilling programs aimed at industrial electricians.

Many companies have an intuitive understanding of the need to embrace the reskilling paradigm shifts discussed in this article, and some, admirably, have already made tremendous commitments to doing so. But their efforts are hampered by two important limitations: a lack of rigor when it comes to the measurement and evaluation of what actually works, and a lack of information about how to generalize and scale up the demonstrably successful features of reskilling programs. To adapt in the years ahead to the rapidly accelerating pace of technological change, companies will have to develop ways to learn – in a systematic, rigorous, experimental, and long-term way – from the many reskilling investments that are being made today. Only then will the reskilling revolution really take off.

✳✳✳✳✳✳✳✳✳✳✳✳✳✳✳✳✳✳✳✳✳✳✳✳✳✳✳✳✳✳✳✳✳✳✳✳✳✳✳

Your Workforce Is More Adaptable than You Think

Joseph Fuller, Judith K. Wallenstein, Manjari Raman, and Alice de Chalendar

In 2018 the Project on Managing the Future of Work at HBS teamed up with the BCG Henderson Institute to survey 6,500 business leaders and 11,000 workers about the various forces reshaping the nature of work. The responses revealed a surprising gap: While the executives were pessimistic about their employees' ability to acquire the capabilities needed to thrive in an era of rapid change, the employees were not. The employees were actually focused on the benefits that change would bring and far more eager to learn new skills than their leaders gave them credit for.

This gap highlights a vast reserve of talent and energy firms can tap into: their own workers. How can a company do that? By creating a learning culture; engaging employees in the transition instead of shepherding them through it; developing an internal talent pipeline for the entire workforce; and collaborating with outside partners to build the right skills in the labor pools it hires from.

Many managers have little faith in their employees' ability to survive the twists and turns of a rapidly evolving economy. "The majority of people in disappearing jobs do not realize what is coming," the head of strategy at a top German bank recently told us. "My call center workers are neither able nor willing to change."

This kind of thinking is common, but it's wrong, as we learned after surveying thousands of employees around the world. In 2018, in an attempt to understand the various forces shaping the nature of work, Harvard Business School's Project on Managing the Future of Work and Boston Consulting Group's Henderson Institute came together to conduct a survey spanning 11 countries – Brazil, China, France, Germany, India, Indonesia, Japan, Spain, Sweden, the United Kingdom, and the US – gathering responses from 1,000 workers in each. In it we focused solely on the people most vulnerable to changing dynamics: lower-income and middle-skills workers. The majority of them were earning less than the average household income in their countries, and all of them had no more than two years of postsecondary education. In each of eight countries – Brazil, China, France, Germany, India, Japan, the United Kingdom, and the US – we then surveyed at least 800 business leaders (whose companies differed from those of the workers we surveyed). In total we gathered responses from 11,000 workers and 6,500 business leaders.

What we learned was fascinating: The two groups perceived the future in significantly different ways. Given the complexity of the changes that companies are confronting today and the speed with which they need to make decisions, this gap in perceptions has serious and far-reaching consequences for managers and employees alike.

Predictably, business leaders feel anxious as they struggle to marshal and mobilize the workforce of tomorrow. In a climate of perpetual disruption, how can they find and hire employees who have the skills their companies need? And what should they do with people whose skills have become obsolete? The CEO of one multinational company told us he was so tormented by that last question that he had to seek counsel from his priest.

The workers, however, didn't share that sense of anxiety. Instead, they focused more on the opportunities and benefits that the future holds for them, and they revealed themselves to be much more eager to embrace change and learn new skills than their employers gave them credit for.

The Nature of the Gap

When executives today consider the forces that are changing how work is done, they tend to think mostly about disruptive *technologies*. But that's too narrow a focus. A remarkably broad set of forces is transforming the nature of work, and companies need to take them all into account.

In our research we've identified 17 forces of disruption, which we group into six basic categories. Our surveys explored the attitudes that business leaders and workers had toward each of them. In their responses, we were able to discern three notable differences in the ways that the two groups think about the future of work.

***

The Forces Shaping the Future of Work

Accelerating Technological Change
-   New technologies that replace human labor, threatening employment (such as driverless trucks)
-   New technologies that augment or supplement human labor (for example, robots in health care)
-   Sudden technology-based shifts in customer needs that result in new business models, new ways of working, or faster product innovation

- Technology-enabled opportunities to monetize free services (such as Amazon web services) or underutilized assets (such as personal consumption data)

Growing Demand for Skills
- General increase in the skills, technical knowledge, and formal education required to perform work
- Growing shortage of workers with the skills for rapidly evolving jobs

Changing Employee Expectations
- Increased popularity of flexible, self-directed forms of work that allow better work-life balance
- More widespread desire for work with a purpose and opportunities to influence the way it is delivered (for example, greater team autonomy)

Shifting Labor Demographics
- Need to increase workforce participation of underrepresented populations (such as elderly workers, women, immigrants, and rural workers)

Transitioning Work Models
- Rise of remote work
- Growth of contingent forms of work (such as on-call workers, temp workers, and contractors)
- Freelancing and labor-sharing platforms that provide access to talent
- Delivery of work through complex partner ecosystems (involving multiple industries, geographies, and organizations of different sizes), rather than within a single organization

Evolving Business Environment
- New regulation aimed at controlling technology use (for example, "robot taxes")
- Regulatory changes that affect wage levels, either directly (such as minimum wages or Social Security entitlements) or indirectly (such as more public income assistance or universal basic income)
- Regulatory shifts affecting cross-border flow of goods, services, and capital
- Greater economic and political volatility as members of society feel left behind

***

The first is that *workers seem to recognize more clearly than leaders do that their organizations are contending with multiple forces of disruption, each of which will affect how companies work differently.* When asked to rate the impact that each of the 17 forces would have on their work lives, using a 100-point scale, the employees rated the force with the strongest impact 15 points higher than the force with the weakest impact. In comparison, there was only a nine-point spread between the forces rated the strongest and the weakest by managers.

In fact, the leaders seemed unable or unwilling to think in differentiated ways about the forces' potential for disruption. When asked about each force, roughly a third of them described it as having a significant impact on their organization today; close to half projected that it would have a significant impact in the future; and about a fifth claimed it would have no impact at all. That's a troubling level of uniformity, and it suggests that most leaders haven't yet figured out which forces of change they should make a priority.

Interestingly, workers appeared to be more aware of the opportunities and challenges of several of the forces. Notably, workers focused on the growing importance of the gig economy, and they ranked "freelancing and labor-sharing platforms" as the third most significant of all 17 forces. Business leaders, however, ranked that force as the least significant.

The second difference that emerged from our survey was this: *Workers seem to be more adaptive and optimistic about the future than their leaders recognize.*

The conventional wisdom, of course, is that workers fear that technology will make their jobs obsolete. But our survey revealed that to be a misconception. A majority of the workers felt that advances such as automation and artificial intelligence would have a positive impact on their future. In fact, they felt that way about two-thirds of the forces. What concerned them most were the forces that might allow *other workers* – temporary, freelance, outsourced – to take their jobs.

When asked why they had a positive outlook, workers most commonly cited two reasons: the prospect of better wages and the prospect of more interesting and meaningful jobs. Both automation and technology, they felt, heralded opportunity on those fronts – by contributing to the emergence of more flexible and self-directed forms of work, by creating alternative ways to earn income, and by making it possible to avoid tasks that were "dirty, dangerous, or dull."

In every country workers described themselves as more willing to prepare for the workplace of the future than managers believed them to be (in Japan, though, the percentages were nearly equal). Yet when asked what was holding workers back, managers chose answers that blamed employees, rather than themselves. Their most common response was that workers feared significant change. The idea that workers might lack the support they needed from employers was only their fifth-most-popular response.

That brings us to our third finding: *Workers are seeking more support and guidance to prepare themselves for future employment than management is providing.*

In every country except France and Japan, significant majorities of workers reported that they – and not their government or their employer – were responsible for equipping themselves to meet the needs of a rapidly evolving workplace. That held true across age groups and for both men and women. But workers also felt that they had serious obstacles to overcome: a lack of knowledge about their options; a lack of time to prepare for the future; high training costs; the impact that taking time off for training would have on wages; and, in particular, insufficient support from their employers. All are barriers that management can and should help workers get past.

What Employers Can Do to Help

The gap in perspectives is a problem because it leads managers to underestimate employees' ambitions and underinvest in their skills. But it also shows that there's a vast reserve of talent and energy companies can tap into to ready themselves for the future: their workers.

The challenge is figuring out how best to do that. We've identified five important ways to get started.

1. Don't just set up training programs – create a learning culture.
If companies today engage in training, they tend to do it at specific times (when onboarding new hires, for example), to prepare workers for particular jobs (like selling and servicing certain products), or when adopting new technologies. That worked well in an era when the pace of technological change was relatively slow. But advances are happening so quickly and with such complexity today that companies need to shift to a continuous-learning model – one that repeatedly enhances employees' skills and makes formal training broadly available. Firms also need to expand their portfolio of tactics beyond online and offline courses to include learning on the job through project staffing and team rotations. Such an approach can help companies rethink traditional entry-level barriers (among them, educational credentials) and draw from a wider talent pool.

Consider what happens at Expeditors, a *Fortune* 500 company that provides global logistics and freight-forwarding services in more than 100 countries. In vetting job candidates, Expeditors has long relied on a "hire for attitude, train for skill" approach. Educational degrees are appreciated but not seen as critical for success in most roles. Instead, for all positions, from the lowest level right up to the C-suite, the company focuses on temperament and cultural fit. Once on staff, employees join an intensive program in which every member of the organization, no matter how junior or senior, undertakes 52 hours of incremental learning a year. This practice supports the company's promote-from-within culture. Expeditors' efforts seem to be working: Turnover is low (which means substantial savings in hiring, training, and onboarding costs); retention is high (a third of the company's 17,000 employees have worked at the company for 10 years or more); most senior leaders in the company have risen through the ranks; and several current vice presidents and senior vice presidents, along with the current and former CEOs, got their jobs despite having no college degree.

2. Engage employees in the transition instead of herding them through it.
As companies transform themselves, they often find it a challenge to attract and retain the type of talent they need. To succeed, they have to offer employees pathways to professional and personal improvement – and must engage them in the process of change, rather than merely inform them that change is coming.

That's what ING Netherlands did in 2014, when it decided to reinvent itself. The bank's goal was ambitious: to turn itself into an agile institution almost overnight. The company's current CEO, Vincent van den Boogert, recalls that the company's leaders began by explaining the why and the what of the transformation to all employees. Mobile and digital technologies were dramatically altering the market, they told everybody, and if ING wanted to meet the expectations of customers, improve operations, and deploy new technological capabilities, it would have to become faster, leaner, and more flexible. To do that, they said, the company planned to make investments that would reduce costs and improve service. But it would also eliminate a significant number of jobs – at least a quarter of the total workforce.

Then came the how. Rather than letting the ax fall on select employees – a process that creates psychological trauma throughout a company – ING decided that almost everybody at the company, regardless of tenure or seniority, would be required to resign. After that, anybody who felt his or her attitude, capabilities, and skills would be a good fit at the "new" bank could apply to be rehired. That included Van den Boogert himself. Employees who did not get rehired would be supported by a program that would help them find jobs outside ING.

None of this made the company's transformation easy, of course. But according to Van den Boogert, the inclusive approach adopted by management significantly minimized the pain that employees felt during the transition, and it immediately set the new, smaller bank on the path to success. The employees who rejoined ING actively embraced its new mission, felt less survivor's remorse, and devoted themselves with excitement to the job of transformation. "When you talk about the *why*, *what*, and *how* at the same time," Van den Boogert told us, "people are going to challenge the *why* to prevent the *how*. But in this case, everyone had already been inspired by the *why* and *what*."

3. Look beyond the "spot market" for talent.

Most successful companies have adopted increasingly aggressive strategies for finding critical high-skilled talent. Now they must expand that approach to include a wider range of employees. AT&T recognized that need in 2013, while developing its Workforce 2020 strategy, which focused on how the company would make the transition from a hardware-centric to a software-centric network.

The company had undergone a major transformation once before, in 1917, when it launched plans to use mechanical switchboards rather than human operators. But it carried that transformation out over the course of five decades! The Workforce 2020 transformation was much more complex and had to happen on a much faster timeline.

To get started, AT&T undertook a systematic audit of its quarter of a million employees to catalog their current skills and compare those with the skills it expected to need during and after its revamp. Ultimately, the company identified 100,000 employees whose jobs were likely to disappear and several areas in which it would face skills and competency shortages. Armed with those insights, the company launched an ambitious, multiyear $1 billion initiative to develop an internal talent pipeline instead of simply playing the "spot market" for talent. In short, to meet its evolving needs, AT&T decided to make retraining available to its existing workforce. Since then, its employees have taken nearly 3 million online courses designed to help them acquire skills for new jobs in fields such as application development and cloud computing.

Already, this effort has yielded some unexpected benefits. The company now hires far fewer contractors to meet its needs for technical skills, for example. "We're shifting to employees," one of the company's top executives told CNBC this past March, "because we're starting to see the talent inside."

4. Collaborate to deepen the talent pool.

In a fast-evolving environment, competing for talent doesn't work. It simply leads to a tragedy of the commons. Individual companies try to grab the biggest share of the skilled labor available, and these self-interested attempts just end up creating a shortage for all.

To avoid that problem, companies will have to fundamentally change their outlook and work together to ensure that the talent pool is constantly refreshed and updated. That will mean teaming up with other companies in the same industry or region to identify relevant skills, invest in developing curricula, and provide on-the-job training. It will also require forging new relationships for developing talent by, for instance, engaging with entrepreneurs and technology developers, partnering with educational institutions, and collaborating with policy makers.

US utilities companies have already begun doing this. In 2006 they joined forces to establish the Center for Energy Workforce Development. The mission of the center, which has no physical office and is staffed primarily by former employees from member companies, is to figure out what jobs and skills the industry will need most as its older workers retire – and then how best to create a pipeline to meet those needs. "We're used to working together in this industry," Ann Randazzo, the center's executive director, told us. "When there's a storm, everybody gets in their trucks. Even if we compete in certain areas, including for workers, we've all got to work together to build this pipeline, or there just aren't going to be enough people."

The center quickly determined that three of the industry's most critical middle-skills jobs – linemen, field operators, and energy technicians – would be hit hard by the retirement of workers in the near future. Together, those three jobs make up almost 40% of a typical utility's workforce. To make sure they wouldn't go unfilled, CEWD implemented a two-pronged strategy. It created detailed tool kits, curricula, and training materials for all three jobs, which it made available free to utility companies; and it launched a grassroots movement to reach out to next-generation workers and promote careers in the industry.

CEWD believes in connecting with promising talent early – very early. To that end, it has been working with hundreds of elementary, middle, and high schools to create materials and programs that introduce students to the benefits of working in the industry. These include a sense of larger purpose (delivering critical services to customers); stability (no offshoring of jobs, little technological displacement); the use of automation and technology to make jobs less physically taxing and more intellectually engaging; and, last but not least, surprisingly high wages. Describing the program to us, Randazzo said, "You're *growing* a workforce. We had to start from scratch to get students in the lower grades to understand what they need to do and to really be able to grow that all the way through high school to community colleges and universities. And it's not a one-and-done. We have to continually nurture it."

5. Find ways to manage chronic uncertainty.
In today's world, managers know that if they don't swiftly identify and respond to shifts, their companies will be left behind. So how can firms best prepare?

The office furniture manufacturer Steelcase has come up with some intriguing ideas. One is its Strategic Workforce Architecture and Transformation (SWAT) team, which tracks emerging trends and conducts real-time experiments on how to respond to them. The team has launched an internal platform called Loop, for example, where employees can volunteer to work on projects outside their own functions. This benefits both the company and its employees: As new needs arise, the company can quickly locate workers within its ranks who have the motivation and skills to meet them, and workers can gain experience and develop new capabilities in ways that their current jobs simply don't allow.

Employees at Steelcase have embraced Loop, and its success illustrates an idea that came through very clearly in our survey results. As Jill Dark, the director of the SWAT team, put it to us, "If you give people the opportunity to learn something new or to show their craft, they will give you their best work. The magic is in providing the opportunity."

That's a lesson that all managers should heed.

✳✳✳✳✳✳✳✳✳✳✳✳✳✳✳✳✳✳✳✳✳✳✳✳✳✳✳✳✳✳✳

Internal Talent Mobility Programs Can Advance Gender Equity. Do Yours?

Nithya Vaduganathan, Colleen McDonald, and Gabrielle Novacek

Companies are facing a moment of reckoning in the workplace. They are struggling to find talent to advance their strategic priorities, and they are seeking to improve gender equity and open pathways for women to grow and develop. In the process, most are overlooking an asset that can help with both priorities: their internal talent mobility program (ITM).

But some companies are reinventing their ITM programs to go beyond the traditional ways of tapping in-house talent for promotions and evolving business priorities. This new generation of ITM programs is democratizing access to opportunity and helping employees chart their careers at a micro level – both of which have particular value for women.

Access and agency are important for women's retention and advancement. Recent studies by researchers at the Massachusetts Institute of Technology and New York University have found that lateral career opportunities are more than twice as effective as compensation in predicting employee retention. And while stretch assignments can be critical for career advancement, studies have found that women are less likely than men to report receiving those opportunities – even when they explicitly say they are interested in working on more challenging projects.

The new ITM programs are deeply embedded in talent operating models and career development processes. They are also designed to make the most of innovative HR technologies,[20] such as digital talent marketplaces. These programs are thus better equipped than their predecessors to normalize skills-based career mobility as part of the development journey for women.

The catch? Many business leaders haven't yet updated their ITM models. Once they do, they will be better equipped to provide equitable career-growth opportunities, which will help attract and retain diverse talent in today's increasingly dynamic environment.

---

20 https://www.bcg.com/publications/2022/billion-dollar-opportunity-in-hr-technology

Equal Access to Opportunity

Data gathered recently by BCG, in collaboration with the talent marketplace provider Gloat, confirms that the new ITM programs can increase assignments for women. Four attributes are key to success:

- **Making All Opportunities Visible to All.** Historically, many corporate opportunities have been allocated on the basis of "who you know, not what you know." But the new ITM programs help address gender inequities by encouraging or requiring opportunities to be posted publicly, making them visible to a broader slate of candidates and giving women an equal opportunity to apply. Publicly posted opportunities typically reveal a wide variety of pathways, including linear promotions, lateral job transfers (such as moving employees from customer service positions into sales roles), and special project assignments (such as setting up product launch teams) that draw employees from several functions.
- **Identifying Potential Matches on the Basis of Skills and Preferences.** To address gender inequities at the speed and scale of business today, ITM programs are increasingly using two-way talent marketplaces. Managers post opportunities on these marketplaces, which suggest potential matches to both posting managers and employees on the basis of employees' profiles. The platform can identify employees' skills given their work experience and training history. By suggesting good-fit possibilities, a talent marketplace can help encourage women to apply and expand the pool of potential candidates for managers seeking recruits. When such marketplaces are in place, data from Gloat suggests that women tend to apply for internal opportunities at an equal or higher rate than men – and are matched accordingly. In more traditional in-house labor markets, women, compared with men, participate at a disproportionately lower rate and are typically given fewer opportunities.
- **Explicitly Working to Mitigate Bias.** To reduce bias, talent marketplaces can hide bias-forming parameters, such as gender, in employee profiles. In addition, talent marketplaces can make personal qualities easier to track and report, making it easier to intervene and mitigate bias in hiring decisions. Seagate Technology has implemented such a talent marketplace. It suggests jobs to employees on the basis of their skills and aspirations. Characteristics such as location, age, gender, and ethnicity do not factor into the platform's suggestions, and it has mechanisms to mitigate the risk of bias in internal hiring. The new marketplace has led to a 58% increase in the participation and assignment of women to open internal positions.
- **Reducing the Risks Associated with Switching Jobs.** To increase the use of ITM programs, employees must be able to look for opportunities without first alerting their manager. This is important, especially for women. A recent

study of exiting employees found that women were less likely than men to ask about internal opportunities, perhaps because they fear repercussions or worry that their manager will pressure them to stay put. When companies configure their talent marketplaces to provide visibility into all opportunities, employees can browse open positions without those concerns.

In addition to advancing women's access to career opportunities, there are many other benefits to the new generation of ITM programs. For example: employee engagement and satisfaction tend to improve; companies can typically save money by reducing their reliance on external recruiting and contracting; and teams become more diverse, as employees are from a variety of backgrounds and ones that may be different from their team leader.

Because more than half of the matches in new ITM programs are across regions and functions, these programs also help break down organizational silos, enable better use of talent across a company, and offer individuals opportunities that they would not have in a model based on who employees know. Equally beneficial, managers can find talent in their company that they never would have encountered without these programs.

Companies are finding it easier to implement and support new ITM programs on a broader scale in part through their use of internal talent marketplaces (such as those provided by Eightfold AI, Fuel50, Gloat, and Hitch).

Embedding ITM Programs in Talent Models and Processes

Findings from BCG's demand-centric growth analysis of more than 3,000 US professional women[21] suggest that new ITM programs can play a role in increasing women's job satisfaction and retention levels. Our analysis looked at employees as if they were customers making decisions about their careers. Thus, it got to the root of the emotional and functional needs involved in making those decisions.

We found a strong correlation between the satisfaction of needs and key indicators of positive employment outcomes: happiness, motivation, and long-term retention. At an aggregate level, the top five drivers of positive employment outcomes have to do with emotional needs: feeling valued, supported, fairly treated, respected, and important. Comparatively, functional needs, such as compensation and benefits, were less determinative on decisions to stay or leave, although they

---

21 https://www.bcg.com/publications/2022/reinventing-gender-diversity-programs-for-a-post-pandemic-world

are table stakes and must, at a minimum, be competitive with other employment options.

Thoughtfully constructed ITM programs, deeply embedded in talent operating models and career development processes, will provide women with better growth opportunities and make the process of identifying them more seamless. This shift can change women's experience navigating their careers, so that they feel valued, supported, and respected in the process. In short, by normalizing career mobility and creating a programmatic approach, companies can give women more agency and strengthen their connections in moments of truth.

ITM programs can enable women to broaden their horizons, sample new experiences, develop new skills, and expand their networks. These programs can also help women accommodate changes in life circumstances, such as caregiving responsibilities, that may require more flexibility at times. Unlike many current mobility experiences for women that take the form of accommodations that inadvertently stall their advancement, more broad-based and skills-based ITM programs can aid career advancement and skill development.

Consider the hypothetical example of Claire, a rising leader in a company without a strong ITM program. She has led initiatives, has great performance reviews, and is on track for a promotion. But she's frustrated that she must exhaustively network to land opportunities to work on stretch projects. Though she'd like more flexibility after she returns from maternity leave, she's worried about creating the impression that she's getting special treatment.

Now, let's imagine an alternative: Claire works for a company with a strong ITM program. She was introduced to the concept of internal mobility when she joined. She knows women at all levels who have signed up for various mobility opportunities.

Claire's company encourages her to share her goals and aspirations broadly, so others can support her in identifying pathways that can help her realize them. In addition, in career conversations, her advisor regularly asks about her progress toward her goals. Such discussions are a standard part of the career-planning conversations that advisors have with employees at least once per quarter. Claire's advisor informs her about training opportunities to aid her transitions, and as she embarks on new assignments, her office invites her to share what she learns with others, just as others have shared their experiences with her.

When ITM programs are integrated with talent operating models, talent mobility options are typically discussed as part of career-planning sessions, and learning and development offerings are designed to support lateral career moves. By creating a foundation of job matching based on skills, ITM programs can also serve as a starting point for rethinking career paths and compensation approaches. And their success can potentially lead to a more strategic approach to diversity and inclusion.[22]

The consumer products company Unilever is an organization that has tried to get out in front on internal mobility. The company rolled out its talent marketplace to its global workforce from 2018 through 2019. The results so far have been promising. More than 80% of the roughly 65,000 eligible members of its online workforce have completed so-called rich profiles on the platform. During the first eight months of the pandemic, Unilever moved more than 9,000 employees into new jobs and unlocked close to 1 million hours of trapped work capacity. Most new assignments have been cross-functional and across countries, and more than 60% of those opportunities have been assigned to women.

Unilever has embedded talent mobility into its company-wide employee development practices. For example, employees participate in purpose workshops, where they share stories about hobbies, childhood passions, and their proudest moments. In the process, they identify the threads that tie their motivations together and point to their personal purpose. Each employee's purpose statement becomes the core of that person's career journey and is reflected in their Future Fit plan. These plans outline ambitions, skills that need development, and potential opportunities for learning, inside and outside the company. Unilever's ITM program then helps employees find ways to realize their aspirations.

✳✳✳

Given today's talent challenges and the uneven progress on women's advancement in the workforce, companies can no longer afford to overlook their ITM program. Companies can use it as a starting point to embed gender equity into their culture and people processes. With a full-scale ITM program in place, companies will be better equipped to manage talent in today's increasingly dynamic environment – and create a more equitable workplace in the process.

✳✳✳✳✳✳✳✳✳✳✳✳✳✳✳✳✳✳✳✳✳✳✳✳✳✳✳✳✳✳✳✳✳✳

---

22 https://www.bcg.com/capabilities/diversity-inclusion/gender-equality

Reinventing Gender Diversity Programs for a Post-Pandemic World

Gabrielle Novacek, Jean Lee, and Matt Krentz

US companies have serious work to do to heal the US female workforce that has been so badly fractured by the COVID-19 pandemic. And although it may be tempting to turn to traditional diversity, equity, and inclusion[23] (DEI) programs, those programs were not designed to address the current challenges.

DEI programs have long been the corporate "home" for strategically driving better outcomes for women. They tend to focus on eliminating discriminatory behaviors, achieving workplace equity, and increasing the representation of women in leadership positions. Complementary human resources policies and benefits have also aimed to level the playing field and nurture high-potential talent on the path to the executive suite.

These programs and policies are insufficient to solve the wide-scale attrition and hiring difficulties of the so-called great resignation. As the pandemic unfolded, the soaring demands of work and home strained women's roles as primary caregivers in most families. Even as of November 2021, women's participation in the workforce remained at a 33-year low. The great resignation forced a reckoning among all employees, not just mothers, and not just women. In November 2021, 4.5 million workers quit or changed jobs – the fourth time in 2021 that the number of workers quitting set a record.

As we look forward to a postpandemic workplace, strong signals suggest that workforce challenges will persist long term. Recent surveys have found that only 35% of working mothers say that they are planning to work as they did before the pandemic. More than half of female knowledge workers have said that they are open to looking for a new job in the next year. Armed with new-found clarity about priorities and values, many women have fundamentally altered their expectations of their work, employers, and lives.

Companies need to find new ways to address the breadth and magnitude of today's challenges. They need to understand women's motivations and how they make decisions about jobs and careers. Companies must also reach far more women across the organization and broaden their objectives and actions (see Figure 2.2). As the chief diversity officer of a financial services organization said, "We've been working diligently to put all of the best practices in place, but they aren't going to be enough to deal with what we're seeing now."

---

23 https://www.bcg.com/capabilities/diversity-inclusion/overview

	Before the pandemic	After the pandemic
Who	Focused workforce efforts mainly on high-potential talent	Focus on women across the organization to address the systemic talent risk in the post-pandemic world
What	Addressed bias and advanced the representation of women at senior levels	Create a motivating work environment for all women that prompts them to stay
How	Continuously improved benefits, training programs, and policies	Develop interventions that address the needs of women and influence their job decisions

Sources: BCG's US Workforce Survey, 2021; BCG analysis.

Figure 2.2: To Address New Workforce Challenges, Companies Must Rest Their Focus, Objectives, and Actions.

Reinventing the Foundation for DEI

DEI programs have made progress in reaching their original goals, but they need to be far bolder and more ambitious to address the new mandate of the post-COVID-19 environment. In seeking to understand how to advance these programs, we surveyed 3,345 US female employees and 4,019 US male workers, and we started with five hypotheses:

- Employees have agency, as they are demonstrating vividly today. Companies need to understand and address the underlying causes of employees' departures and discontentment.
- Employees will make career decisions that satisfy both their functional needs (such as work-life balance and compensation), as well as their emotional needs (such as feeling challenged, secure, or valued at work).
- A broad set of drivers – demographic identities, life context, work context, and attitudes – can all potentially be important in influencing needs. An employee's diverse demographic identities may not be the most important or even a significant driver of needs. And needs will almost certainly change over time.
- By identifying patterns in combinations of needs and isolating the drivers of needs, we can unlock a new segmentation of the workforce that is grounded in commonality and relevancy, rather than outside-in assumptions or essentialism.
- This needs-based segmentation can serve as the foundation to create employee value propositions that improve employees' happiness, create a motivating work environment, encourage them to stay, and, ultimately, boost employee outcomes.

In testing these hypotheses, we drew inspiration from BCG's state-of-the-art consumer research methodology: demand-centric growth.[24] The DCG methodology breaks away from the simple, insufficient consumer-segmentation approach that uses broad demographic groups (such as millennials, women, and Asians). Instead, DCG uses a comprehensive segmentation approach that factors in additional drivers (such as attitudes) that emerge from quantitative research and are examined using advanced analytics. By understanding individuals' needs, DCG uncovers what truly drives decision making in different circumstances.

We adapted the survey-based DCG methodology to understand the workplace needs of our representative sample.[25] Applied to an organizational context, the DCG approach allowed us to assess the importance and interplay of a comprehensive menu of potential demographic, attitudinal, and contextual drivers in creating discrete patterns of functional and emotional needs (see Figure 2.3). And because the methodology recognizes human complexity, we were able to determine that not all dimensions that shape an employee's identity, beliefs, and life situation are equally important in driving the person's functional and emotional needs at work.

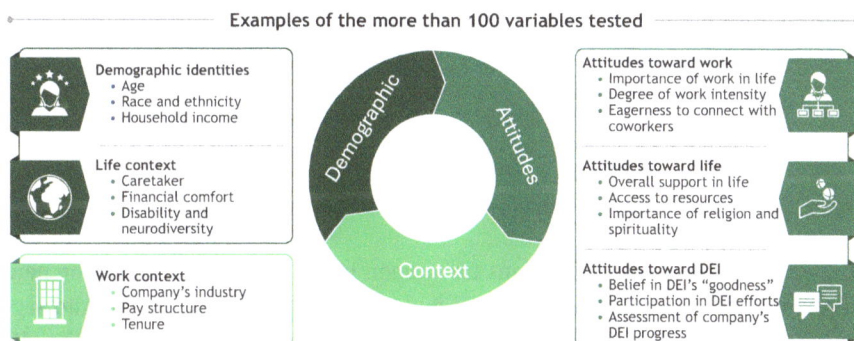

Examples of the more than 100 variables tested

Demographic identities
- Age
- Race and ethnicity
- Household income

Life context
- Caretaker
- Financial comfort
- Disability and neurodiversity

Work context
- Company's industry
- Pay structure
- Tenure

Attitudes toward work
- Importance of work in life
- Degree of work intensity
- Eagerness to connect with coworkers

Attitudes toward life
- Overall support in life
- Access to resources
- Importance of religion and spirituality

Attitudes toward DEI
- Belief in DEI's "goodness"
- Participation in DEI efforts
- Assessment of company's DEI progress

Source: BCG's US Workforce Survey, 2021; BCG analysis
Note: DEI = diversity, equity, and inclusion.

Figure 2.3: A Broad Set of Drivers Influence Workplace Needs.

24 https://www.bcg.com/capabilities/customer-insights/customer-demand
25 The survey consisted of 8,805 full-time female and male workers in nongovernment, for-profit companies with 500 or more employees. The sample was balanced at the population level for representation, with key demographics balanced to within 3% of US labor statistics. A subset of 1,433 respondents were oversampled to ensure sufficient representation for Black and LGBTQ+ workers, and 8 participants identified as other, rather than women or men.

We then delved further into human motivation and behavior by establishing the relative importance of more than 20 potential functional and emotional needs in decision making (see Figure 2.4). We conducted a series of statistical tournaments in which participants were asked to make a series of tradeoffs. For example, would they rather connect with coworkers or have better benefits, and would they rather have better benefits or feel valued and appreciated. This technique uncovered the real drivers of choice that can be impossible for employees to determine and articulate directly.

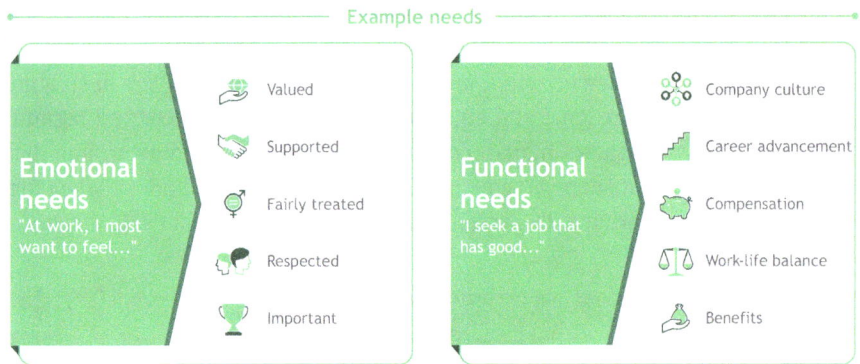

Sources: BCG's US Workforce Survey, 2021; BCG analysis.

Figure 2.4: Our Research Assesses the Importance of Both Emotional and Functional Needs.

The analysis has three implications for women in the workforce.[26] First, the new segmentation enables companies to de-average their female population into segments that are grounded in what women revealed as the real reasons for the differences among them. Second, by surfacing both the functional and emotional needs that affect decision making, companies can tap into the broader set of issues that underlie the great resignation of women – issues that are much harder to articulate than a desire for more money or other functional benefits. And third, as organizations wage the indefinite battle between aspirations and resources, they can balance nuance with executional pragmatism, target the needs that matter most, and build programs that will be more successful at attracting, retaining, and advancing women. (For a summary of the insights that we derived from this analysis, see "Six Quick Takeaways.")

∗∗∗

---

26 https://www.bcg.com/capabilities/diversity-inclusion/gender-equality

Six Quick Takeaways

Our approach to DEI is fundamentally different from what companies have done in the past.

Addressing needs matters. There is a strong statistical correlation between satisfying women's needs and improving leading indicators of positive employee outcomes, specifically, happiness, motivation, and retention.

Emotional needs matter more. Although more difficult for women to articulate than functional needs, emotional needs correlate more strongly with leading indicators of positive employee outcomes.

One size does not fit all. While a core set of mostly functional needs are generally shared among women, their emotional needs are diverse. A nuanced approach to segmentation is needed.

Needs are not static. The primary variables that drive diverse needs are dynamic in nature; the needs for any individual will shift over time.

Intersectional identities other than race generally are not discrete drivers of needs. Most traditional intersectional identities do not drive unique needs but rather affect women's abilities to fulfill the needs that they share with others.

The programs that companies have aren't the ones they need. The traditional DEI focus on eliminating discrimination, improving equity, and increasing the representation of women in leadership won't alone deliver what is needed today. To address the great resignation, companies need programs that influence the work and career choices of many, not just a select few.

***

Addressing Needs, Especially Emotional Ones, Matters

Our research suggests that a needs-based DEI strategy has the potential to significantly improve outcomes for women. Across our survey population, we found a strong statistical correlation between the satisfaction of needs and the key indicators of positive employee outcomes: happiness (R-squared of 80%), motivation (R-squared of 50%), and long-term retention (R-squared of 50%) (see Figure 2.5). In other words, the more likely female employees were to say that their most important needs, especially emotional ones, were being met, the more likely they were to be happy and motivated at work and to stay in their jobs. Among women who expressed the strongest satisfaction of needs, they were 15 percentage points (pp) more likely to say they were very happy than the average respondent, 33 pp more likely to say they were highly motivated, and 9 pp more likely to say that they would definitely be at their company in three years. Stated simply, by focusing on

Sources: BCG's US Workforce Survey, 2021; BCG analysis.

Figure 2.5: Satisfying Needs Strongly Correlates with Improved Employee Happiness, Motivation, and Retention.

satisfying women's needs, companies have significant potential to influence their decision making and drive positive employee outcomes.

A great deal of DEI work is unsurprisingly focused on addressing women's functional needs – including compensation, benefits, and work-life balance. In a world in which pay and caretaking responsibilities remain unequal, this is to be expected. Satisfying functional needs is also easier to do and measure, and women often rank these needs as most important. But our analysis shows that the fulfillment of emotional needs – such as feeling valued, supported, and respected – correlates more strongly with women's happiness at work and in shaping positive employee outcomes. In other words, money can't buy happiness (see Figure 2.6).

Importance of needs[1]

Need	Rank
	1
	12
	7
	5
	15
	21
	14
	16
	9
	10
	8
	19
	3
	17
	13
	18
	2
	6
	22
	11
	23
	20
	4

The needs that women often rank as most important, including compensation and benefits, are typically not the biggest drivers of happiness

Correlation of satisfied needs with women's overall happiness

Values	63
Supported	60
Fairly Treated	59
Respected	58
Important	57
Company Culture	52
Career Advancement	51
Impactful	50
Secure	49
Content of work	48
Control	47
Company performance	47
Compensation	46
Able to be myself	46
Challenged	45
Quality of talent	45
Work-life balance	42
Competent	41
Work space	39
Flexibility	38
Being among people like me	37
Connections	37
Benefits	32

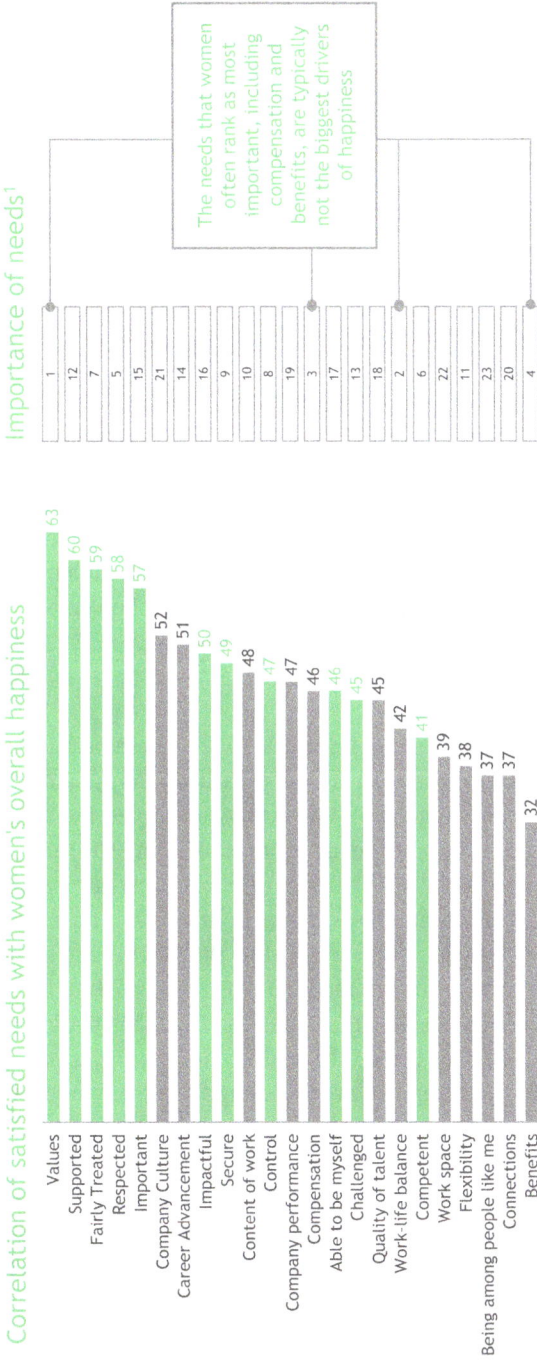

Sources: BCG's US Workforce Survey, 2021; BCG analysis.
Note: n = 3,345 full-time working women.
[1]Average MaxDiff scores.

Figure 2.6: Emotional Needs Are Harder to Articulate, but They Correlate More Strongly with Women's Happiness.

One Size Does Not Fit All When Needs Are Diverse and Dynamic

The systemic challenges of pay equity, leadership representation, and day-to-day discriminatory experiences demand ongoing focus. But companies must do more. They must ask whether today's approaches and interventions are tapping into the diverse sets of needs that influence outcomes across the women in their workforce. (See "Looking Beyond the Woman Label.")

∗∗∗

Looking Beyond the Woman Label
Tanya is a Black woman who was recently hired out of a top college by a prestigious investment bank. "I'm incredibly ambitious – I'm the first person in my family to go to college, and this is my chance to change things for my whole family," she said. "But I didn't grow up rich. A senior recently made fun of my [urban] accent. It is just so hard to fit in."

Barbara, a middle-aged white woman, works as a financial analyst at a major industrial goods manufacturer. "What am I going to do with a workshop on building my executive presence? My family depends on my salary and my health insurance. How about instead helping me not worry that I was going to get laid off during the pandemic."

Julie is a relatively junior executive on the fast track. "I came here because of the program for emerging leaders. I'm barely out of business school, and I'm already working on an initiative that is one of our CEO's top strategic priorities. I've got a very clear goal to be the chief marketing officer of a major corporation," she said.

Finally, Sara, a senior executive in the health care industry, was recently named to lead a large corporate function after a career in line roles. "I couldn't be more thrilled. Some of my colleagues were surprised by the move. They interpreted it as a step back in my career. But I'm ready to put in the work to learn something new, and it's a part of the business that could really use the dedicated energy of somebody who is excited to be there," she said.

The experiences of these four women (we are not using their real names) illustrate the wide variety of contexts and needs that women bring to the workplace – and the limitations of current DEI programs. Most DEI programs are designed to drive greater representation of women in leadership and are aimed at the Julies of the workforce – young, ambitious, and on the fast track. For the Tanyas, Barbaras, and Saras – the vast majority of working women – these programs are much less accessible and effective.

∗∗∗

Therefore, reshaping DEI programs so that they drive different outcomes depends on de-averaging female workers into segments. A one-size-fits-all approach will be insufficient. This is especially true because needs are dynamic, changing over the course of a woman's life and career.

So, what factors lead to the most significant differences in needs among women?

Age and Seniority. Our research found that age and relative seniority drive the most significant differences in needs among women. Put simply, 25-year-old women are likely to have different needs from 50-year-old women, just as junior staff are likely to have different needs from senior executives. In other words, the trajectory of a woman's life and career is central in shaping a woman's workplace needs.

While these findings may seem intuitive, few DEI programs recognize and support this evolution of needs as women move through the stages of life. As the chief human resources officer of a consumer packaged goods company said, "We focus a great deal on young high-potential employees, but rarely do we think about how we should be supporting the older employee in a nonmanagement role, or even our most senior executive women once they've made it to the top."

The Importance of Work in a Woman's Life. Is work a day job or a mission? Is a profession a central part of a woman's identity, or is receiving a paycheck most critical? Answers to these questions can influence the tradeoffs that a woman is willing to make for a job, for public signals of success (such as a company's reputation), and for the content of the work. As with age and seniority, these answers can change over time.

Motherhood. Motherhood naturally surfaces important differences in needs between women with and without children at home. Many DEI programs address motherhood but often stop short of recognizing the changing needs of older women. With more free time, senior empty nesters are often eager to find new purpose and experiences at work, yet traditional DEI programs emphasize the needs of younger women and generally do not provide ongoing support.

Salaried Versus Hourly. How women are paid and, often by extension, their economic position within the company are the fifth variable. Current DEI efforts rarely address the needs of women who are hourly and frontline workers – needs that are very different from those of women who are emerging leaders. The desire for safety and security has been especially acute among hourly female employees during the pandemic, as it ravaged key sectors of the US economy – such as retail, service, and travel – that are heavily represented by women. Some women were forced to work when the virus was widespread and unchecked, while others found that their economic security was suddenly at risk.

Race. The one intrinsic variable that drove significant differences in needs among younger women is race, reflecting the broader challenges of achieving gender and racial equity[27] in the US. In general, all women place outsized emphasis on fair treatment. Additionally, younger women of color disproportionately seek the opportunity to get ahead but are skeptical that they have an equal chance to succeed. This intersectional cohort clearly has discrete needs and deserves focus. (See "The Role of Intersectionality.")

✳✳✳

The Role of Intersectionality

Many factors that may seem to be important in influencing discrete needs turn out not to be as critical as age, seniority, and the other four major drivers. For example, women in different industries and in different types of companies (such as startups and incumbents) within the same industry expressed similar functional and emotional needs.

Perhaps most notably, a set of common intersectional identities, such as LGBTQ+ and having a disability, also did not emerge in aggregate as primary determinants in driving the needs of women in the workforce. These identities, of course, matter, and many organizations are working to increase their representation in the workforce, but our analysis suggests that other factors are often more important in shaping needs for these individuals.

This may explain why women-specific LGBTQ+ programs, for example, successfully serve a general purpose of affiliation or advocacy, but they often struggle to maintain the long-term engagement of these employees. In the words of a young manager in the tech industry, "At this point in my career, I'm well past the point of it being worth my time to talk about how to come out as a lesbian at work. Help me figure out how I'm going to keep my career on track when I become a mom later this year."

The variation in the needs of LGBTQ+ women are too great to be treated as if they are similar. It makes more sense to address the basic experiences shared by LGBTQ+ women, but then to serve these groups within the broader framework of the needs that they share with others.

Individuals with intersectional identities often do experience different barriers in realizing important needs. For example, a woman who grew up in a different socioeconomic environment than her peers did may find it more difficult to realize a need to connect with colleagues. Groups of intersectional women may also confront increased incidences of unconscious bias or discriminatory behavior.

✳✳✳

---

27 https://www.bcg.com/capabilities/diversity-inclusion/racial-equity

A New Needs-Based Segmentation

Collectively, the most significant factors generate 11 key segments of women (see Figure 2.7). Each segment is based on a hierarchy of needs unique to the individuals who populate it. Since we determined this needs-based segmentation by conducting a broad survey of women in the US workforce, it describes patterns and archetypes in the general working population and yields valuable universal insights. Contrasting the needs of women in two demographic groups helps to demonstrate why companies need this new segmentation.

Younger, Junior Women. This broad grouping of women occupying non-leadership roles breaks down into four distinct segments based on the women's needs. It's instructive to look at two segments in particular (see Figure 2.8).

The first segment (striving racial minorities) comprises women of color who see work as important, but it does not define their lives. Their differentiating needs are more functional than emotional. Relative to their go-getter counterparts, they care disproportionately about compensation, benefits, and fair treatment. Work may not be central to their identity – it's not what they lead with at a party of strangers – yet they want to advance in their careers, often articulated as a desire to go beyond the world in which they grew up. They give poor scores to their company's DEI efforts and are skeptical that they have an equal chance to succeed. These women also reported among the lowest levels of happiness and motivation at work as well as likelihood of staying at their company.

These findings suggest that racial equity initiatives established in the wake of George Floyd's murder are not working as intended. "We were under a lot of pressure from our board to make public statements, but as a black woman, I can tell you that all the statements and book clubs in the world don't change the fact that our younger employees look up and see that there aren't many people that look like me at my level," said the chief diversity officer of a major retailer. "We have a lot of work to do to fix some fundamental problems in how we recognize and support people of color moving up through the organization."

By contrast, younger go-getters are more likely to value feeling important, successful, competent, and confident and having the opportunity to do work that they care about. This group, which includes both white women and women of color, unsurprisingly reports higher overall sentiment than most other segments. Most current DEI programs, which have been designed to drive greater representation of women in leadership, often address the needs of the go-getters through access to executive leaders and mentors, coaching and development programs, and the opportunity to take on high-profile assignments. These programs work specifically because they are directly targeting the most important needs of these women.

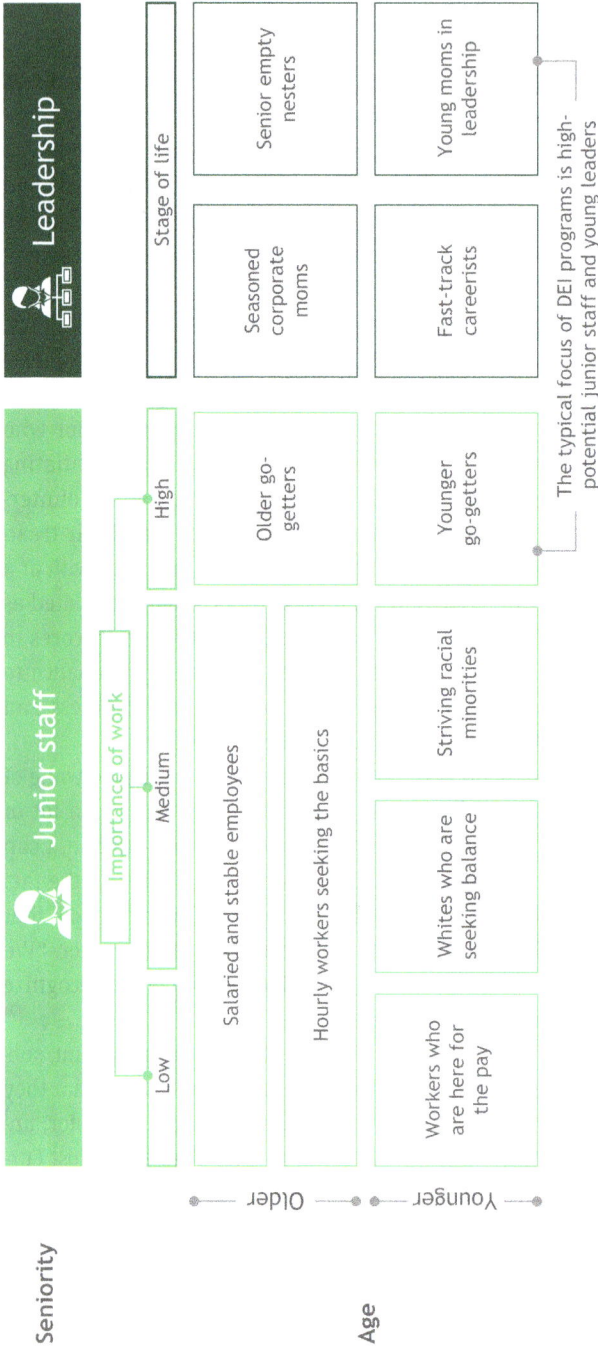

Figure 2.7: Eleven Segments Emerge from an Analysis of the Needs of the Female Workforce.

Sources: BCG's US Workforce Survey, 2021; BCG analysis.
Note: DEI = diversity, equity, and inclusion.

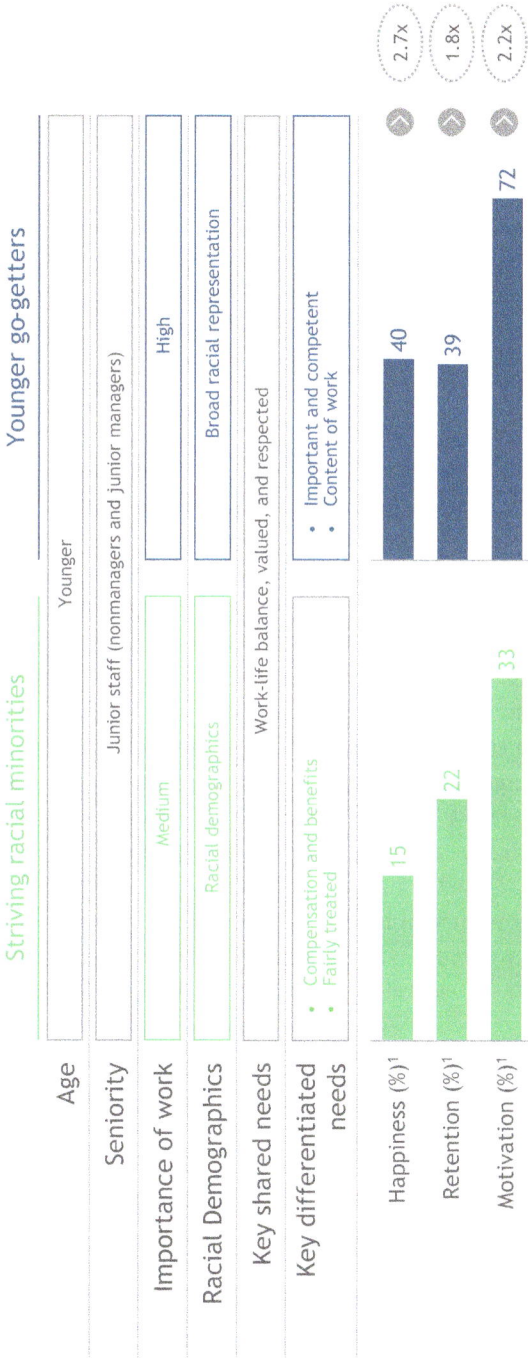

	Striving racial minorities	Younger go-getters
Age		Younger
Seniority	Junior staff (nonmanagers and junior managers)	
Importance of work	Medium	High
Racial Demographics	Racial demographics	Broad racial representation
Key shared needs	Work-life balance, valued, and respected	
Key differentiated needs	• Compensation and benefits • Fairly treated	• Important and competent • Content of work

| | | 2.7x | 1.8x | 2.2x |

	Striving racial minorities	Younger go-getters
Happiness (%)[1]	15	40
Retention (%)[1]	22	39
Motivation (%)[1]	33	72

Sources: BCG's US Workforce Survey, 2021; BCG analysis.

Note: n = 207 striving racial minorities; n = 247 younger go-getters.

[1]Percentage of the sample responding that they are very happy, they will definitely still be at the company in three years, and they are very motivated, respectively; the participants responded on a scale of one to five.

Figure 2.8: A Comparison of Two Segments of the Younger, Junior Staff.

Older Women. This broad grouping of women, covering frontline workers to CEOs, breaks into five segments using the new approach. Two segments vividly show the contrast in needs of women of similar ages: senior women in leadership who no longer have children at home (senior empty nesters) and junior older women in salaried positions (salaried and stable employees) working in nonmanagerial roles such as analysts and administrative assistants (see Figure 2.9).

Senior women in leadership demonstrate a significant shift in needs as their children leave home. These women want to focus their time and energy on work that delivers impact. For many, the chance to write a third act of their careers energizes them as they seek new knowledge and challenges at work.

A great many of today's DEI initiatives targeting senior women in leadership focus on networking opportunities or leveraging them as mentors for younger go-getters. This role does not go over well. Only 21% indicate that they personally benefit from their company's gender programs, and only 31% believe that leadership is held accountable for their company's DEI outcomes. Older women do not want to carry the load of solving their company's challenges.

Although the needs of less-senior older women are different, they also often go unrecognized and unresolved. The cohort grades their company's DEI efforts poorly – just 8% indicate that they benefit from their company's gender programs, and they have the lowest participation in these programs across all women, potentially in part due to a lack of relevance or even eligibility.

Not surprisingly, these women care more about the functional basics – pay, benefits, work-life balance, flexibility, and control – than do executive women at a similar life stage. They also want to feel secure and fairly treated, and they want to feel valued. An administrative assistant from a professional services firm said, "Over the last month, I've worked around the clock to support my manager and his team on a major deal. I went well beyond what's expected of me in my job, spending my evenings and weekends with my computer in my lap. But then when the team had a big dinner to celebrate the deal closing, I wasn't invited. I felt completely invisible."

Applying This Methodology in the Real World. In order to be actionable for individual organizations, more targeted research must be done to determine where and how best to subdivide segments. Furthermore, there is a pragmatic tradeoff in terms of how deeply to subdivide segments; while each additional segmentation may bring further granularity, DCG methodology is designed such that those nuances are increasingly less significant in shaping outcomes and thus less likely to be worth the added implementation complexity. Each company will have its own unique answers to these questions.

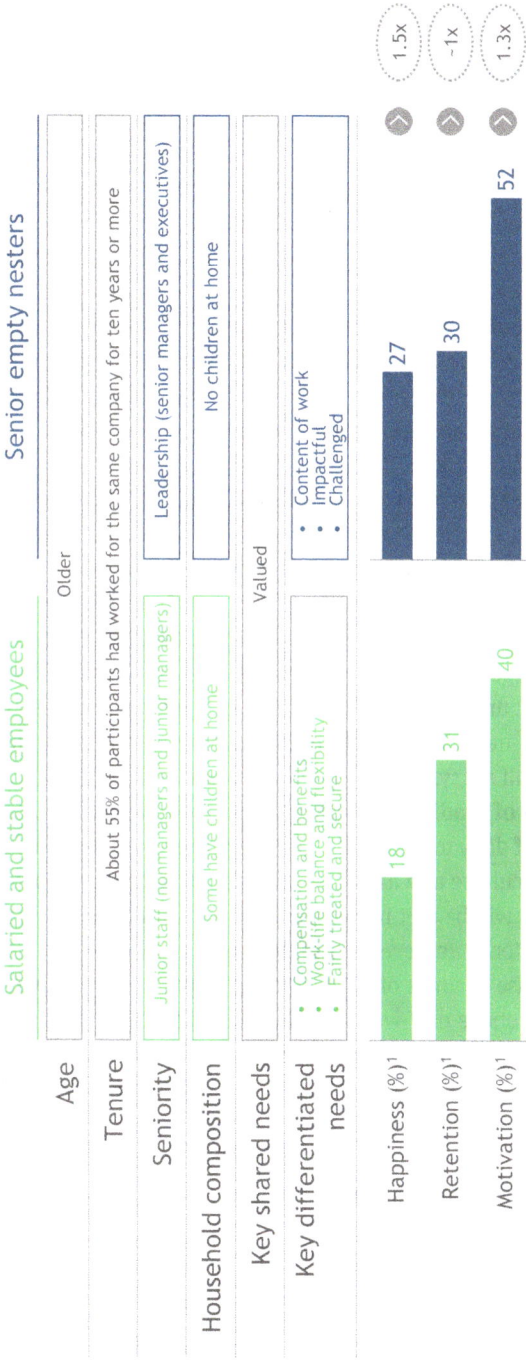

	Salaried and stable employees	Senior empty nesters
Age		Older
Tenure	About 55% of participants had worked for the same company for ten years or more	
Seniority	Junior staff (nonmanagers and junior managers)	Leadership (senior managers and executives)
Household composition	Some have children at home	No children at home
Key shared needs		Valued
Key differentiated needs	• Compensation and benefits • Work-life balance and flexibility • Fairly treated and secure	• Content of work • Impactful • Challenged

Bar values:
Happiness (%)[1]: 18 / 27 — 1.5x
Retention (%)[1]: 31 / 30 — ~1x
Motivation (%)[1]: 40 / 52 — 1.3x

Sources: BCG's US Workforce Survey, 2021; BCG analysis.
Note: n = 524 salaried and stable employees; n = 143 senior empty nesters.
[1]Percentage of the sample that responded they are very happy, they will definitely still be at the company in three years, and they are very motivated, respectively; the participants responded on a scale of one to five.

Figure 2.9: A Comparison of Two Segments of Older Staff.

A New Approach to DEI

The great resignation provides companies with a crisis too valuable to waste. The systemic talent risk across industries is large and lingering. We need to find ways to motivate women and encourage them to stay. Companies cannot continue doing what they are doing because their DEI programs were not designed to serve this purpose. Instead, companies need to take steps toward a new DEI approach that tackles the bigger talent challenge – giving women what they are currently missing at work.

– **Customize the needs-based segmentation.** Companies need to analyze their own workforce to understand which segments apply to their female employees. Companies also need to determine if different segments or subsegments are needed, identify any gaps relative to key needs, and determine the starting points for addressing them.

– **Broaden core DEI offerings so they satisfy functional and emotional needs.** Traditional solutions – such as expanding benefits, providing training programs, implementing codes of conduct, and adopting policies – must also address emotional needs. For example, a part-time option that provides the functional needs of flexibility and work-life balance may not serve a woman's emotional needs if the company does not respect her off-hours or if it does not provide meaningful, secure, long-term career options for part-timers. In other words, organizations need to understand how women experience the solutions to ensure that a full ecosystem of support maximizes their efficacy.

– **Expand beyond the scope of traditional DEI.** A woman's workplace experience is shaped by millions of daily touch points, grounded in a company's invisible yet powerful corporate culture and amplified through its leadership model. A woman's emotional needs will be met in myriad ways – through interactions with a supervisor, the milestones and events that the company chooses to celebrate, the company's response in times of crisis, and the opportunities employees have to excel. Factors outside of a woman's diverse demographic identity influence these experiences. As such, truly addressing emotional needs will require stepping outside the boundaries of what has historically been considered DEI and focusing on the broader employee value proposition.

This powerful approach can solve underlying emotional needs, unlock happiness and motivation, and improve retention – and not just for women. It also has the potential to be applied to the male workforce as well. (See "What About Men?")

***

What About Men?

How different is a segmentation of the male workforce? Without diving too deeply into the needs of men, and recognizing the limitations of broad generalizations, several grounding insights are worth mentioning.

As with women, age and seniority are the two most important drivers generating diverse needs in the male workforce in the US. The importance of work in life and the stage of life are also important drivers of men's needs, just as they are of women's needs.

Upon closer inspection, however, important differences emerge. First, race does not drive differences in workplace needs among younger, junior men to the same degree that it does for their female counterparts. But while white men and men of color share a common set of fundamental needs, the barriers to fulfilling those needs can be profoundly different.

Second, unlike for women, having a disability influences the needs of younger men in leadership roles. Our hypothesis is that a strong presence remains important to career and leadership success for men, as described extensively by other researchers.

Beyond these two key differences, the importance of some needs looks different across genders, on average, even when the drivers that generate a discrete segment are the same. For example, women generally place more importance on wanting to feel valued and appreciated, respected, and fairly treated. Among functional needs, work-life balance (likely a reflection of their traditional role as

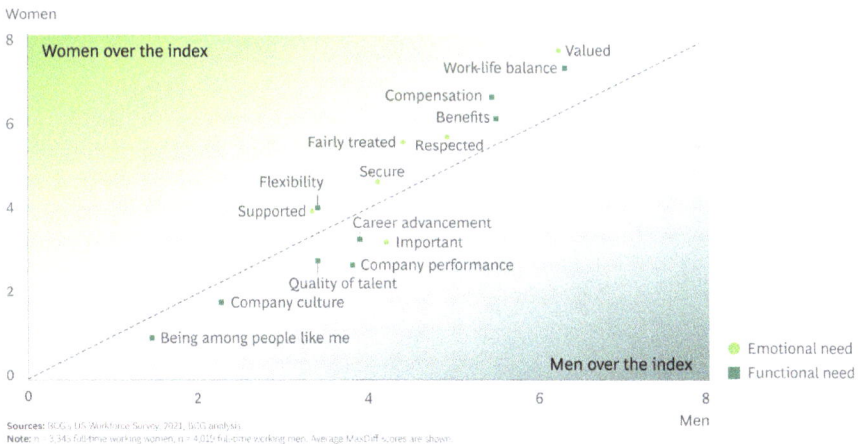

Figure 2.10: Some Notable Differences Emerged Between Women and Men, on Average.

caregiver) and compensation (likely owing to the legacy of the gender pay gap) stand out for women. Meanwhile, on an emotional level, men value feeling important and successful more than women do. Men also place a higher value on the company's performance as a functional need, reflecting the larger proportion of men in leadership roles (see Figure 2.10).

Recognizing these differences is critical, especially in companies where a gender imbalance persists at the leadership level. What may be resonant, motivating, and meaningful for male leaders and managers may not be so for their female counterparts or direct reports.

$$***$$

Though our findings may seemingly complicate efforts to improve gender diversity, they chart a powerful path for companies seeking to support women in a way that stretches beyond the boundaries of traditional DEI functions. By de-averaging women into segments that are grounded in the real drivers of needs, organizations can begin to reinvent their DEI efforts to improve happiness, motivation, and retention for far more women than is done today.

By recognizing the limits of money, flexibility, and other functional benefits as organizational glue that retains women, companies can start to develop more meaningful interventions, programs, and employee value propositions and make a difference in the work lives of many more women. And in doing so, they will start to humanize the work experience and work itself.

Chapter 3
Embracing New Models of Work

Does Your Hybrid Strategy Need to Change?

Deborah Lovich and Rosie Sargeant

Companies continue to struggle to design and implement a post-COVID return-to-office strategy that works for employees. To find the most workable alternative, they should focus on four factors: the needs of the work, the needs of the people, how work gets done, and the new managerial muscle required to manage a hybrid workforce.

This fall, companies are once again pushing workers to return[1] to the office, continuing the debate over how many days employees should work together in person.

This debate continues to miss the point.

One-size-fits-all mandates can succeed only if work is a universal task executed by a homogenous workforce. Of course, we know neither is true. Instead of threatening[2] employees, CEOs should empower and enable their managers – especially those on the front line – to gain a deep and nuanced understanding of the work their teams do, the working style of their team members, and how that work best gets done. They must also consider the impact of generative AI, which will change all of these factors.

Our research, experience working with company leaders, and surveys of workers around the world show how considering these factors can lead to better outcomes for everyone.

Companies Are at a Crossroads

We can empathize with CEOs. Leaders must justify office rents despite record-low occupancy levels and build a culture of collaboration in a place with empty halls.

---

1 https://www.wsj.com/articles/zoom-other-remote-work-champions-call-employees-back-to-the-office-e5a78c2d
2 https://edition.cnn.com/2023/08/29/business/amazon-jobs-return-to-office/index.html

---

https://doi.org/10.1515/9783111369921-004

They are grappling with quiet quitting,[3] quiet cutting,[4] pressure from city governments to restore the vibrance of business districts, and the impact of generative AI.

But the answer to these pressures is not return-to-office mandates that essentially use face time as a performance management tool – think badge-swipe monitoring, which has elicited notable backlash.[5] Monitoring the time employees spend online doesn't work, either. A recent survey of 18,149 desk workers and executives conducted by Slack[6] revealed that 32% of employees' time is spent on performative work, and 63% try to keep their status active online even if they're not working at that moment.

The inclination to associate physical presence or time active online with productivity is a symptom of a broader issue, as many of today's leaders struggle to embrace ways of working that are radically different from how they grew up. They proved themselves in a culture where commuting to the office to work from 9 to 5 was the norm, and where anyone who tried to work flexibly was marginalized – such as those on the "mommy track."[7]

The most successful organizations will recognize that there is too much complexity to set rigid, top-down mandates, and that the managers who are at the rock face of the work, the team, and the customers are best positioned to make such decisions when they are empowered with the right skills and tools.

CEOs and executive teams who focus on the following four actions can make work *work better* for everyone.

---

3 https://hbr.org/2022/09/when-quiet-quitting-is-worse-than-the-real-thing

4 https://www.wsj.com/lifestyle/careers/youve-heard-of-quiet-quitting-now-companies-are-quiet-cutting-ba2c326d

5 https://www.cnbc.com/2023/06/13/google-rto-crackdown-gets-backlash-check-my-work-not-my-badge.html

6 https://slack.com/intl/en-gb/blog/news/state-of-work-2023

7 https://www.themuse.com/advice/mommy-track-what-to-do

Recognize the Needs of the Work

When we asked more than 1,500 office-based workers[8] when they wanted to be in person, we learned that they want to come to the office to do tasks and activities they consider best done there. For instance, participants were eight times more likely to prefer being in-person for affiliation and development, compared with doing work that requires focus or tackling administrative tasks, which are better done remotely.

But where employees feel most effective doing certain types of work is only one side of the coin. We also explored how much time they spend doing these tasks. We found that individual contributors spend 37% of their time on work they believe is done most effectively in person; for managers and executives, this jumps to 49%. But this is on average across organizations. It is important for leaders to spend time investigating what those preferences look like based on the nature of work and people across their organization.

It becomes even more critical to recognize which types of work are best done in different settings in the age of generative AI. When doing focus work, our survey data suggests that 65% of employees want to be remote – but some of this work can be greatly enhanced with the use of generative AI. A field experiment that our BCG colleagues conducted[9] with the support of a group of academics from HBS, MIT, Wharton, and the University of Warwick found that for tasks that involve creative ideation, GenAI generates output that should be considered as a final draft (versus a first draft that humans need to take time to edit). This means that for some employees, the mix of work that they do may start to shift, as they hand over some of the focus work they would have preferred to do remotely and pick up other tasks beyond the frontier of generative AI's competence. As a result, their work models may also need to shift, depending on what these new tasks are.

Recognize the Needs of the People

In our survey, roughly 90% of employees who identify as female, caregivers, LGBTQ+, or as having a disability consider flexible work options an important factor when deciding whether to stay in or leave their job. That is 30% higher than employees who did not identify with these categories. In other words: If you care about diversity, equity, and inclusion, you need to get your working model right.

---

8 https://www.bcg.com/publications/2023/flexible-working-models
9 https://www.bcg.com/publications/2023/how-people-create-and-destroy-value-with-gen-ai

We saw a particularly wide gap when it comes to gender: Female employees are 1.5 times more likely than their male counterparts to prioritize flexibility. And this is not just a working-mom phenomenon. We found only a marginal difference (3%) among women when comparing caregivers with noncaregivers.

Our biological cognitive differences also indicate preferences toward certain work environments. In some situations, groups of people doing the same job may have similar cognitive profiles. For example, a team of software engineers is more likely to be "analytical/tough-minded"[10] and therefore might work best when allowed to maintain focus and prefer to have routines in how they do their day-to-day work.

But teams with high cognitive diversity will need more options to maintain optimum performance and happiness. We found outliers in our survey, for example – those who prefer to do interactive work remotely, and administrative or focus work in person. Some of their preferences are likely linked to cognitive characteristics such as introversion/extraversion.

Leaders struggling with how to think about getting the best out of employees with different cognitive profiles would do well to remember that your people are just as diverse as your customers.[11] Just as successful companies obsess about their customers and the decisions they make, it may be even more important for them to obsess about their employees. By doing so, they can reveal the root of the emotional and functional needs involved in making decisions about their careers – and create work environments that fulfill these needs.

Rethink How Work Gets Done

"Place" is just another tool for getting work done. As HBS professor Tsedal Neeley has observed,[12] "I talk about using the office as a tool, the same way we use various technologies as tools to communicate and engage. If you see the office as a tool, you determine what specific uses it has for collaborations that require people to be physically present together."

Yet 62% of our survey respondents told us that they do not have a say in their work model policy. Instead, it is dictated either by company-wide guidelines or by their manager. Of all participants, 39% reported that their company decides

---

10 https://www.frontiersin.org/articles/10.3389/fpsyg.2015.01098/full
11 https://www.forbes.com/sites/deborahlovich/2022/03/02/its-past-time-to-treat-all-employees-like-customers/?sh=4e65e14126ff
12 https://www.bcg.com/publications/2023/stop-tracking-employee-attendance-start-trusting-people

where they work. In these companies, 24% of employees were unhappy with their work location policy; this figure decreases to 14% if the manager decides, and to 6% if the team decides. The closer to the executors of the work the policy gets set, the more satisfied employees are.

Companies like Cisco[13] and Dropbox[14] are redesigning their office space to make it more amenable to collaboration. Such moves are consistent with their respective work model policies, which enable employees to do focus work remotely and encourage employees to come together for key events such as all-hands meetings. As Cisco's CEO Chuck Robbins put it, in today's world you have to offer a compelling "return on commute" to get your employees bought into coming into the office.

Redesigned work models also need to consider the ways in which we communicate. For example, we worked with Verizon[15] to improve the way they run meetings, such as scheduling 25- or 50-minute meetings with a 5- or 10-minute lagged start time to give people breathing room. We also identified meetings that could be replaced by asynchronous modes of work (such as email, chat, shared documents, or offline review) and clarified what "required" and "optional" meant. In our experiments, 90% of participants reported overall meeting effectiveness had improved and 78% felt they wasted less time sitting in meetings where their live participation wasn't required.

Leaders will also need to monitor the impact of new technologies that they introduce. The generative AI experiment mentioned above also revealed that overreliance on generative AI can lead to a loss of collective diversity of ideas. As leaders seek to benefit from the value creation opportunities of generative AI, they'll need to consider where and how people collaborate most effectively to ensure they retain their creativity and innovativeness.

Invest in Building a New Managerial Muscle

The orchestration of these factors needs to come from managers – those at the front line, working with the teams. They are closest to the needs of the work, the people, and how that work gets done.

---

13 https://fortune.com/2023/05/05/cisco-ceo-chuck-robbins-rebranding-office-collaboration-center-slashing-private-workspaces-coax-employees-back/?utm_source=email&utm_medium=newsletter&utm_campaign=chro-daily&utm_content=2023081413pm&tpcc=NL_Marketing
14 https://blog.dropbox.com/topics/work-culture/the-shifting-dimensions-of-work#:~:text=At%20Dropbox%2C%20we've%20decided,a%20daily%20basis%20post%2DCOVID.
15 https://www.verizon.com/about/news/verizon-study-focus-meeting-accomplish-more

However, this orchestration requires two new managerial muscles.

The first is one that was not needed before COVID, when work was done in the office by default, nor during COVID, when remote work was predominant for many office-based professionals. Managers now need to facilitate discussions with and align their teams on where, when, and how work gets done. They need to hold weekly retrospectives on what worked, what didn't, and what to change in how they work the next week.

The second muscle is one that managers arguably needed before COVID, since working with distributed teams isn't new. Managers need to build their ability to create connection and culture as well as develop, inspire, mentor, and coach across distributed and hybrid teams. They must also meet employees' emotional as well as functional needs. A recent BCG survey[16] on employee expectations about leadership at work conducted across nine countries revealed that the top four qualities characterizing great leaders are recognition, people coaching and development, empathetic listening, and care.

Building these new managerial skills requires work, but the rewards are worth it: better performance, engagement, and retention, to name but a few. And just like any muscle, it needs investment of time and practice to strengthen. However, every organization can take positive steps starting from within: Identify your best managers – the ones who are already doing some of these things. Determine the specific habits and behaviors that set them apart, then follow a "best teach the rest" approach to help others learn how to develop similar capabilities. This is beyond simple training; it is about teaching, coaching, role modeling, and rewarding new ways of working every day.

In short: Instead of setting top-down mandates and expecting frontline managers to enforce them, leaders ought to focus on empowering those managers to co-create ways of working with their teams that are best suited to the needs of the people and the work they do, as well as the digital and GenAI tools at their disposal.

While it may be easier to follow the crowd and issue blanket return-to-office policies, the potential upside of implementing thoughtful changes based on the four categories above is not only worth it – it will soon become an imperative for businesses that want to create and sustain work and talent advantages into the future.

---

16 https://www.bcg.com/publications/2022/all-about-generative-leadership-and-its-benefits

Making Flexible Working Models Work

Deborah Lovich and Rosie Sargeant

The pandemic broadened the aperture on flexibility, unlocking unprecedented shifts in where, when, and how we work. For a significant subset of employees – largely those who are office-based and whose work can be done anywhere with a laptop and the internet – flexibility became standard practice. Moreover, it has become an expectation that workers have of their employers: an expectation that is currently being challenged by a wave of return-to-office policies.

The question "What is the right work model policy?" looms large for leaders today. But that is not the right question to be asking. The right one is "How do we construct work to optimize both productivity and joy?" And the answer to that question can be found only through a deep understanding of how people do their best work – across all categories of responsibilities and tasks. This is the key finding from our surveys of more than 1,500 global office-based workers' behaviors and preferences, which complement our research on how to make work *work* better for deskless workers.[17]

Employees want flexibility for many reasons. They need to balance personal responsibilities such as caregiving. They also need to concentrate on work tasks that open-concept offices can complicate. At the same time, they need to gather in person with colleagues to do more collaborative and creative work because they crave community and opportunities for development. And at the highest level, all workers see flexibility as an indicator of a trusting culture.[18]

So yes, there are multiple reasons employees want flexibility and most are ready to quit if it isn't offered. But the reality of how to deliver flexible work effectively is much more nuanced.

Flexible Work Doesn't Mean Remote Work

Flexible work has a definition problem. All too often, it is conflated with fully remote work, but this is not what's happening in most organizations. The majority of our respondents reported working in a hybrid model. And even in fully remote models, one in seven employees are choosing to come into the office on some days.

Conflating prescribed hybrid models with flexibility is also misguided. The employees who told us they work in hybrid models with set office days do not

---

17 https://www.bcg.com/publications/2022/how-to-retain-deskless-workers
18 https://www.bcg.com/capabilities/organization-strategy/organizational-culture

feel like they have flexibility. In fact, only 28% of them said they feel like they have significant flexibility in where they work, compared with 100% of employees working in less prescribed hybrid models.

One-Size-Fits-All Work Policies Don't Work

When employees come into the office, they want to know that their time is being used meaningfully. For example, respondents were eight times more likely to want to work in person for affiliation and development compared with doing focus work (such as analysis, emails, and writing reports) and administrative tasks; they often perceive the latter two categories to be more efficient when carried out remotely.

And the amount of time spent varies by role type. On average, individual contributors spend a little more than one-third (37%) of their time on work they believe is done most effectively in person (such as training, social events, and collaboration). Meanwhile, managers and executives spend close to half their time (49%) on work they believe is done most effectively in person (such as onboarding new hires and giving feedback).

The most effective work models reflect these preferences and behaviors, which can be unique to individual organizations, functions, and teams.

Top-Down Decrees Lead to Dissatisfaction

Nearly two-thirds (62%) of our respondents told us that they do not have a say in their work model policy. Instead, it is dictated by either company-wide guidelines or their manager. Of all participants, 39% reported that their company decides where they work. In these companies, 24% of employees were unhappy with their work location policy. That 24% goes down to 14% if the manager decides and 6% if the team decides. In other words, the closer to the work the policy gets set, the more satisfied employees are with it.

Employees want agency. Keep in mind that before COVID, most office-based employees would travel to their place of work every day by default. During COVID, remote became the default. Only now do organizations find themselves in the position of telling employees when and where to work.

Leaders need to proceed cautiously. Flexible work policies have become to employees an indication of their company's culture of trust and accountability for results. And low-trust environments have major implications for worker engagement and productivity.

Employees Are Ready to Vote with Their Feet

The stakes are high: nine in ten respondents consider flexible work options important when looking for a job. Moreover, many employees are willing to quit if they aren't happy with their flexible work options. Of the employees we surveyed, those who were dissatisfied with their work model were more than 2.5 times more likely to consider leaving their organization in the next year compared with those who were satisfied.

Additionally, flexible work is critical for diversity, equity, and inclusion. Roughly 90% of surveyed women, caregivers, LGBTQ+, and people with disabilities consider flexible work options important or very important in staying in or leaving their job. We saw a particularly wide gap when it comes to gender: female employees are 1.5 times more likely than their male counterparts to prioritize flexibility this way. Notably, we found only a marginal difference (3%) among women when comparing caregivers with noncaregivers. In other words, this is not just a working-mom phenomenon.[19]

The Next Steps for Company Leaders

There are five things organizations need to do[20] to start getting flexible work right:
1. Align as leaders on the company's needs and priorities ("what are we solving for?"), as well as the degree of freedom that managers and teams will have to decide how to work.
2. Empower business unit and functional leaders to segment the work that their teams do and identify models suited to the needs of their specific types of work.
3. Enable all team leaders to work with their teams to further customize work models according to specific tasks, individual preferences, and team requirements. And be flexible with the models themselves – they may need to change from week to week as work (and personal) priorities shift.
4. Invest in the key enablers to make the models work, namely, manager upskilling, collaboration tools (both physical space and technology), and modeling by senior leaders. Working this way is new for most organizations – it requires rewiring how people work, how leaders lead, and how they all are supported.

19 https://www.bcg.com/publications/2023/reinventing-the-childcare-industry-for-the-workforce-of-today
20 https://www.forbes.com/sites/deborahlovich/2023/05/31/five-prerequisites-for-high-performance-hybrid-work-how-do-you-measure-up/?sh=7bc186d27011

5. Identify the KPIs that reflect what you want to achieve. The focus should be on impact, not inputs; measure quality, innovation, productivity, growth, and engagement, versus monitoring badge swipes to track days in the office or hours online. Review these KPIs often to learn and adapt as you go.

∗∗∗

It would be convenient to assume that the return-to-office debate can be resolved with a corporate missive. Instead, leaders in the future of work[21] need to take the time to understand how to enable employees to do their best work – so that they can create value *and* thrive.

∗∗∗∗∗∗∗∗∗∗∗∗∗∗∗∗∗∗∗∗∗∗∗∗∗∗∗∗

---

21 https://www.bcg.com/capabilities/people-strategy/future-of-work

Tapping into Fluid Talent

Nithya Vaduganathan, Colleen McDonald, Allison Bailey, and Renee Laverdiere

Rapidly changing workplace dynamics over the past decade and especially during the Great Resignation are forcing company leaders to tap into what we call "fluid talent." Rather than just drawing from traditional sources, they should look to former employees and freelancers as well as talent that is hidden elsewhere in the company, borrowed from other companies, or working in other geographic markets.

While nearly all companies understand the urgency to find new sources of talent, few are going about it systematically. According to a BCG survey of more than 700 executives responsible for digital transformation,[22] fewer than one-third of companies today go beyond traditional talent acquisition channels (see Figure 3.1).

The portion of companies in each cohort that go beyond traditional talent acquisition channels

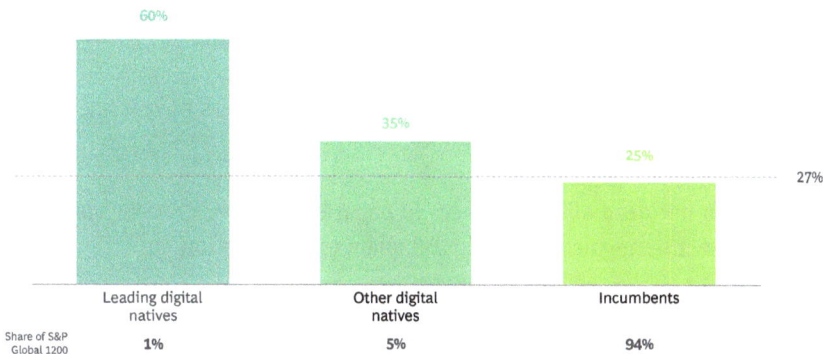

	Leading digital natives	Other digital natives	Incumbents
	60%	35%	25% 27%
Share of S&P Global 1200	1%	5%	94%

Sources: 2021 BCG Global Digital Transformation Survey; BCG Analysis.
Note: The leading digital natives are companies with strong global competitive advantage based on access to privileged high-volume, high-value data and platforms and total shareholder return (TSR) that is about three times higher than average. Other digital natives are emerging digital-first companies that are generating TSR about 2.5 times higher than average. Incumbents are traditional companies, including both those that have successfully built some digital capabilities and those that have yet to digitally transform.

Figure 3.1: Most Companies Could Source Talent More Expansively.

Companies struggle to identify where to look within and beyond their organizations to find fluid talent. They are overwhelmed by the exploding number of digital talent platforms[23] – such as Fiverr, Toptal, and Upwork – and the complexity of managing so many talent sources and solutions. Even companies that embrace

---

22 https://www.bcg.com/capabilities/digital-technology-data/digital-transformation/overview
23 https://www.bcg.com/publications/2020/a-strategic-approach-to-on-demand-talent

fluid talent may not fully adapt their operating models to get the most from new sources of talent.

A fluid talent approach requires a fundamental shift in people management.[24] It blurs the lines between external and internal talent sources, asks HR to play new roles and engage differently with technology, and subtly shifts the dynamics between companies and their workers. It also asks managers to shift their thinking about their teams and ways of working, moving from "owning" to "accessing" talent. How can companies take fluid talent from a nice concept to a concrete set of actions that create business value?

On the basis of dozens of interviews with Fortune 500 leaders, a detailed survey of more than 100 HR and business leaders, analysis of the HR technology landscape, and our work with clients, we find that companies aiming to make this transition should take three actions:

- Identify where a fluid talent model will deliver the most value for the organization.
- Create an ecosystem of partners, including talent matching platforms and solutions for upskilling and reskilling employees.
- Develop a fluid talent operating model that reengineers how work is done and careers are built.

Companies do not need all the answers to begin their journey. Their early steps can generate wins on which to build a full talent transformation.

The Promise of Fluid Talent

Finding and retaining the right talent is growing more challenging. The skills gap is widening, while the half-life of skills shrinks and the need for expertise in areas like digital expands. At the same time, workers' expectations have changed. People put a greater premium on workplace flexibility, autonomy, and purpose, a shift that is contributing to high levels of attrition. These dynamics are encouraging companies to experiment with a range of fluid talent initiatives (see Figure 3.2).

Alumni and Workforce Returnee Programs. Companies such as Amazon and Goldman Sachs are increasingly offering return-to-work, or returnship, programs that ease the path back into the workforce for alumni and other experienced workers. The programs offer combinations of pay, training, and mentorship. Unilever's U-Work program, for example, aims to break the compromise between gig

---

24 https://www.bcg.com/capabilities/people-strategy/overview

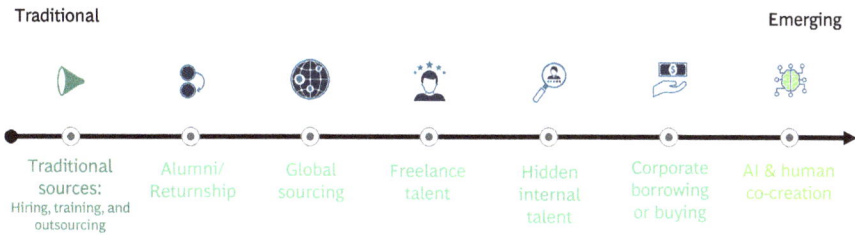

Figure 3.2: Companies Experiment With New Talent Sources.

and traditional work models, enabling alumni and even current employees to work on specific assignments like a contractor or freelancer but have guaranteed pay and benefits. Parents who took time off to care for children are one of many target populations of these programs. Both alumni and returnees are attractive to employers:[25] Alumni already know the organizations, and returnee populations include individuals with strong prior work experience.

Global Talent Sourcing. Organizations, including the customer service division of one of the world's largest tech companies, are removing location constraints for job openings and opening hubs near attractive talent pools. Automattic, the creator of Wordpress.com, has more than 1,980 employees in 96 countries and has had a fully remote work model for more than 15 years. Once a rarity, models like this are becoming more common as companies rethink work models amid COVID-19. The list of companies that have announced plans to allow employees to work from anywhere indefinitely continues to grow. Salesforce, for example, has shifted to posting jobs by time zone, rather than by city.

Hidden Internal Talent. Companies like Seagate Technologies are creating internal talent mobility programs to better match existing employees with internal project needs and job opportunities, unlocking hidden capacity, helping their organizations respond more quickly to market opportunities, and enhancing career development for their teams. Nearly 90% of all eligible employees registered for Seagate's Career Discovery platform within 45 days of its launch, and the company estimates that it unlocked 35,000 hours and saved over $1.4 million in external contractor costs in the first four months of the program. Unilever used its internal talent mobility platform to move more than 9,000 employees from one job to another in the early days of the pandemic and estimates that it unlocked close to 1 million hours through the program.

---

25 https://www.bcg.com/publications/2018/two-groups-you-cannot-ignore-war-talent

Freelancers. In past work with Harvard Business School's Managing the Future of Work program, we discovered that nearly two-thirds of companies report medium to extensive use of freelance platforms and that almost 90% of business leaders expect that digital talent platforms will be at least somewhat important to their organization's competitive advantage.

Bridgestone, for example, worked with Toptal, a network of freelance software developers, designers, finance experts, and project managers, to streamline the process of retreading, or adding rubber, to tires to extend their life. The arrangement allowed Bridgestone to access skills that it did not require full-time.

Corporate Borrowing or Buying. During the early days of the COVID pandemic, Sysco, the world's largest food distributor, and Kroger, the supermarket chain, entered a talent-sharing agreement in which furloughed Sysco workers were offered temporary employment at Kroger distribution centers. And Royal Philips, a leading health technology company, and Walt Disney Company partnered to test the use of storytelling, animation, and cartoon characters during MRIs performed on children – softening the hard edge of a loud, often claustrophobic experience.

Human-AI Co-Creation. Airbus, an aerospace manufacturer, teamed up with Autodesk, the design and engineering software company, to create an airplane partition that is 45% lighter but just as strong as current models. The companies relied on "generative design," an AI-enabled process in which humans give design parameters to the software, which in turn creates thousands of alternatives, learning from each iteration.

These initiatives suggest the potential of a fluid talent model to better meet talent needs today and adapt to changing skill requirements tomorrow. Managed carefully, fluid talent approaches may also create more equitable opportunity and diverse teams. Digital talent platforms, for example, can remove elements such as race and appearance from the hiring decision. And companies that make opportunities broadly visible often see greater applicant diversity. Since Schneider Electric implemented its Open Talent Market, for example, women have received 55% of the assignments.

Fluid Talent in Action

If the promise of fluid talent is clear, bringing it to life is not. Executives often talk about the need for fluid talent, but at most companies no one takes responsibility for it – or has clear ideas about developing it.

Some companies, however, have broken away from the pack. In particular, a handful of leading digital natives – including Alphabet, Amazon, Apple, Meta, Microsoft, and Netflix in the US as well as Alibaba, Baidu, and Tencent in China – more commonly go beyond traditional talent acquisition channels. In BCG research, about 90% of survey respondents from these companies reported the ability to rapidly adjust to changing talent demands across teams.

How can more companies be like this group? We found that there are three keys for companies to unlock fluid talent advantage:

Identify the highest-value use cases. Five use cases represent high-value opportunities for many companies. The most well-known are quickly finding specialized talent and managing fluctuations in demand for talent. These are opportunities for many companies to experiment with new talent sources while maintaining a flexible cost base. For example, Microsoft partnered with Limitless Technology to help manage surges in customer service queries. Limitless developed a network of Microsoft brand advocates to respond to customer queries. Given the experts' existing product knowledge, they quickly became effective in their roles. Microsoft observed faster response times, lower cost, and similar customer satisfaction with the Limitless workers.

Companies are also using fluid talent in other, less well-known ways. Some companies are relying on fluid talent to provide expert advisory on projects and new ventures, innovation, and skill development and career advancement. Strategy and corporate finance functions, for example, often use the expert advisory model for special projects. In another approach, the Italian energy company Enel partnered with crowdsourcing platform InnoCentive to enlist the help of hundreds of thousands of potential problem solvers to identify more than 5,000 new ideas.

Many of these use cases are applicable within specific industries or corporate functions. Figure 3.3 provides a broad overview of where use cases may find a home and the sources of talent within which companies can search.

Depending on their maturity, market position, and location, companies will have different needs. Companies should pursue the use cases that meet their specific needs, rather than those that are popular or those that have been adopted by competitors. Allianz, for example, launched its internal talent mobility platform after surveys showed that workers believed career opportunities were not transparent. The platform helped increase retention and employee development. Meanwhile, Seagate Technology launched an internal talent marketplace when it shifted its business model and needed to redeploy talent to new areas of the business.

Curate a partner ecosystem. The landscape for fluid talent has changed enormously over the past two years. Venture investors poured more than $12 billion into HR tech companies[26] in 2021, more than three times the amount invested in 2020.

---

26 https://www.bcg.com/publications/2022/billion-dollar-opportunity-in-hr-technology

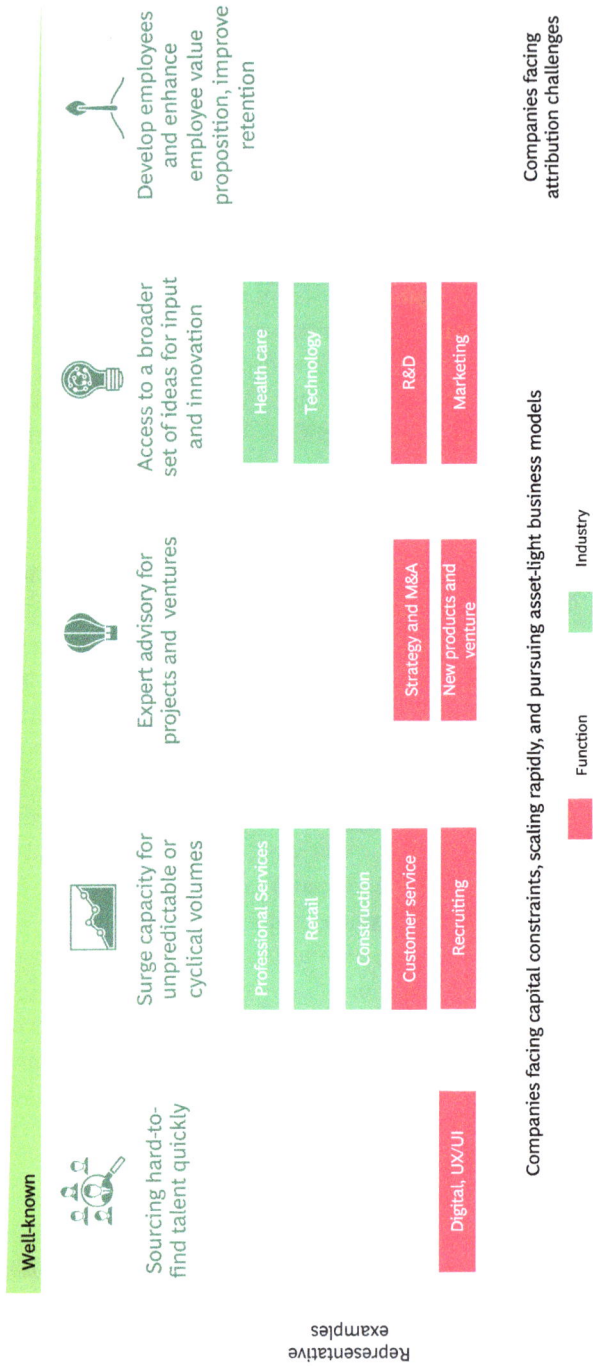

Figure 3.3: Five Fluid Talent Use Cases.

Source: BCG analysis.
Note: Each use case draws on more than one of the talent sources shown in Exhibit 2, as applicable.

Companies are offering more sophisticated AI-powered tools for anticipating talent needs, skills assessment and inferencing, talent matching, and talent sourcing.

Even as they expand their offerings, none of these HR tech companies offers an integrated, end-to-end solution for fluid talent management. Consequently, companies need to work with several HR tech partners to meet their talent needs, coordinating with labor market data and assessment companies, recruiting partners, external and internal talent platforms, upskilling providers, and others.

In so doing, companies must consider the strength of tools from vendors, their product roadmaps and integrations with other offerings, and ease of use, especially when many enterprise users will be working with the solution. They also should evaluate how well vendors work with clients to enable employee onboarding and encourage adoption.

Support fluid talent with a new operating model. Companies that have experimented with fluid talent understand the need to adapt legal and procurement frameworks, rewire HR processes like performance management, build cross-functional project teams, and invest in change management. But to really unlock value from fluid talent, companies also need to rethink their ways of working and how they deploy and onboard talent.

BCG research has found that fewer than one-third of companies report that they can rapidly adjust to changing demands across teams. This is more than a sourcing challenge; it suggests that, beyond looking more broadly for talent, companies need to adjust their operating models to deploy talent more flexibly.

Beyond deployment, companies can help freelance, contract, and other fluid-talent workers learn the company culture and norms. They can develop a system of onboarding that spells out the unwritten rules – for example, by defining detailed norms at the start of a project – and ensure that managers model the desired behavior. They can also create programs to support new hires, such as assigning a peer to be a "culture buddy." And they can use technology to make work processes more explicit. ByteDance's Lark technology, for example, integrates software and collaboration tools so that work is visible to others in real time. Automattic uses its own collaboration space along with tools like Slack to improve transparency, broaden accessibility, and enable asynchronous and distributed work.

Of course, as companies revamp their operating models, they should build in controls to mitigate risks. This could mean more frequent reviews of the work conducted by freelancers and contractors or rerouting of the queries that gig workers cannot resolve to other teams.

✳✳✳

Models for tapping into fluid talent continue to evolve as companies seek a broader range of talent sources and address the growing pains of a new working model. The matchmaking and enterprise contracting models for freelance talent, for example, are still a work in progress. Managers also need help redesigning workflows so that outsiders, whether they are alumni or freelancers, can pick up discrete assignments in a much longer stream of work. We expect to see more companies experimenting with their own novel programs, such as Unilever's U-Work, that aim to capture the best of internal and external talent.

Whatever the mix of talent sources that they adopt, organizations that unlock fluid talent will be more competitive in a transforming market. They will create knowledge based on a richer and more diverse set of expertise, develop their people more effectively, and emerge ready to respond to market opportunities.

But before they can activate fluid talent, companies need a strategy for fluid talent. The leaders in the field have a clear understanding of how fluid talent will enable their strategy and purpose and a willingness to go beyond familiar partners and technologies to explore the art of the possible. They are also open to changing how they work, because it can unlock the value of fluid talent.

The authors thank colleagues Patrick Forth, Romain de Laubier, Saibal Chakraborty, Tauseef Charanya, and Matteo Magagnoli, whose work on digital transformation[27] informs this article. Figure 3.1 relies on heretofore unpublished research conducted by that team.

****

---

27 https://www.bcg.com/publications/2022/rise-of-digital-incumbents-building-digital-capabilities

Making Work Work Better for Deskless Workers

Vinciane Beauchene, Julia Dhar, Katie Lavoie, Deborah Lovich, Chris Mattey, Nick South, and Sebastian Ullrich

At a time of massive labor shortages in industries that rely on factory workers, nurses, cashiers, restaurant servers, teachers, call-center operators, truck drivers, and other "deskless workers," more than four in ten of these job holders are at risk of quitting – and pay isn't the reason why.

Deskless workers in health care,[28] retail, manufacturing, hospitality and logistics, and many similar industries represent 70% to 80% of the world's labor force. While many people with office jobs switched to working remotely during the height of the COVID-19 pandemic, most deskless workers remained onsite. Now, more than half of them say that they are burned out, and 43% are either actively or passively looking for a new job, according to BCG's latest survey of deskless workers.

The primary reason that deskless workers look for a new job, our survey found, is not because of unsatisfactory compensation but because their emotional needs are not being met. When members of this workforce group don't feel respected, appreciated, treated fairly, or valued at work, they are willing to walk.

The findings are part of BCG's research on the future of work,[29] culled from a survey of more than 4,600 deskless workers in France, Germany, the UK, and the US. The respondents were almost evenly split between men and women, and they differed widely in age, level of seniority and job experience, and employment status.

Meeting Emotional Needs Is Key to Keeping Employees Onboard

Conventional wisdom holds that deskless workers' pay determines their sentiments about their jobs – and when asked, deskless workers themselves say that compensation is the aspect of their jobs that matters most to them. But our analysis of this group shows that when deskless workers consider leaving, the primary factors are emotional. In fact, eight of the top ten factors that motivate deskless workers to quit involve emotional rather than functional needs. At the top of that list: feeling fairly treated and respected, feeling valued and appreciated, doing work that's meaningful and enjoyable, and having a good relationship with a manager or boss.

---

28 https://www.bcg.com/industries/health-care/overview
29 https://www.bcg.com/capabilities/people-strategy/future-of-work

Emotional factors are not the only workplace factors that deskless workers care about. Among the top ten considerations that contribute to a decision to leave a job are day-to-day work environment, opportunities for career advancement, and employer performance and reputation.

Younger Workers and "Quick Quitting"

Gen Z workers are by far the most eager to pursue a job change. Nearly two-thirds (63%) of 18- to 24-year-old deskless workers say that they feel burned out from work, and 55% are either actively looking for a new job or would consider switching if the right opportunity came along. Younger workers are substantially more likely than their older counterparts to be on the lookout for work elsewhere. By comparison, only 30% of deskless workers who are 55 or older say that they are job hunting, and 38% of deskless workers who are 45 to 54 say so.

The phenomenon of workers leaving a new job after a relatively short period of time has come to be known as "quick quitting." Our data confirms that the quick-quitting trend is most prevalent among deskless workers who have the least amount of time on the job. Among deskless workers, 52% of those whose tenure is less than 12 months are either actively or passively job hunting.

Attitudes Differ by Geography and Industry

Deskless workers' feelings about burnout and about quitting their jobs differ depending on their location and industry. Of the four countries in our survey, the UK has the largest portion of people in deskless jobs who say that they are open to a new opportunity – 49%, including 8% who are actively looking and 41% who are passively looking for work.

In Germany, 43% of deskless workers are looking for a different job, 38% of them passively and 5% actively. In the US, 6% are job-searching actively and 37% passively. The situation in France appears to be the least volatile, with 4% of deskless workers actively searching for new employment and 33% looking more casually.

At the height of the pandemic, the health care industry and the public sector[30] were among the industries that experienced the fewest layoffs or reduced

---

30 https://www.bcg.com/industries/public-sector/overview

work schedules.[31] Nurses, teachers, and other deskless workers in those sectors continued to work, often under severely challenging conditions. This may explain why a disproportionate number of those workers now feel burned out and ready to quit. In health care, 41% of deskless workers are either actively (7%) or passively (34%) looking; among education providers, 4% are actively looking and 36% are passively looking.

Other industries at high risk of employee loss include retail, transportation and warehousing, and manufacturing.

What Employers Should Do

When deskless workers quit, employers[32] lose a lot more than just the time and money it takes to replace them and get new hires up to speed in their roles. If enough top performers follow more attractive offers out the door, their departure can leave an organization without the quality and quantity of talent it needs to carry out strategic plans and deliver for its customers and other stakeholders.

Our survey findings offer clues about how employers can retain deskless workers, starting with understanding what the workers see as important and then meeting those needs.

Find out what workers want. The survey findings clearly indicate that deskless workers overall want the functional basics of a good job, including competitive pay and acceptable work-life balance, and the emotional benefits of feeling valued, recognized, and respected, doing work they enjoy, and having a positive relationship with their manager. What deskless workers at any individual organization want may be slightly different, however – and the only way to know is to ask. Invest in finding out through surveys, focus groups, and one-on-one conversations. Then use those insights to adjust practices to meet deskless workers' needs while also ensuring that any new practices align with strategies and policies for the entire workforce, including office-based and remote workers.

Build great managers. Managers are the glue that binds all workers to their jobs and to the organization. Our research shows that deskless workers who are dissatisfied with their managers are 50% more likely to feel burned out, three times more likely not to recommend their employer as a place to work, and twice as likely to leave. Organizations must ensure that their managers have the capa-

---

31 https://web-assets.bcg.com/93/b6/11ba136841189e51cc50486f1340/bcg-decoding-global-reskilling-and-career-paths-apr-2021.pdf

32 https://www.bcg.com/capabilities/people-strategy/overview

bilities they need to deliver a great work experience. Companies that have successfully done so have identified top-performing managers, found out how they work, engaged those managers to teach their peers, and incorporated better ways of working[33] into day-to-day routines. Great managers may not be able to stop active job seekers from looking, but they can keep passive job seekers in the organization.

Invest in making work better. Just as companies commit to investing when they roll out new products or enter new markets, they must dedicate real effort to making work better for deskless workers. After an organization identifies potential changes to explore as possible ways to improve work, it must invest in the technology, upskilling, governance, and other enablers needed to support the new practices; then it must pilot and make necessary adjustments before rolling out and scaling the workplace changes. Investments don't end there. If younger workers with less time on the job are the group most inclined to leave, employers need to invest in improving onboarding and career planning so that the people who represent the future of their workforce feel connected to and engaged with the organization, knowing that they have the attention and support of managers who can help them thrive even before they walk through the door.

✳✳✳

Organizations must look beyond what deskless workers say is important in a job to understand the factors that may actually keep them from leaving in search of something better. By reading between the lines of what people say and do, forward-thinking employers can restructure work to provide members of this vital sector of the global workforce the support they crave. Companies should take the time to understand deskless workers' true needs, build great managers, and work together with their employees to identify and invest in scaling best practices that truly make work better.

✳✳✳✳✳✳✳✳✳✳✳✳✳✳✳✳✳✳✳✳✳✳✳✳✳✳✳✳✳✳✳

---

[33] https://www.bcg.com/publications/2020/why-you-need-new-approach-learning

The $12 Billion Opportunity in HR Technology

Nithya Vaduganathan, Colleen McDonald, Allison Bailey, Renee Laverdiere, David Allred, and Sesh Iyer

Talent management is a large and growing challenge at many organizations, and talent management providers are racing to roll out new offerings that can help business leaders and managers improve how they recruit, oversee, develop, and retain human capital. Many HR tech companies that formerly specialized in a single aspect of the talent management value chain are building out more comprehensive offerings, and others are growing through consolidation. Dozens of companies are competing to expand their offerings, causing significant confusion in the market.

To create clarity for solution providers, we recently surveyed more than 100 CHROs and other business leaders to understand their current pain points and unmet needs in human capital management (HCM) technology. For technology providers and the investors that back them, the results offer real insights into what businesses want. We have also identified several ways that HCM technology companies can create advantage by focusing on differentiated data, skill taxonomies, and a position that connects or orchestrates multiple parts of the talent value chain.

The next 18 to 24 months will be a critical window for providers to stake out their positions in this crowded and highly active market. Those that understand the needs of the market and design smarter solutions to meet those needs will find the odds in their favor.

An Explosion in Activity

The past few years have seen an explosion in activity for talent management technologies. Companies are wrestling with the growing challenge of managing talent amid changes in work norms due to COVID, the gig economy, and other factors. But this challenge brings opportunity, too. In 2021, more than $12 billion in venture capital poured into the HR technology market, with the rate of investment more than tripling from 2020 to 2021, as investors back companies whose ideas are promising (see Figure 3.4).

BCG breaks the talent management value chain into six steps, with specific providers specializing in each:

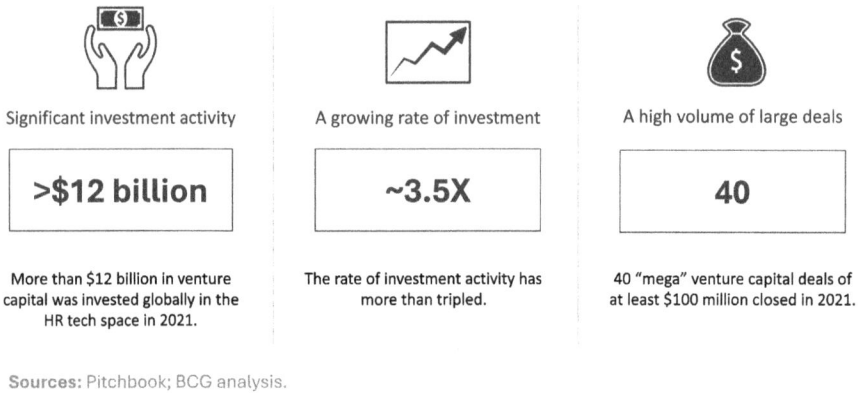

Significant investment activity	A growing rate of investment	A high volume of large deals
>$12 billion	**~3.5X**	**40**
More than $12 billion in venture capital was invested globally in the HR tech space in 2021.	The rate of investment activity has more than tripled.	40 "mega" venture capital deals of at least $100 million closed in 2021.

Sources: Pitchbook; BCG analysis.

Figure 3.4: The Market for Talent Management Solutions is Seeing Major Investment Activity.

–   **Anticipate** future talent needs.[34] Labor market analytics solutions like Emsi Burning Glass offer rich data about talent supply and demand at the skill level to inform workforce planning.
–   **Assess skill levels.** Companies including EmPath and SkyHive use AI-powered solutions to assess and infer skills and proficiency levels in a more robust manner and at scale.
–   **Source talent and match internal candidates to opportunities.** In addition to continued innovations in recruiting technology (such as HireVue's video interviews and chat-based candidate interactions), we have seen new digital sourcing platforms like Catalant, InnoCentive, Toptal, and Upwork emerge to offer access to highly skilled labor "on demand." Talent marketplaces provided by companies such as Gloat, Hitch, Fuel50, and Eightfold AI are emerging to better identify and manage internal talent and enable employees to move throughout the organization.
–   **Develop the skills and capabilities of the current workforce.** A growing suite of learning and development companies like Degreed, EdCast, and BetterUp enable reskilling and upskilling and help managers identify internal candidates for specific roles.
–   **Embed workers in the organization.** Solutions like Starmind and Microsoft Viva Topics promise to help workers navigate the organization and quickly get up to speed.
–   **Manage employee performance and engagement.** Companies like Lattice and 15Five offer continuous performance management solutions with inte-

---

34 https://www.bcg.com/publications/2021/strategies-for-building-hr-function-of-future

grated performance appraisals, goal setting, and real-time feedback. Other competitors, including Perceptyx, help employers keep a pulse on employee sentiment through surveys and sensing and by crowdsourcing solutions.

Enterprise Customers Want an Integrated Solution

Despite all the activity, in many ways the field is still evolving and maturing. For example, skill taxonomies are of mixed quality and do not always align with each other, requiring significant adaptation to specific industries and individual companies. Solutions still have only a limited ability to accurately infer employee skill levels, and even sophisticated matching platforms rely almost exclusively on skills to create matches; they don't consider factors like personalities or work preferences that we know are important in building teams. And applications that rely on analytics need to build controls to identify and dismantle bias – rather than amplifying it as some early-stage use cases have done.

More broadly, companies struggle to keep up with the variety of disconnected solutions for individual aspects of the value chain. That has led to a kind of arms race in the industry, as providers that are strong in one area of the value chain seek to address other areas. For example, Microsoft announced a partnership in early 2020 with Oracle to track job applicants more effectively by integrating LinkedIn employee profile data with the Microsoft Viva platform. Similarly, staffing agency Randstad launched a new offering in June 2021, called RiseSmart BrightFit, which combines labor market data with skill assessments to recommend roles and courses for transitioning employees on the basis of skill gaps and proficiency levels.

Other companies are building out their offerings through acquisition. For example, Workday made several acquisitions to expand its offerings, including Peakon ($700 million), which offers a tool to measure employee sentiment and engagement. That follows a bigger deal in 2018, for enterprise performance management platform Adaptive Insights ($1.6 billion).

Over the long term, these innovations and investments will transform how companies manage talent, creating more equitable opportunities and unlocking fluid talent to meet some of their most pressing challenges. In the short term, however, there is significant confusion in the market. HCM software players, traditional staffing companies, strategic advisory firms, HR tech disruptors, and big tech are all playing in the space, looking to establish a favorable position as the ecosystem matures. To enterprise customers, it can seem as if everyone is trying to do everything, and there's no clear winner just yet. According to one survey, a staggering 94% of HR decision makers struggle to keep up with the latest technology trends and developments.

This confusion comes through clearly in BCG's survey results as well. We asked more than a hundred HR and business leaders for their thoughts about HCM technology and their most pressing pain points. Among the most important:

–   Managing multiple sourcing functions, which leads to significant complexity
–   Planning processes that fail to identify the skills needed to meet future business requirements
–   Coordinating the ecosystem of various upskilling and reskilling providers or solutions

Our conversations with HR leaders suggest that the most important coordination needs to happen across the value chain, as companies look for solutions that integrate disparate data sources, talent sources, and functionality to manage talent more seamlessly.

Three Strategies for Talent Management Providers to Create an Edge

To create advantage in the fast-moving HR tech market, our analysis suggests three main strategies that talent management providers can apply to create a defensible advantage.

Develop differentiated data to power predictive analytics and insights. In a world powered by AI, data is king, and the scale, richness, differentiation, timeliness, and quality of the data all matter. Accurately identifying skill requirements and assessing capabilities requires working with macroeconomic data, job postings, résumé and career histories, candidate profiles, the hiring pipeline, training records, performance data, and even "on the job activity" – for example, data about which programs and applications people use in their day-to-day work. Incumbent HCM players – which have entrenched systems and already serve as central HR data repositories for most companies – have a strong position from which to expand and capture more value. Staffing companies have proprietary data derived from their activities – information about who needed what in terms of staff and when, how that staff performed, and how that staff was paid – that they can use to predict future talent needs and improve candidate matching, creating a positive feedback loop.

Another control point for data are talent marketplaces, which have an advantage because they actually *create* data through transactions. Learning platforms know who is learning what and how well individuals are mastering new skills, so these platforms can offer in-depth data on skills to aid matching. Finally, access to tools and applications that workers use in their day-to-day jobs can serve as a control point to yield richer data than external scraping alone. For example, Microsoft Viva Topics uses AI to determine topic expertise in an organization by scanning employees' documents and emails.

Create a strong skill taxonomy, with the capability to adapt it for industry and company context. Almost every talent platform and external data provider has its own skill taxonomy or ontology to enable talent matching, but some are better than others. In our work with clients, we have found that most companies will need to invest in making their skill taxonomies fit for purpose (even those that are based on troves of data). Developing usable taxonomies can require aligning them with multiple external taxonomies, simplifying them using machine learning, and refining them further with functional and industry experts to unearth the common skills at the right level of granularity. For global organizations, this process also requires understanding the way that languages can have different terms for similar types of skills. And skill taxonomies aren't static – they need to evolve over time as needed skillsets change more quickly than ever before.

Establish a position that connects or orchestrates multiple parts of the talent management value chain. Companies are eager for more-integrated solutions. An offering that first helps companies anticipate workforce needs and identify potential matches from across internal and external talent sources and then connects them with a set of reskilling and upskilling solutions will quickly become "sticky" to customers. Establishing such a position does not require owning all of the solution components – indeed, our research suggests that companies overwhelmingly want to be able to access a suite of upskilling providers rather than operating in a closed ecosystem. But companies that establish a position early in key points of the value chain – talent matching, for example, or even becoming the storefront for a variety of skilling activities – can create an advantage through strong customer relationships and by setting the terms of engagement for other ecosystem suppliers.

Implement Must Go Beyond the Technology Itself

Last, the change management[35] component of implementation is critical. Providers that treat talent management technology as a plug-and-play solution are setting themselves up for failure. Instead, BCG research has found that the real value of digital technology[36] comes from realigning business processes and ways

---

35 https://www.bcg.com/capabilities/business-transformation/change-management
36 https://www.bcg.com/capabilities/digital-technology-data/overview

of working. A good rule of thumb is that 70% of the value comes from changes to the business, 20% from the technology itself, and 10% from the underlying algorithms. In fact, many enterprise companies looking at this market report that an intuitive user interface and a strong client success team are key considerations in their choice of solution partners.[37]

But implementation needs go well beyond the technical domain. Companies also need partners that can work with them to adapt their skill taxonomies for industry and company specifications, help them learn from other companies' journeys, and partner with them to envision their own future of work. More than any platform implementation, this journey is about changing an organization's culture. Enterprise customers will flock to providers who can help them do just that.

The next 18 to 24 months will be a critical window of opportunity for talent management providers to stake out their positions, establish their role in emerging talent ecosystems, and claim share. Players and investors should keep a focus on enterprise customer needs and key control points and tailor their strategies accordingly.

The authors thank Sibley Lovett, Max Santinelli, JinK Koike, Andreas Liedtke, and Lena David for their thought partnership and contributions to this article.

✳✳✳✳✳✳✳✳✳✳✳✳✳✳✳✳✳✳✳✳✳✳✳✳✳✳✳✳✳✳✳✳

37 https://www.bcg.com/capabilities/people-strategy/overview

Next-Generation HR Is Connected and Value Centered

Jens Baier, Rainer Strack, Philipp Kolo, Martin Twesten, Ádám Kotsis,
Pierre Schatlowski, and Pragya Maini

A fast-changing global business environment is pressuring companies to rethink their internal and external customer-delivery models and accelerate their transformation agendas. The HR function[38] can serve as the catalyst for such transformation by helping to create future-ready organizations – the kind of businesses that can keep pace with rapid technology advancements, manage a gig economy that demands flexible and remote work options, and retain the best talent.

To meet these expectations, HR departments must first be willing to transform themselves. They need to reexamine their own people strategies,[39] organization structures, processes, and staff capabilities while leading by example in embracing technology. By doing so, HR can play a central role in building customer-centric organizations, driving business priorities, and delivering value.

Five Key Priorities

As we look to the future, we see five priorities that will guide businesses through the changes to come – principles that, in turn, should define the strategies of HR functions everywhere.

Employee Centricity. Adopt a people-first approach to meet current and future talent demands and to offer a seamless employee experience. Organizations are in a war to attract, develop, and retain the best talent. They need to meet the expectations not only of current employees but also potential new hires by providing hassle-free, digitized experiences that are supported by self-service options, chatbots, and quick feedback tools. HR functions are essential to ensuring user-centric journeys along the entire employee life cycle.

Cost Efficiency and Value Delivery. Focus on value creation and controlling costs to drive overall standardization and process simplification. As businesses strive to increase process efficiencies in order to deliver sustainable financial results, HR needs to play its part in cost reduction through effective resource utilization. It can do this by automating transactional tasks and flexibly adopting new ways of working. The function must be able to conquer the people challenges that emerge from shifting business models – especially in times of economic slow-

---

38 https://www.bcg.com/capabilities/people-strategy/digital-human-resources
39 https://www.bcg.com/capabilities/people-strategy/overview

down, when organizations face intense recessionary pressures on business activity and cash flow.

Skills, Capabilities, and End-to-End Process Responsibility. Develop experts to foster global collaboration and robust process harmonization along the entire HR value chain. Conquering today's business challenges demands a dedicated shift in how HR is organized, resourced, and staffed. To unleash a best-in-class HR department, organizations increasingly need to move away from a generalist model to one powered by specialists who spend all of their time on a specific process, supported by state-of-the-art tools and global, up-to-date best-practice frameworks. Such functional experts should then work with HR business partners and local points of contact to design and implement HR and business priorities together, which will promote efficiency and ensure end-to-end responsibility for key processes.

Agility and Scalability. Encourage new ways of working and cross-functional collaboration by responding fast and flexibly to changing business priorities. HR must keep pace with the unprecedented speed of change and serve as the driving force behind an organization's transformation. The function is uniquely positioned to steer this transformation; by enabling and advocating for firm-wide change, HR can shape how work is done and equip all employees with the right skills. It can also set the right communication and program-management metrics to ensure the transformation's success.

Data and Digital Readiness. Tap the potential of disruptive technologies and leverage advanced data analytics to make people decisions and enhance overall employee management. To drive higher productivity and engagement, HR functions must look beyond basic employee data to harness nuanced insights on individual working preferences, career goals, and attrition risk, as well as data beyond its organization's boundaries. The function should also leverage cloud solutions and cutting-edge technology to enable streamlined and automated HR processes, such as talent sourcing, compensation management, and other operations. A data-driven HR function that can make objective decisions, predict workforce trends, and flag areas of concern is critical to creating a people-first organization that aligns with employee needs.

Future-proofing the HR Function

To prepare their businesses for the future – and help them undertake critical transformation projects along the way – HR departments must themselves be ready to face the challenges of tomorrow. Businesses will have to reshape the following elements of their HR departments to become future-proof:

- **People Strategy.** HR departments must establish the right priorities to determine how to generate the most business value. Having a well-defined people strategy that aligns with the organization's overall strategy is important, as are performance metrics for business-critical initiatives, the employee experience, internal customer satisfaction, technological integration, and cost reduction.
- **Organization Structure.** HR must collaborate with other functions and stakeholders to address the growing complexity of their organizations. It needs to adapt existing ways of working to create comprehensive process accountabilities through appropriate centralization, bundling, outsourcing, and the automation of activities.
- **Processes and Governance.** HR processes need to be well-connected to other parts of the business and designed with an employee-centric approach to ensure seamless end-to-end experiences. Governance mechanisms should be optimized to define clear responsibilities, reduce handovers, and enable global consistency while adhering to local regulatory requirements.
- **IT, Analytics, and Digital Tools.**[40] Organizations must upgrade existing legacy HR platforms – which are often expensive and cumbersome to integrate – to modern cloud-based solutions that can easily be used with self-service platforms and best-of-breed digital solutions.
- **Staff Capabilities.** The ability to reshape the HR function of any business will significantly depend on whether its people are able to take on new roles and responsibilities. The HR workforce needs to be quick in acquiring skills that mirror the function's new purpose, vision, and mission.
- **Business Case.** For each new process it undertakes, HR must identify a holistic future-state vision that realistically outlines the required investments and provides clarity on the savings that can be achieved. Documenting an ongoing efficiency-and-effectiveness summary will be critical to the success of the function's evolution.
- **Change Management**[41] **and Stakeholder Communication**. The department must set up a program management office to create an implementation action plan, flag areas of concern, and track the success of its transformation. Continuous employee-centric communication initiatives – with a clear "what's in it for me" change narrative for impacted employees – will ensure alignment with relevant stakeholders and are critical to sustaining the change.

---

40 https://www.bcg.com/capabilities/digital-technology-data/overview
41 https://www.bcg.com/capabilities/business-transformation/change-management

Looking Ahead

Well-connected, value-centered HR departments that can meaningfully contribute to enhancing organizational effectiveness are needed now more than ever. The secret to adapting to the changing landscape of work is to pursue essential priorities aimed at improving employee journeys, retaining top talent, and updating processes and technology systems.

Meanwhile, HR professionals will need to expand and refresh the skills and strategies of their own departments, ensuring that each element is ready to support the business of the future. Ultimately, the mission of any HR function is to develop an organization's greatest asset – its people.

✶✶✶✶✶✶✶✶✶✶✶✶✶✶✶✶✶✶✶✶✶✶✶✶✶✶✶✶✶✶✶✶✶✶✶✶✶✶✶

Transforming Technology Companies: Putting People First

Nicole Bennett, Ruba Borno, Sebastian DiGrande, Jim Hemerling, and John Wenstrup

Technology companies today face unprecedented change. Consider some of the major shifts now under way: from hardware to software, from point products to platform positions, from on-premises to cloud computing, from waterfall to agile software development, from selling products to selling solutions. As throughout the broader economy, in technology, traditional products are becoming commoditized, and nimbler emerging companies with stronger business models are routinely and readily outpacing dominant market players.

To compete in the maelstrom of today's markets, established technology companies must transform. Now. And swiftly. As one chief human resources officer (CHRO) told us, "It's insane to think that you have 18 months to make a transformation stick."

If transformation is urgent, so is the realization that it's not only about strategy and processes. It's about the most crucial asset technology companies have: people. And the impacts of change in the industry on people and the organization are enormous.

The implications of these changes and the challenges they pose for HR organizations are equally enormous. From talent needs to organization structure, the pressures to transform the role of the CHRO – and the entire HR function – are escalating. Yet in all too many technology companies, HR struggles to meet these challenges. It's time for technology companies to formulate a new view of HR and forge a deeper partnership between HR and the business. Doing so will require a fundamental change in HR strategy and operations.

The Impacts on People and Organizations

Industry shifts are straining technology companies' operating models, ways of working, and talent needs to the breaking point. Consider the following trends.

The Economic Imperative: Driving Growth While Preserving Margins. Although overall industry growth is a modest 3%, certain spheres are growing briskly: notably, public cloud services (projected compound annual growth rate from 2013 through 2018: 17%) and mobile-enterprise security (projected CAGR from 2012 through 2017: 23%). However, core businesses (such as on-premises applications and hardware) increasingly face commoditization. Companies must therefore boost investment in high-growth areas (such as cloud computing) as they squeeze out costs from their mature business lines. Since the commoditized businesses subsidize the new high-growth areas, the challenge is to recoup margins in those areas faster than they are being lost in the commoditized areas.

The Emergence of Hybrid Business Models. Managing the core (legacy) business alongside new growth areas requires maintaining two different operating models: one (legacy) optimized for efficiency and one (growth) optimized for speed to market. Larger companies must decide whether to integrate or segregate the two disparate models. Regardless of its size, any company with a hybrid operating model must compete for talent against pure-growth companies.

Another challenge for hybrids: managing two employee value propositions without friction. Layoffs in the mature business lines make it hard to keep talent. Meanwhile, the unrelenting demand for talent in the fast-growth areas calls for an irresistible value proposition that competitors can't match.

The War for the Right – and Best – Talent. Skill shortages are rampant: in security (200,000 unfilled positions in the US alone), enterprise applications, systems engineering, and cloud storage. Programmers skilled in certain languages, as well as technical and specialized salespeople, are also in short supply. (See Code Wars: The All-Industry Competition for Software Talent,[42] BCG Focus, May 2014.)

But the problem isn't just skill shortages. An even bigger issue is the war for the best and the brightest – what Google calls smart creatives. Attracting, deploying, and retaining such talent, simultaneously addressing specific skill shortages, dramatically escalates the war for talent. It's tough for mainstream companies to compete against high-growth companies, with their innovation appeal and tempting compensation packages. Furthermore, Millennials are more motivated by a sense of mission and leaders who make them feel appreciated than by an extra $300 in the monthly paycheck. (See Decoding Global Talent,[43] BCG report, October 2014.)

The Need to Collaborate Across Boundaries. Many well-established technology companies have grown on the back of a single flagship product. Today, companies are competing across product categories, and with the rise in integrated solutions, silos are merging. Employees must be able to easily navigate functional and product boundaries to achieve the collaboration needed to deliver these more holistic solutions. Then, as boundaries begin to dissolve, and once-separate groups combine into single teams (a services, sales, and engineering team, for example), roles will need to be redefined.

The Need for New Ways of Working. Agile development and solution-based selling are forcing the development of new processes and new operating models.

---

42 https://www.bcg.com/publications/2014/hardware_software_human_resources_code_wars_all_industry_competition_software_talent
43 https://www.bcg.com/publications/2014/people-organization-human-resources-decoding-global-talent

Core business processes – such as product development – are following new rhythms, creating new handoff points, and dictating new deliverables. Development deadlines, sales cycle times, service feedback loops, and other timelines will inevitably compress. It is essential to ease collaboration across product teams and functions, with customers, and even with ecosystem partners. As product teams broaden, spans of control will likewise broaden, necessitating changes in evaluation and compensation models.

Rising to the Challenge: The New HR Manifesto

HR's role must fundamentally change. No longer can HR be a supporting player. It must assume a leading role as a strategic partner in driving and orchestrating transformation.

HR must understand the requirements of the transformation and how these impact HR. It must craft its own vision of how people and the organization will enable the strategy. HR must anticipate the people and organizational implications of every change initiative. It must know whether the company has the capability and the capacity to meet its strategic goals. All the while, HR must keep pace with the organization as the transformation unfolds, operating with agility and in real time.

An Expanded Role

HR cannot shed its traditional responsibilities, such as performance reviews, talent searches, and benefits. But it must move far beyond the role of service provider and take on broader and deeper organizational challenges.

As Figure 3.5 shows, HR's expanded role involves more than a linear change. Each step requires a deepening of capabilities. For example, increasing cost pressures require greater efficiencies in providing services. HR must also fortify its functional expertise so that it can serve the business more effectively. Professionals must work side by side with line leaders, providing them with the support they need in organization design, change management, and other critical activities.

Because people and talent are the key – or the key obstacle – to growth, HR must be proactive in the transformation effort. In that way, it will win the confidence and trust of senior leaders and elevate its position to that of partner.

The challenge for many HR organizations is winning the credibility to take on this expanded role. This can present a chicken-and-egg dilemma. Many HR professionals aren't viewed as true partners by CEOs. Traditionally, their role hasn't re-

As a strategic partner

- Participates in senior-leadership discussions and helps shape the strategy and transformation agenda
- Frames and elevates strategic people-and-organization issues and priorities
- Adapts the HR operating model to enable HR to engage with the business as a strategic partner

As a transformation enabler

- Understands the business transformation and how it will impact roles, skills and behaviors, and the HR disciplines
- Assesses its capability and capacity to respond across each HR discipline and address any gaps
- Mobilizes HR resources and operates in an agile mode to enable the transformation

As a functional expert

Focuses on providing expertise and advice in core HR disciplines, including:
- Recruiting
- Compensation and benefits
- Learning and development
- Performance management
- Mobility
- Occupational health and safety

As a service provider

Focuses on reliable and efficient execution of core HR services, including:
- Payroll
- Employee data and record keeping
- Training administration
- Time and expense management

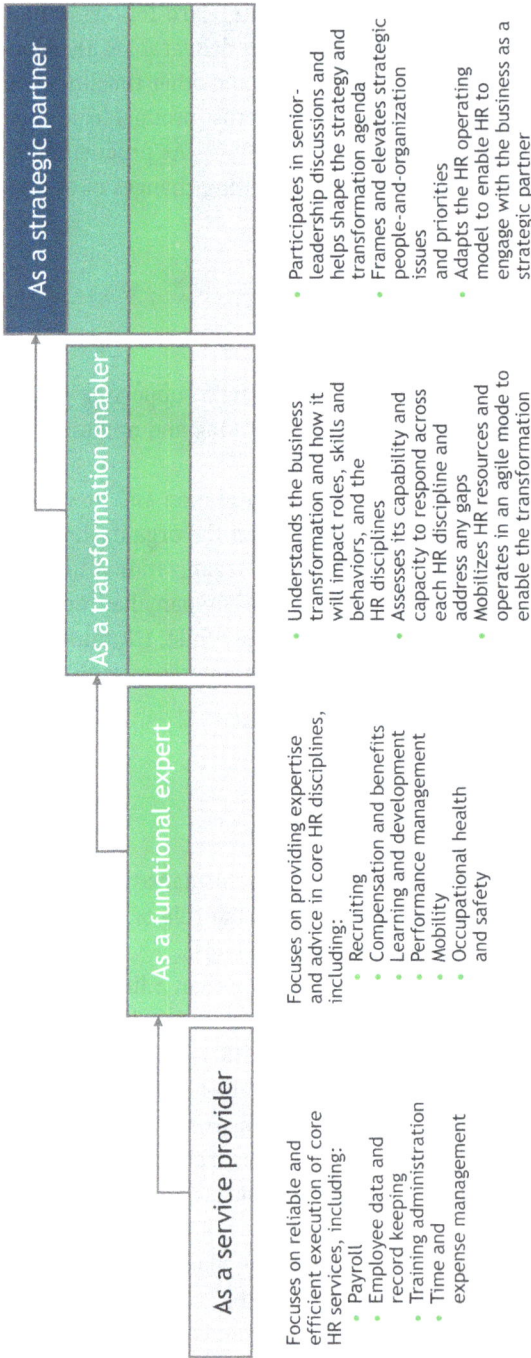

Sources: BCG experience

Figure 3.5: HR's Expanded Role.

quired that they perform in these new ways, so they'll need to demonstrate their ability and willingness to earn a seat at the table.

HR will also need the capacity to evolve in real time. Constantly changing customer and market demands aren't the exclusive province of the business functions. The HR organization needs its finger on the pulse of the dynamics of both the company and the industry. It needs its eye on the future. And it needs the ability to anticipate and adapt to change. A CHRO for a social-media company recently told us that HR's mandate in the transformation goes beyond its traditional role. "HR is the ignition for the innovation engine," he said. It can be the unbiased arbiter in some of the more contentious decisions that accompany a transformation.

A New Operating Model

To broaden its role and develop new capabilities, HR must alter how it operates in several areas, including the following (see Figure 3.6).

HR's Engagement with the Business. To keep pace with the many changes in the business, HR will need to be more proactive, responsive, and flexible. HR must be integrally linked to the business at higher levels. Netflix is a noteworthy example: CEO Reed Hastings and Patty McCord, who was at the time the chief talent officer, collaborated on a piece defining how Netflix shaped culture, motivated performance, and managed talent. The document (which went viral) exemplifies HR's partnership with the business – at the highest level, both in leadership and strategic import.

HR's Own Way of Working. HR organizations are just as silo afflicted as the line businesses. Worse, each client-facing group tends to serve its silo at the expense of working in concert with the larger HR organization to leverage HR's efforts. For example, in many cases, local HR departments, mistrusting centers of excellence, do the work themselves. So activities that demand a consistent, enterprise-wide approach (such as strategic workforce planning) are undermined. Instead, HR needs to change from loose confederation to "one HR."

HR's Own Talent. The traditional skill set of HR professionals can leave them unprepared for the more strategic challenges they face. They'll need more high-performance skills and behaviors, such as the ability to counsel business leaders as partners and the capacity to manage the people elements of any business change, whether it is a restructuring or a new-system implementation. Above all, the CHRO needs to determine what talent is needed to fill all of HR's roles and ensure that everyone works together to create a more effective HR organization.

The Use of Analytics, Measurement Systems, and Related Tools. It's time for HR organizations to get "religious" about data. Powerful tools and methodologies

HR's own talent

What talent, competencies, and qualifications are needed in HR?

HR structure and collaboration

How should HR leaders and staff be organized and work together?

HR operational planning

What is HR's holistic operational plan?

HR's engagement with the business

How does HR engage and interface with the business?
Is the HR operational plan in sync with the business cycle?

HR analytics, measurement systems, and related tools

Which technological solutions are needed to support HR's work?

HR processes and capabilities

What HR processes and capabilities are required to support the business?

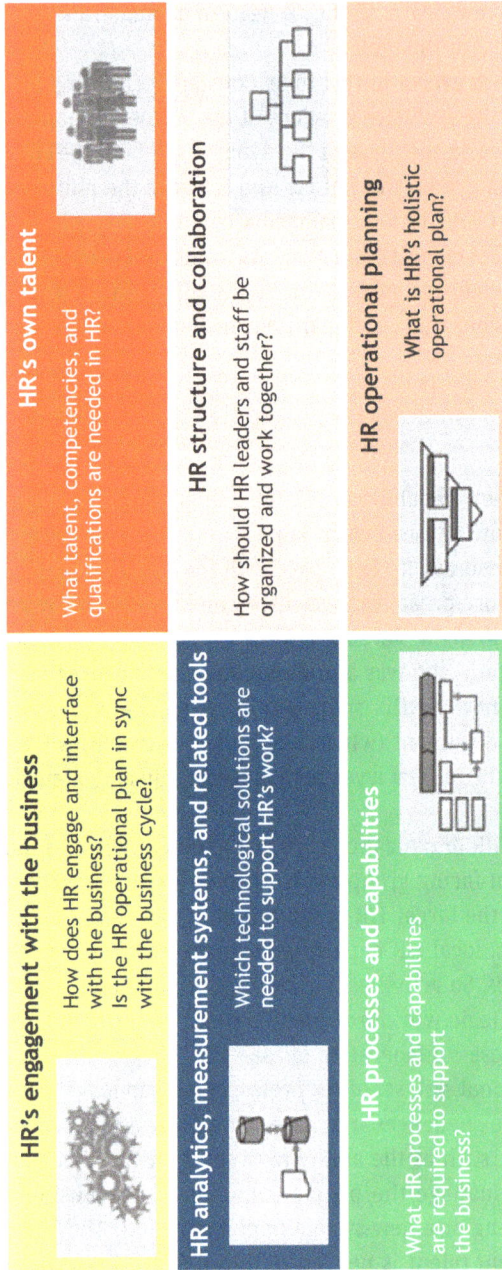

Sources: BCG experience

Figure 3.6: HR's Broader Role Calls for a New Operating Model.

can inform and improve people decisions. Analytics can be used to create a profile of the most innovative employees or to pinpoint the reason for high attrition among a particular cohort (both, Google practices). Other tools can help analyze future talent requirements or track the efficiency and effectiveness of service delivery.

Retooling Processes, Upgrading Capabilities

To fulfill its new role as transformation enabler, HR will also need to retool core processes and upgrade its capabilities. Seven critical areas will need attention.

Organization Design. Frequent product and strategy shifts will call for regular modification of the organization structure. Line business leaders, together with HR, should decide how the organization needs to change. Then, HR should orchestrate the process, bringing the right people together and ensuring that they address the critical questions and their implications. HR also needs to be proactive in managing surge capacity within the organization design, analyzing and guiding decisions about whether to outsource or develop internal capability.

The greater challenge, though, is associated with the increased complexity of organization design. Traditionally, HR professionals have had little experience designing organizations that address the major shifts now under way. Now, as functional dividing lines crumble and hybrid operating models become more prevalent, HR must be able to drive and orchestrate the needed changes in organization design.

Employee Engagement and Culture. Establishing a high-performance culture is crucial for aligning people with the strategy and securing employee engagement, as well as for attracting and retaining the best talent. HR must ensure that the company's cultural identity includes such critical attributes as customer focus, the willingness to take risks, collaboration, and agility. Although culture change happens within the business lines, HR is responsible for fostering it through leadership role modeling, performance management policies and practices, rewards and incentives and people policies, and even the physical workspace design. (See High-Performance Culture,[44] BCG Focus, June 2013.)

Strategic Workforce Planning. In a more volatile operating environment, strategic workforce planning is a continuous process – one that HR must instigate and coordinate. HR must also take the lead in assessing and anticipating emerging skill gaps and in developing site strategies to fulfill future talent needs. That in-

---

[44] https://www.bcg.com/publications/2013/people-organization-behavior-high-performance-culture

cludes determining which levers – training, sourcing, or acquisitions – to activate to fill talent gaps.

Talent Acquisition and Retention. Acquiring talent will require new, unconventional, and more far-reaching pipelines and strategies. Among them: recruiting college freshmen and sophomores with the aim of securing talent earlier and implementing programs that seed the supply of science, technology, engineering, and mathematics talent for the future. Managing the company's brand (by, for example, promoting its appearance on best-places-to-work lists) will remain important. But increasingly, companies will need more creative targeted tactics, such as sponsoring "hackathons" to discover technical talent and offering scholarships to lock in the best of the best.

Retention will also call for fresh approaches that satisfy Millennials' need for intrinsic rewards. Google, for instance, structures small teams around its high-impact smart creatives. These teams thrive in an environment of open dialogue and brainstorming.

Learning and Development. Companies have to either invest in learning and development or form a strategy that can support perpetual personnel churn. More important, companies need to abandon the traditional notion that learning and development equal training. Experiential learning is vital. Leading companies orchestrate rotations – or simply put smart people into jobs at which they learn by doing.

Leadership Development. To help leaders drive growth, lead transformation, and develop future leaders, HR needs to define the critical competencies and devise a way to assess them. HR also needs to coach managers with agility and vision who are adept at navigating change. (See "Adaptive Leadership,"[45] BCG Perspective, December 2010.)

Compensation and Performance Management. These areas require a complete overhaul. New incentive models are needed to promote new growth businesses and solution selling. Targeting specific talent pools will call for developing differentiated compensation strategies and creative new perks, such as leave-of-absence policies.

To adapt to the motivation profile of Millennials, some companies are abandoning annual reviews and stack rankings. They're adopting performance management systems that feature more regular feedback, less emphasis on ratings, and more measurements pertaining to "living the culture."

---

45 https://www.bcg.com/publications/2010/leadership-engagement-culture-adaptive-leadership

The Leadership Imperative

Putting people first in transforming technology companies is not a lofty idea; it is a matter of practical necessity.

HR is naturally positioned to be a critical enabler of transformation. But answering that call means that HR must change. It must contribute to shaping people strategies and setting the transformation agenda. It must fortify its own core capabilities and transform the way it operates. HR needs its own version of "agile," experimenting and learning as it grows.

CHROs today should possess creativity, vision, and their own form of operational expertise. They must be decisive and confident in their business judgments if they (and their organizations) are to act as – and be seen as – strategic partners of business leaders. To govern a transformational function, CHROs need to have transformational leadership abilities: the capacity to envision the future, an entrepreneurial mindset, agility, and the willingness to take risks.

Because putting people first is paramount, CEOs should lead the charge in calling for HR's expanded role. It is no longer acceptable for CEOs to hold onto low expectations about HR's potential contributions or to overlook its role. Such attitudes only threaten a company's ability to operate in a world of constant disruption.

What might a changed HR look like? One CHRO's experience captures it perfectly. When called in for her annual review, she was surprised (and encouraged) by the CEO's approach: "First," he said, "let's talk about our company's plan for the coming year. Where do you think we should be headed?"

Ultimately, putting people first in transforming technology companies is a call to leaders: CEOs must revise their view, reset expectations, and advance partnership; line business leaders must engage; and CHROs must embrace the challenge and step up to become transformation partners. Nothing less than the enterprise's ability to compete and win depends on it.

Chapter 4
Building the Workplace of the Future

What's Fueling Burnout in Your Organization

Rob Cross, Karen Dillon, and Martin Reeves

Many people believe burnout is driven by excessive work demands. In fact, it's driven by a specific type of demand–work that requires too much collaboration between individuals or teams of employees. To reduce this collaboration overload, ask these four questions: Can we reduce structural complexity? Does our workflow make sense? Has the profusion of teams spiked employees' microstress? And have we built a sense of purpose in our employees' everyday interactions?

Organizations around the world are experiencing unprecedented levels of burnout,[1] which is creating a significant – and under-recognized – cost to organizations in the form of quiet quitting, reduced innovation, and even spiraling health care costs. Many people are quick to point to an increase in overall workload as the culprit. But our research shows that the work itself has not increased so much as the *collaborative demands*[2] of the work.

By that, we mean the volume and frequency of the collaborations that people have to engage in to complete the work – what we call the collaborative footprint – have risen over the past decade and a half, bringing exponential opportunities for stress. This comes through the increased potential for misunderstanding, misalignment, and imbalances of workload and capacity, among other things. All of this combines to create a battering of everyday stresses.

One form of this stress is the one we call "microstress" – small moments of stress from interactions with colleagues that feel routine but whose cumulative toll is enormous. Our research[3] into high performers has made clear the destructive impact of unchecked microstress, both on individuals and on teams. At the team level, this form of stress propagates through networks and relationships.

---

1 https://www.gallup.com/workplace/349484/state-of-the-global-workplace.aspx#ite-506900
2 https://hbr.org/2021/09/collaboration-overload-is-sinking-productivity
3 https://hbr.org/2023/02/the-hidden-toll-of-microstress

---

https://doi.org/10.1515/9783111369921-005

It may seem challenging to find ways to reduce stress on teams that are over-loaded with deliverables, but leaders have more tools at their disposal than they may realize. Instead of relying only on coaching on individual coping strategies, leaders can look for systemic improvement in the collective working environment. We have identified four overlooked collective strategies that leaders can implement for reducing microstress. Here are the four key questions you need to ask.

Can We Reduce Structural Complexity?

For decades organizations have been building organizational complexity – not only in expanding spans and layers in traditional hierarchical structures (expanding the number of direct reports to reduce layers between the front line and the C-suite), but also in moving to matrixed, networked, or other more agile ways of working. While new these structures can be effective at increasing flexibility, they have also unintentionally introduced complexity by multiplying the required number of interactions per employee. We routinely see organizations adopting advice to move to structures with consistent spans of control (the number of people one is responsible for managing) of eight people. But such efforts to improve efficiency don't consider the collaborations required to do the work. The collaborative footprint of work – which has risen 50% or more in the past 15 years, according to Rob Cross's research[4] – is creating exponential opportunities for small stresses to run rampant in any organization. Unchecked, such complexity, can easily accumulate, triggering a proliferation of microstresses.

De-layering might seem to be a solution, but in embracing it many organizations have moved to spans of control that really are not feasible given the collaborative intensity of the work. (We've even seen some organizations scaling up to spans of control of 12 or more.) Such flat hierarchy can create stress for employees balancing competing objectives of multiple leaders to whom an employee might report, formally or informally.

Removing layers, while appealing on cost analyses and decision-making flows, also often introduces other less visible inefficiencies around work. Many teams are underperforming today due to priority overload where too many uncoordinated asks are coming into the teams from disconnected stakeholders[5] and failures of co-ordination and prioritization at high levels in the organization.

---

4 https://hbr.org/2016/01/collaborative-overload
5 https://sloanreview.mit.edu/article/when-collaboration-fails-and-how-to-fix-it/

One way to fix that is to have explicit processes to remove excessive complexity. It may not be possible to rewind all of these efforts at de-layering organizations, but there are a few simple practices[6] you can employ to root out the potential for unnecessary stress from structural complexity. Most companies have many ways of introducing new complexity, but no systematic continuous effort to remove it. Netflix is one of a handful of firms known for prioritizing identifying and removing unnecessary complexity.[7] As their company policy states, "We work hard to . . . keep our business as simple as possible . . . you don't need policies for everything." If you must introduce new teams or procedures, consider making them temporary. Create them with an explicit sunset clause, such that it is dissolved when no longer useful, avoiding the gradual ratcheting of complexity over time.

Companies can also control complexity by continually simplifying the product portfolio, which is often a key driver of complexity. Trader Joe's has a such a policy for controlling the number of SKUs[8] to maintain the number at less than 10% of the industry average. Similarly, LEGO controls the number of colors and brick types in its products, to control manufacturing and logistical complexity.

Above all, don't just think about on paper efficiency, think about the collaborative asks being placed on human beings who execute these tasks day in, day out. When we have asked top teams in offsites who in the room wants another email, meeting, or phone call in their lives, we have yet to see a single hand shoot up. The more complex, the more matrixed, the more required communication and connection between employees, the more ad hoc the more microstresses are going to be impeding the effectiveness of work.

Does Our Workflow Make Sense?

Organizations have had an unrelenting push into agile, network-centric structures executing through teams that are formed and disbanded at increasingly rapid pace. These efforts are providing speed, but taken to an extreme, they are starting to sacrifice the benefits of scale and efficiency that came from the process revolution. Forming and reforming project teams requires increasing coordination, often relying on the heroics of individual employees to get work done. But that is not a sustainable strategy – and triggers endless opportunities for burnout.

---

6 https://hbr.org/2020/01/taming-complexity
7 https://jobs.netflix.com/culture
8 https://d3.harvard.edu/platform-rctom/submission/trader-joes-food-for-thought/

"It's better to rely on a process than just people," Don Allan, CEO of Stanley Black & Decker observed[9] of one of the key HR lessons of the pandemic, "so you do not create unnecessary stress and even burnout for your organization."

The proliferation of technologies in the workplace promises to streamline work and communication, but instead can often became a source of additional complexity, required work and stress. Often, we find organizations using between six and nine means of collaborating to get work done – meetings (virtual and face-to-face), email, instant messaging (such as Slack), team collaborative spaces, phone calls, texting, etc. Inefficiencies invariably creep in as people use these modalities differently – for example, who doesn't have a colleague who loves to write elaborate emails, hiding what they want in the 10th paragraph! Or at the other extreme, some people use one modality (e.g., IM) to solve problems quickly, but lack of transparency into the interaction creates misalignment with other teammates who have no idea a decision was made over IM.

One way to limit this stress is to agree on collaborative norms. For example, a team might agree to only use bullets on email. And if a longer explanation is required or a disagreement seems to be brewing, the team agrees to meet face to face. We find a simple exercise of asking teams to agree to three positive norms across all modes of collaboration that they want to sustain and three negatives they want to stop (e.g., emailing at night, hitting reply to all on mundane responses, etc.) can generate 8% to 12% time savings across teams, allowing them more time to focus on the actual work. Technology itself is not necessarily a bad thing, but the culture that springs up around using that technology is where microstress creeps in.

Teams can also limit the set of tools they're using and bake them into the work in a way which reduces human transaction costs. Focus on maximizing technology that helps eliminate or reduce the costs of mundane tasks, e.g., setting up workflows on Slack or recurring meetings to ensure appropriate check ins don't slip through the cracks because they're relying on a team member to set up and coordinate. Encourage the team to invest time in learning the tools and share their productivity tips and tricks. And avoid new tools or multiple tools that inadvertently becoming new sources of work or complexity, e.g., through cumbersome sign on procedures or lack of mutual compatibility. Too often teams aren't consulted about which tools will actually help their productivity.

---

9 https://hbr.org/2023/03/has-your-organization-acted-on-what-its-learned-in-the-pandemic

Has the Profusion of Teams Spiked Employees' Microstress?

One of the unintended consequences of organizations relying on teams that are assembled for projects is that teams have less time to build the kind of trust that is essential for efficient collaboration. And that happens repeatedly because many organizations require employees to contribute to five or six team efforts (in addition to their primary team) and have often let these groups grow too large,[10] with the average team size hovering around 15.

To avoid team growth from causing trouble, don't let "flexible" turn into inefficient. Some organizations trying to attract and retain top talent during the great resignation (and quiet quitting) have implemented talent marketplaces[11] which allow employees to locate projects they would like to work on or roles they want to fill as they chart their own career progression. Though well-intended as a talent retention tool, these shifts create inefficiencies in the network that most organizations do not account for. These programs are well-received by the employees but induce microstresses on both the team the employee is leaving and the one they are ported into, as they suddenly have to redirect and shape key working relationships with new people. One life sciences organization we worked with modeled the relational cost (the "switching costs" on work relationships and productivity of continually rotating teams) and determined that it didn't make sense for anyone to switch roles or teams in less than fifteen months because both the team and the rotating employee would fail to optimize the opportunity.

Companies must also ensure that their return-to-office plan doesn't create hidden stress. About 80% of companies are opting to require employees to be in the office three days a week, according to research from i4cp (the Institute for Corporate Productivity). To soften the blow and ensure flexibility, about half of those companies are allowing employees to pick the days they want to return.

Unfortunately, this well-intentioned effort has also created a new set of microstresses when the people who an organization needs to work together pick different days. Leaving this up to chance will not only hurt employee morale, but innovation and productivity. To prevent this, some organizations are using a technique called organizational network analysis[12] (a methodology that maps employees' working relationships) to specify specific groups of employees that need to be in the office at a given interval. Such an analysis can help leaders answer three critical questions in a return-to-office strategy:

---

10 https://hbr.org/2013/11/the-new-rules-of-breakthrough-collaboration
11 https://hbr.org/2023/05/how-to-design-an-internal-talent-marketplace
12 https://sloanreview.mit.edu/article/optimizing-return-to-office-strategies-with-organizational-network-analysis/

– *Who* should be brought back together and in what cadence of in-person and virtual interactions?
– *What* work should be prioritized in the now scarcer in-person time?
– *How* do leaders manage the transition to a hybrid model with the least resistance?

This method also helps motivate employees to resume some in-person interactions by showing them how hybrid work can improve their own effectiveness.

Have We Built a Sense of Purpose in Our Employees' Everyday Interactions?

Organizations have become adept at working efficiently with the help of technologies – what can't be swiftly taken care of on a Zoom call these days? But when work revolves around technology use, it can become transactional, missing the opportunity to make sure that employees understand how their work contributes to that purpose.

To avoid that problem, smart companies create opportunities to discuss purpose and how each group contributes to it. It is your role as a leader to shape and communicate the goal that you're all working toward. Don't let that get lost in the sea of microstress. With a clear understanding of how they are contributing to purpose, employees can more easily prioritize their work. Discuss what work is essential (and what is not) in contributing to purpose and use this to help your team prioritize and redesign work accordingly.

While many organizations focus on rallying employees around a collective corporate purpose, our research also suggests that purpose can be found in positive everyday interactions with colleagues,[13] too. For example, employees can find meaningful purpose in "co-creating" (involving the aha moments that emerge as people build on each other's ideas) which helps builds a sense of *We are in this together.* Small moments of working on something together create an authentic connection, a kind of antidote to the flood of microstresses that otherwise fill employees' days.

Finally, as leaders, don't underestimate the impact of your own microstress, both on you and your team. Look for interactions in which you are unintentionally creating microstress for your team – for example, being slightly unpredictable in

---

[13] https://sloanreview.mit.edu/article/a-noble-purpose-alone-wont-transform-your-company/

your expectations, failing to communicate deliverables clearly, or continually micromanaging their work. The microstress we create for others inevitably boomerangs back on us. If you recognize where you are the source of unnecessary microstress and try to course-correct, you will not only help reduce stress on your team, but you'll be also reducing stress on yourself, as well.

✳✳✳✳✳✳✳✳✳✳✳✳✳✳✳✳✳✳✳✳✳✳✳✳✳✳✳✳✳✳

We Can't Outrun Our Biology

Parneet Pal and Martin Reeves

It's tempting to conceive of businesses as economic islands that can be independently optimized by considering only a handful of operational variables, like product performance, efficiency, and financial returns.

But increasing awareness of how economic activity is encroaching on the limits of finite planetary resources has overturned this simplistic view. Most businesses now clearly acknowledge their dependence on and embeddedness within the larger systems of society and nature and have expanded their conception of strategy accordingly.

Recent science further deepens this "multi-systems" view of business by illuminating the deep connectedness among work environments, cellular biology, human health, and decision making. This requires companies to expand their conception of "sustainability" inwardly and reconsider how work is structured and managed, beyond the much discussed issue of flexibility of time and location.

Our Bodies, Our Minds, Our Jobs

Good decision making lies at the core of successful business strategy and execution. Though much attention is given to the financial and behavioral aspects of making wise choices, less attention has been given to the invisible biological foundations – and limits – we hit up against each day that directly shape our decision-making ability.

These biological limits are dependent on the interactions between our cellular health and our work environment.

The Limits of Cellular Health

Healthy cells in every organ in our body rely on a delicate balance in our metabolism, the hundreds of thousands of life-sustaining chemical reactions that convert food to energy, use that energy to build and maintain the body, and eliminate waste.

As with other natural systems, this cellular balance between growth and repair maintains a safe operating zone (a narrow range of temperature and pH) through a process called homeostasis, beyond which cellular function breaks down.

These evolved cellular mechanisms effectively rely on principles of energy conservation and efficiency, minimizing waste and recycling old or damaged parts, and maintaining stability through an intricate web of cell-to-cell communications mediated by various hormones and metabolites.

One of the key regulators of cellular metabolism is mitochondria. These organelles are descendants of ancient bacteria that symbiotically co-evolved in multicellular organisms. Though popularly known as simple "cell batteries" converting the food we eat into ATP (adenosine-triphosphate, the unit of cellular chemical energy), recent scientific advances in systems biology now point to their ubiquitous role in almost every aspect of cellular health and disease.

Inflammation and Disease

Inflammation is the body's natural immune response to any kind of injury and is an integral part of the process of healing, for example, if we scrape our hand, there is bleeding, redness, and swelling, followed by scab formation and repair of skin.

However, injury comes in many different forms. Think of the onslaught of physical, environmental, mental, emotional, and social stressors – big and small – that we navigate each day.

When the capacity of mitochondria to mitigate this stress load is exceeded – when we don't pay attention to how we eat, move, sleep, or manage psychological strain, or to the environmental pollutants we expose ourselves to, it precipitates a low-grade response called chronic inflammation. This disrupts cellular metabolism and energy production, resulting in cellular damage, and creates a self-perpetuating cycle of even more inflammation.[14]

This kind of internal cellular energy crisis often simmers in the body subclinically, without any overt symptoms that we are aware of in our daily lives.

However, it is reflected in several blood biomarkers indicating dysregulation of blood sugar, insulin resistance, reduced biodiversity of the gut microbiome, hormonal imbalance, elevated blood pressure, deposition of visceral fat around abdominal organs, and narrowing of arteries that carry blood to the heart and brain.

Inflammation is the starting point of almost all lifestyle-related chronic diseases, such as heart disease, obesity, diabetes, many cancers, strokes, auto-immune disease, and Alzheimer's and Parkinson's disease, as well as mental health disorders like depression and anxiety.

Three out of four people in the US, and increasingly globally, will suffer from one or more of these diseases in their lifetime. They account for upward of 75%

---

14 Furman D, et al. "Chronic Inflammation in the Etiology of Disease Across the Life Span." Nat Med. 2019;25(12):1822–32.

of our health care spend in the US, creating a huge avoidable expense for individual companies and for society as a whole.

Inflammation and Decision Making

Beyond disease, new research shows that even low levels of inflammation also influence our decision making in the moment.[15] Biologically, inflammation is interpreted by our body as a signal that our immediate survival is at stake, and we must grab any resources we can get our hands on, making us impulsive, unable to delay gratification, and prone to short termism.

Lifestyle imbalances such as sleep deprivation add fuel to this fire, by increasing emotional lability, impulsivity and risky decision making while reducing focus, memory, speed, and accuracy.[16]

The Exposome

Mitochondria and cellular health do not function in isolation. They are dependent on the so called exposome,[17] an individual's total cumulative environmental exposures from conception onward.

The exposome includes factors such as climate, air quality, industrial chemicals, pesticides, radiation, urbanization, food and water, tobacco, medications, and microbiome; lifestyle behaviors such as how we eat, move, sleep, and manage stress; and our social support and economic status.

These exposures are interpreted and responded to by our cells and mitochondria through shifts in important biological pathways such as inflammation and epigenetics – mechanisms such as DNA methylation and histone modifications that determine which genes are turned on or off at any given moment.

In other words, our health as well as our ability to think, feel, move, act, collaborate, create, make decisions, and relate – everything we do in our work and

---

15 Gassen J, et al. "Inflammation Predicts Decision-Making Characterized by Impulsivity, Present Focus, and an Inability to Delay Gratification." Sci Rep. 2019;9:4928.

16 Williamson AM, et al. "Moderate Sleep Deprivation Produces Impairments in Cognitive and Motor Performance Equivalent to Legally Prescribed Levels of Alcohol Intoxication." Occup Environ Med. 2000;57:649–55.

Whitney P, et al. "Feedback Blunting: Total Sleep Deprivation Impairs Decision-Making That Requires Updating Based on Feedback." Sleep. 2015;38(5):745–54.

Toschi N, et al. "Sleep Quality Relates to Emotional Reactivity via Intracortical Myelination." Sleep. January 2021;44(1):zsaa146.

17 Vineis P, Barouki R. "The Exposome as the Science of Social-to-Biological Transitions." Environ Int. 2022;165: 4.

personal lives – is an outcome of the interplay between the exposome and cellular metabolism.

The greater the imbalances in the exposome, the worse our cellular health and inflammation.

Paying Attention to the Workplace Exposome

It's now widely appreciated that business decisions have ecological consequences which in turn can have negative business consequences, such as the depletion of input materials, an inability to attract talent, undermining stakeholder trust, social sanction, and restrictive regulation.

In the same way, the working environment has biological consequences which in turn have direct business consequences, including reduced motivation, elevated absenteeism, elevated health care costs, and poor decision making.

As such, we need to extend inward the vision of businesses as systems embedded in, and dependent on other systems (society, nature) to pay more attention to the working environment.

How then in practical terms can we ensure that the business exposome is sustainable for health and decision making?

Embracing Biology as Part of the Future of Work

Given the above links between the human body and organizational effectiveness, leaders should take several steps to mitigate harmful risks – and optimize the way people live and work.

Reframing
We must begin by becoming aware of the importance of the link among the conditions of work, cellular biology, and the consequences for decision making and business health.

Given the new findings of the effects of the exposome on employee health, productivity, and decision making, leaders should now recognize organizational culture as a powerful social, economic, environmental, and psychological exposure for themselves and their teams.

This provides a cogent motivation for prioritizing and tracking employee well-being and the six causes of burnout[18] (work overload, perceived lack of control, insufficient reward, breakdown of community, absence of fairness, and value conflict) as a strategic business imperative.

The "future of work" has received much attention following the disruptions of COVID, but has mainly focused on issues of temporal and locational flexibility and on the impact of AI on jobs and productivity. It needs to expand to deal with the issues of biological sustainability.

Educating

As individuals there is much that we can do to lower our inflammatory load to improve mitochondrial health and metabolism, including:
- Align daily routines with the body's circadian rhythms – eating, moving, and working during the daytime with 7 to 9 hours of time to rest, fast, and sleep at night – allowing for optimal cellular repair and regeneration
- Shift from being sedentary to moving the body daily, which increases focus, learning, and memory through the production of brain-derived neurotrophic factor[19] and a decrease in cellular oxidative stress
- Minimize exposure to air pollution and increase time in nature, which lowers stress hormone levels
- Reduce consumption of sugary, processed foods and increase intake of whole, fiber-rich plant foods to stabilize blood sugar and insulin levels, and increase biodiversity of the gut microbiome

Unlocking this potential requires education to link the latest scientific findings to practical actions and supporting tools for lasting behavior change.

Baking-in

Environmental sustainability was initially treated by most businesses as a set of considerations to be managed separately from core business processes. More recently, there has been much effort to make sure that it is baked into business strategy and operations. Analogously, workplace well-being programs have traditionally been considered mainly as "nice-to-have" and "add-on" offerings for em-

18 Maslach C, Leiter MP. "Early Predictors of Job Burnout and Engagement." J Appl Psychol. 2008;93(3):498–512
19 Walsh EI, et al. "Towards an Understanding of the Physical Activity-BDNF-Cognition Triumvirate: A Review of Associations and Dosage." Ageing Res Rev. 2020; 60: 1.

ployees. This is reflected in the fact that the actual quality and utilization of these services is highly variable, with mixed outcomes.

The COVID pandemic helped to raise awareness of the underlying stress, mental health, and burnout epidemic at work. However, postpandemic, burnout rates continue to rise – up to 48% among employees and 53% among managers.[20] There is also a stark discrepancy between the perception of workforce well-being among executive leadership (three out of four believe it has improved) and the ground reality of their employees (the majority report that well-being has worsened or stayed the same).[21]

While both executives and teams may be individually motivated to improve their well-being, heavy workloads, long work hours, and stressful cultures make this difficult to put into practice. At the same time, most employees recognize the need for more than just a better health benefits program. Well-being needs to be embedded systematically, as part of its core business processes from performance assessment, through sustainability efforts, to leadership training.

In particular, companies need to expand inwardly how they think about sustainability, both through self-interest and collective welfare. Beyond the impact on finite planetary resources, they need to concern themselves with the conditions they create for human biology. Such measures are perfectly feasible for any firm to embrace, as illustrated in the example below.

In short, we are beginning to realize that we can't outrun our biology, however tempting it is to believe that there are no limits to our capacity to handle stress or to produce. Paradoxically, it is only by attending to these limits that we can sustain our effectiveness over time.

∗∗∗

How One Financial Services Firm Addressed Inward Sustainability

A global financial services firm recognized that its current workflow, workloads, and reward systems were the main contributors to the increasing levels of reported burnout and attrition on their teams. This prompted a few changes:

---

20 Microsoft. "Hybrid Work Is Just Work. Are We Doing it Wrong?" *Work Trend Index Report.* 2022.
21 Fisher, J et al. "As workforce well-being dips, leaders ask: What will it take to move the needle?" *Deloitte Insights.* 2023.

- A leadership mind-set shift from well-being being solely an employee's individual responsibility to one that is a by-product of the company's culture and work environment
- Managers regularly checking in with their teams to assess and redistribute workloads; setting clear norms and expectations for email and other internal communication response times; and devoting time to addressing well-being issues during performance reviews
- A department-wide initiative to prune total and individual meeting times, providing more room for uninterrupted, focused, and creative work during the workday
- Adding frequent touchpoints for public recognition (town halls, team meetings) as emotional rewards in addition to its financial incentive system
- Increased adoption by employees of evidence-based guidelines for sleep, movement, and nutrition as part of their daily routines
- A reiteration of their existing organizational value of "entrepreneurialism" and "innovation," in this case, leaders modeling a culture of well-being

****

How to Make Sure Your Employees Enjoy Their Work

Deborah Lovich

There has been a ton of research over the years on why employee engagement matters.

For example, a report earlier this year from Microsoft's WorkLab[22] – which "delves into the latest science and the most innovative thinking" about how and where and why people work" found that "high employee engagement correlates with stronger financial performance."

There are many reasons for this bottom-line impact. We've known about them for years. A 2013 Harvard Business Review article[23] identifies several of them: because companies with highly engaged employees report higher levels of productivity, lower levels of absenteeism and turnover, and fewer safety incidents and quality problems.

Setting aside the concern that correlation doesn't prove causation, let's accept the fact that in this case these and other studies over a long period of time have certainly provided strong circumstantial evidence. But they also raise an important question: What does "engagement" mean?

My home-grown formula for determining engagement is pretty straightforward: Those who enjoy their work will be engaged. Those who see their jobs simply as pay checks, necessary to pay the bills, will be less engaged. And those who consider their jobs drudgery will drag their teams down, chalk up more absences, job-hop more frequently, produce less, and make more mistakes than those who are happy.

The BCG Henderson Institute, Boston Consulting Group's internal think tank, recently conducted a wide-ranging survey that adds some much-needed richness to this discussion.

With more than 1,000 respondents across industries, geographies, work categories, and levels of responsibility, our "Making Work Work" survey (feel free to take it yourself[24]) asked respondents how much time they routinely spend on various types of activities, how they rate their "effectiveness" on these activities (i.e., productivity) and how much they "enjoy" doing them.

---

22 https://www.microsoft.com/en-us/worklab/work-trend-index/the-new-performance-equation-in-the-age-of-ai#:~:text=The%20analysis%20shows%20that%20employee,work%2C%20you%20are%20more%20productive
23 https://hbr.org/2013/07/employee-engagement-does-more
24 https://www.113.vovici.net/se/13B2588B5A0A74E1%5d

The activities we asked them about included administrative work, focus work (thinking, writing), collaborative work (meetings, brainstorming), individual and group development (training) and culture/team building (connecting). For managers and executives, we added overseeing work, mentoring and coaching.

Joy = Retention

Our biggest takeaway was fascinating, but perhaps not surprising: *People who enjoy their work are 40% less likely to look for another job.* That is a huge retention premium.

Overall, the new BCG Henderson Institute data indicate that employers risk losing as many as 69% of their employees who don't enjoy their work. That number goes down to 41% among those who do enjoy their work. That's a 40% reduction in attrition risk. In short, joy pays.

We also dug deeper to see what constitutes joy at work.

Collaboration and Affiliation = Joy

The other big takeaway for leaders is that *the two types of activities linked most closely with enjoying work the most are those involving (1) collaboration with others and (2) team building and affiliation.* Leaders and day-to-day managers should make more time and get much better at such activities.

People get energy out of other people. But a word of caution: Before you drag everybody back into the office to collaborate and connect with their teammates and colleagues, make sure that they have intentional time to do that when they are in person – not spending their time on administrative tasks, focus activities, and so forth – when they come in. In other words, when you want employees to commute, make the commute worthwhile.

Interestingly, the survey found that the respondents now spend, on average, about 25% of their time on administrative work (sending and answering emails, paperwork, scheduling meetings), 17% of their time on interactive work, but only about 3% of their time on team building and affiliation activities.

For those whose jobs are not by definition strictly administrative, the "admin" burden has to end. Why? Because the vast majority of people don't enjoy it. In fact, you might even want to call it demoralizing and soul-sucking.

Administrative work has the lowest enjoyment rating of any work activity. So here is where some real rethinking of work needs to happen: What can we eliminate and how can we use technology and perhaps generative AI to reduce the tediousness of the administrative tasks that can't be eliminated?

Companies everywhere are generating flexible new technology- and GenAI-driven ways to deliver customer value and productivity. The data tell us that we need to add joy at work to the list of goals as well.

****

Enjoying Work Matters More than You May Realize

Deborah Lovich and Rosanna Sargeant

Attrition risk should be on every corporate leader's radar. According to the BCG Henderson Institute's recent survey of 1,000 office-based workers around the world, nearly half (45%) are at least passively job searching. This finding is even more pronounced among younger and more diverse populations, jumping to 51% for people aged 25 to 34 and to 54% for ethnic and racial minorities. All industries are affected, but the travel and tourism (71%), legal (70%), food and beverage (67%), and consumer goods (67%) sectors face the most risk.

Of course, retention is a complex issue unique to each company. But the good news is that our survey insights also suggest a universal solution: doubling down on employee joy. As intuitive as it sounds, the concept of joy has often been left out of the discourse on productivity and retention in the business world. Indeed, while companies are becoming more attuned to issues of health and wellness[25] and employee engagement, they often try to address those challenges by adding benefits without an exploration of the employees' day-to-day work itself. Most company leaders simply aren't thinking deeply – or strategically – about whether their employees find their work interesting, rewarding, or fun. It's a blind spot that could result in the loss of key talent.

Production: Insert Slideshow Here

Joy at Work Cuts Attrition Risk in Half

We designed our latest Making Work *Work* survey to better understand the impact of employees' feelings of enjoyment and effectiveness in their role. We found that joy has an outsized impact on retention: Employees who enjoy their work are 49% less likely to say they would consider taking a new job than employees who don't enjoy their work. This finding echoes insight from another recent BCG study of more than 11,000 workers[26] that identified "doing work I enjoy"

---

25 https://www.bcg.com/publications/2023/workplace-burnout-costing-canadian-companies-billions
26 https://www.bcg.com/press/18december2023-employees-move-on-from-current-jobs

---

Note: The authors wish to thank Jacob Smith, Jessica Lao, Caitlin Arnold, and Sophia He for their contributions to this article.

as the factor with the third strongest correlation with retention at the one-year mark, behind only job security and feeling respected at work.

Among our Making Work *Work* respondents, individual contributors have the highest risk of leaving, and they exhibit the lowest enjoyment ratings. On a scale of zero to 100, where 100 means "I enjoy my job as much as anyone possibly could" and zero means "I do not enjoy my job at all," individual contributors rated their work enjoyment at 55 on average, compared with a score of 76 among executives.

Interestingly, the relationship between joy and retention holds even for employees who don't consider themselves very effective at their job. Roughly a quarter of our individual contributors identified as "high joy and low effectiveness," and this group exhibited a similarly low attrition rate (38%) to their "high joy and high effectiveness" peers (35%). Closer inspection reveals that 60% of these high-joy and low-effectiveness employees work in tech, financial services, and professional services, and they tend to be slightly younger and shorter in tenure than their counterparts in other sectors. It's possible that their self-evaluation results from lack of mastery: roughly one-tenth of the qualitative responses from this cohort indicate newness to the role and lack of training as barriers to effectiveness.

Hybrid is the Answer

Team-driven, hybrid work models – that is, hybrid models in which schedules for on-site or remote work are decided collectively by teams (those closest to the jobs) – yielded the most joy and effectiveness across the different types of activities (for example, administrative, focus, or collaborative work) among our survey participants.

However, while most companies seem to have embraced hybrid models (reported by 58% of our respondents), only 13% of total respondents were part of teams that are able to determine their work models together. By contrast, 59% of respondents say that they receive work model mandates from above. This is a mistake, as team-decided models yield a 13% boost in joy over top-down mandates.

Critically, companies with team-driven, hybrid work models also perform better than their peers across key business metrics. Earlier this year, our analysis of company revenue data alongside work model policies taken from Scoop's Flex Index showed that a structured hybrid work model – meaning companies that allow their employees to work remotely some days and require them to be in the office for others – grew twice as fast from 2020 to 2022 as firms that required their employees to always work in the office.

Driving Joy Requires Getting Specific

In our prior survey, we shared how much time employees spend[27] on different types of tasks. For example, we found that, on average, individual contributors spend just over one-third (37%) of their time on work they believe is done most effectively in person, such as affiliation and collaborative tasks. By contrast, managers and executives spend nearly half their time (49%) on work they believe is best done in person, such as onboarding new hires and giving feedback. We've been able to add a layer of analysis to show how much joy people find in these jobs – and have found that people are spending too much time on tasks that chip away at joy.

This is especially true for individual contributors, who spend only 5% of their time on high-joy work, compared with managers and executives, who spend 56%. To name one particularly egregious example, administrative work takes up 29% of individual contributors' time and yields little joy, while individual development takes up only 5% of their time but yields high joy. Compare this with the experience of managers and executives, who spend nearly one-fifth of their time (19%) on interactive work – a task that consistently gives them joy.

How to Create a More Enjoyable Workplace

These findings should guide efforts to rethink how work gets done. For example, given the volume of administrative work that many employees report doing, firms should consider using technologies like GenAI to automate this type of work while allowing people to reallocate their time toward more joyful tasks.

This is particularly important given organizations' focus on integrating GenAI into their processes. Such efforts are primarily geared toward the technology's potential to boost productivity or creativity, but companies also need to explore its potential to boost employee joy. Preliminary studies seem promising: in the BCG survey[28] of 11,000 employees, 46% of those who used ChatGPT regularly for administrative duties reported being "very satisfied" at work, compared with just 18% of those who did not use GenAI tools for these tasks.

Leaders also need to roll up their sleeves and identify what's standing in the way of their employees' enjoyment of work. Our *Making Work Work* survey revealed that joy and retention have the same top two blockers: motivation and support. With a better understanding of what employees' need – similar to the depth of knowledge that companies seek about their customers – leaders can

27 https://www.bcg.com/publications/2023/flexible-working-models
28 https://www.bcg.com/press/18december2023-employees-move-on-from-current-jobs

start to design programs and policies that flip the script. Joy looks different for everyone.

When virtually every organization today is reshaping work, it's paramount that firms recognize the importance of joy. Their ability to attract and retain top talent depends on it.

****

11,000 People Tell Us What Really Matters at Work and Why We Should Care

Debbie Lovich, Gabrielle Novacek, Christopher Gentile, Jean Lee, Hillary Wool, Nick South, and Nicole Sibilio

The relationship between employers and their employees has shifted fundamentally. BCG research of 11,000 employees reveals that roughly one in four employees are at risk, meaning that they are not planning to be in their current job a year from now. If leaders want to keep their best people, they need to deploy more sophisticated analytics to understand their employee needs and focus investment on priority actions to reduce attrition risk and increase satisfaction, motivation, and feelings of inclusion.

To understand what really matters, we asked over 11,000 employees across the US, Canada, the UK, France, Germany, Australia, Japan, and India from October 6 to 30, 2023 how they felt about various aspects of work.

The results are fascinating and important for leaders defining their workforce priorities.

Workers are still looking for better employment. In fact, when we asked them about their expected retention – whether they see themselves with their current employer within a year – 28% said no, with a range of 19% to 36% depending on the country. That means whether they are actively or passively looking, if a better offer came around, they would take it.

With so much talent at risk of leaving, we need to think about our employees the way we do our customers. Employees are constantly making choices: they choose where to work and how much energy to put into their work every day. As we would with customers, we applied analytical consumer research methods to understand which factors are the biggest drivers of retention.

Meeting emotional needs really matters. We tested over 20 different needs according to how important they were to employees, and their level of satisfaction with each one. Roughly half of the needs were functional, such as pay, hours, career advancement opportunities – and the other half were emotional, such as feeling valued and supported, and doing work you enjoy.

We found that when you ask employees directly whether or not they would take a new job, their answers refer to functional needs. Pay is an overwhelming

Note: The authors would like to thank Katherine Rivet, Gretchen May, Dennis Konczyk, Liliana Diaz, Eileen Donovan, Sherif al-Qallawi, Neftali Gutierrez, Katie Lavoie, Ruth Ebeling, Jennifer Bratton, Cory Kaplin, Vinciane Beauchene, Sebastian Ullrich, Tatsuya Takeuchi, and Neetu Chitkara, whose extraordinary efforts created this important piece of research and findings.

first choice, followed by benefits and perks, then hours and work/life balance, work I enjoy/care about, and better career learning opportunities. But again, this is what employees say they want. This means if you want to lure employees to apply for a new job you should offer materially better pay, benefits, and hours.

If you get a bit more sophisticated and ask employees to make choices between different aspects of work, you get a different answer. This is MaxDiff analysis – it forces a person to make tradeoffs between multiple options, allowing you to see what really matters from a long list of options. When you do this, the top two needs remain the functional benefits of pay and hours and work/life balance – basic requirements for each job. But some emotional needs rise to the top as well – feeling fairly treated and respected, feeling like I have job security, doing work I enjoy. This means, for example, that if you want a prospective employee to accept a job offer, you need to make sure they see in the recruiting process a culture that can meet these emotional needs.

We took this analytical methodology a step further, correlating the 20+ needs with employees' stated expectation to stay at or leave their jobs within a year.

Here, the case for meeting emotional needs becomes strikingly clear. Emotional needs dominated all five top needs identified (when correlated with retention), while functional needs like pay plummeted to the bottom of the list.

The top five needs correlated with attrition globally emerged as:
- Feeling like I have job security
- Feeling fairly treated and respected
- Doing work that I enjoy
- Feeling valued and appreciated
- Feeling supported

If you want your employees to stay with your organization, you should strongly consider delivering against these emotional needs.

When asking employees why they would take a new job, functional needs are at the top

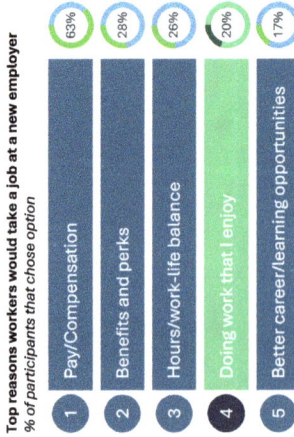

Top reasons workers would take a job at a new employer
% of participants that chose option

1. Pay/Compensation — 63%
2. Benefits and perks — 28%
3. Hours/work-life balance — 26%
4. Doing work that I enjoy — 20%
5. Better career/learning opportunities — 17%

Functional Emotional

When employees have to make a choice, emotional needs rise in importance

Top preferences when forced to pick between options[1]
Preference rank when participants chose option in trade-off

1. Pay/Compensation
2. Hours/work-life balance
3. Feeling fairly treated and respected
4. Feeling like I have job security
5. Doing work that I enjoy

Emotional needs rise in importance

When you look at top needs correlated with attrition, emotional needs dominate

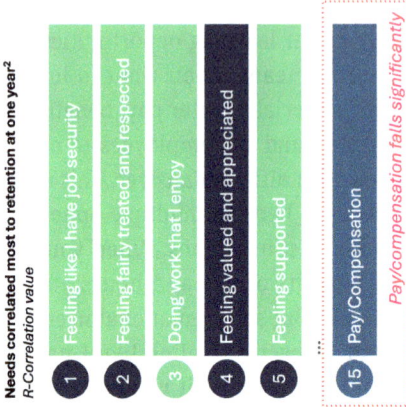

Needs correlated most to retention at one year[2]
R-Correlation value

1. Feeling like I have job security
2. Feeling fairly treated and respected
3. Doing work that I enjoy
4. Feeling valued and appreciated
5. Feeling supported
15. Pay/Compensation

Pay/compensation falls significantly

1. Respondents were asked what they care the most/least about at work and were prompted to select the top and bottom among 22 options in randomized groups of 5
2. Correlation between satisfaction with each listed element and answer to the question "I see myself working at my current employer in 1 year"
Source: BCG Employee Sentiment Survey, October 2023 (N = 11,285 across the US, Canada, UK, France, Germany, Australia, Japan, & India)

In a labor market with unemployment at record lows in many countries – for example, a steady 1.34 job openings per worker looking for a job in the US as of October 2023 – and with, as we found, many workers open to leaving their job, the implications for employers are clear. They need to deliver the basic functional needs like pay, benefits, and hours, but more importantly, they increasingly need to meet their employees' emotional needs of feeling secure in their job, feeling they are treated fairly and respected, enjoying the day-to-day work, and feeling valued, appreciated, and supported.

How to Deliver on the Emotional Needs Your Employees Seek

We know that it's critical for employers to fulfill employees' emotional needs, but how do leaders best do that? In an urgent context with finite resources, which priorities and investments make the biggest difference for retention?

With an immense amount of data at our fingertips, we identified the levers most correlated with resolving these five emotional needs from among 300 workplace characteristics – ranging from upskilling opportunities to working model and leadership. We found four significant, highly correlated characteristics:
1. Great managers
2. Supportive leaders
3. Access to resources to be successful
4. Access to opportunity regardless of background

% who do not see themselves at current organization in 1 year

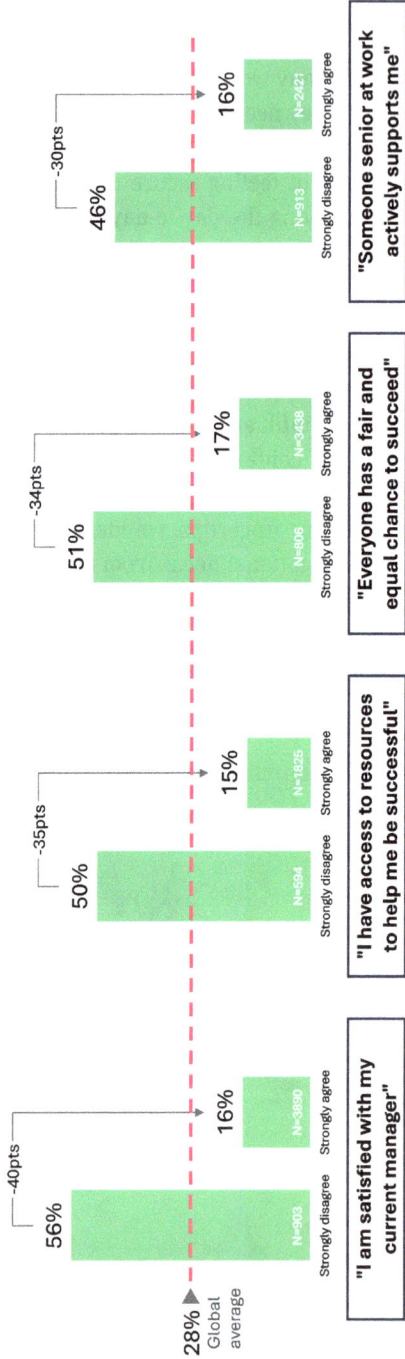

28% ▲
Global
average

"I am satisfied with my current manager"

Strongly disagree
N=903
56%

-40pts

Strongly agree
N=3850
16%

"I have access to resources to help me be successful"

Strongly disagree
N=594
50%

-35pts

Strongly agree
N=1825
15%

"Everyone has a fair and equal chance to succeed"

Strongly disagree
N=806
51%

-34pts

Strongly agree
N=3438
17%

"Someone senior at work actively supports me"

Strongly disagree
N=913
46%

-30pts

Strongly agree
N=2421
16%

Attrition risk is defined as answering "maybe", "unlikely", or "definitely not" to the question: Do you see yourself working at your current organization in 1 year?

Source: BCG Employee Sentiment Survey, October 2023 (N = 11,285 across the US, Canada, UK, France, Germany, Australia, Japan, & India)

Managers Matter – And Have an Outsized Impact on Retention

The most powerful lever for delivering these emotional needs is your day-to-day manager – which was also number one in seven out of eight countries we surveyed (it was number two in India, after ability to see a path to becoming an executive/leader). Managers have the power to make or break an employee's day – they're the ones who play the most influential role in shaping their team's day-to-day experience. They can recognize good work, have your back when something goes wrong, and understand what matters to you – or conversely, they can take credit for something you did, assign blame, or make you feel unseen.

Investing in upskilling to make all managers great is the best investment you can make to retain your best workers. And even if you're not worried about retention – our research found that investing in managers is also linked to higher employee motivation, satisfaction, and feelings of inclusion.

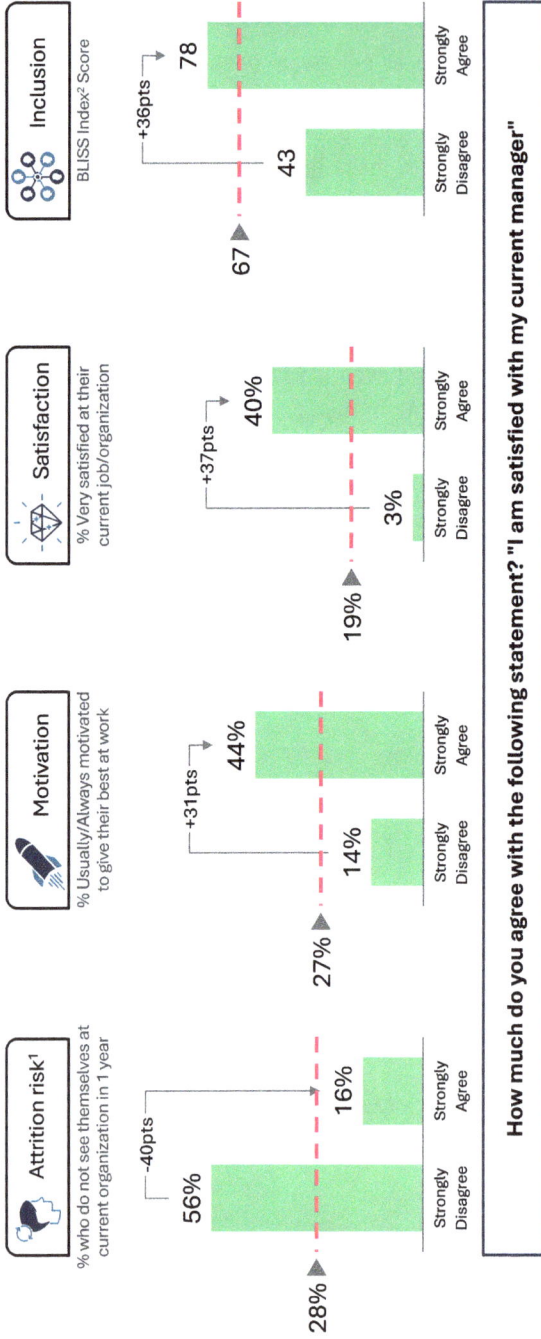

Attrition risk[1]
% who do not see themselves at current organization in 1 year

28% ▲

‒40pts

56% Strongly Disagree

16% Strongly Agree

Motivation
% Usually/Always motivated to give their best at work

27% ▲

+31pts

14% Strongly Disagree

44% Strongly Agree

Satisfaction
% Very satisfied at their current job/organization

19% ▲

+37pts

3% Strongly Disagree

40% Strongly Agree

Inclusion
BLISS Index[2] Score

67 ▲

+36pts

43 Strongly Disagree

78 Strongly Agree

How much do you agree with the following statement? "I am satisfied with my current manager"

1. Attrition risk is defined as answering "maybe", "unlikely", or "definitely not" to the question: Do you see yourself working at your current organization in 1 year?
2. BCG BLISS Index (Bias-Free, Leadership, Inclusion, Safety, and Support) is a comprehensive, statistically rigorous tool measuring factors that influence feelings of inclusion in the workplace

Sample Sizes: Manager Satisfaction: Disagree (903), Agree (3890)

Source: BCG Employee Sentiment Survey, October 2023 (N = 11,285 across the US, Canada, UK, France, Germany, Australia, Japan, & India)

We found that great managers – those whom employees said they strongly agree that they are satisfied with – are associated with a 40-point decrease in attrition risk, a 31-point increase in employee motivation, and a 37-point increase in satisfaction compared with those who were strongly dissatisfied on a five-point scale from strongly disagree to strongly agree on an array of statements. Feelings of inclusion also rose by 36 points on the BCG BLISS index (Bias-Free, Leadership, Inclusion, Safety, and Support), which is a comprehensive, statistically rigorous tool measuring factors that influence feelings of inclusion in the workplace.

The other three levers – supportive leaders, access to resources to be successful, and access to opportunity regardless of background had very similar impacts globally when taken in isolation.

When satisfaction with manager, the single biggest retention lever, is improved, we found it correlated with a 12-percentage point reduction in attrition risk over the global average. Each additional lever you pull is associated with a 2 to 3 percentage point reduction in potential attrition. Pulling all four levers reduces attrition risk from the baseline global average by about two-thirds, from 28% to 9%.

% who do not see themselves at current organization in 1 year

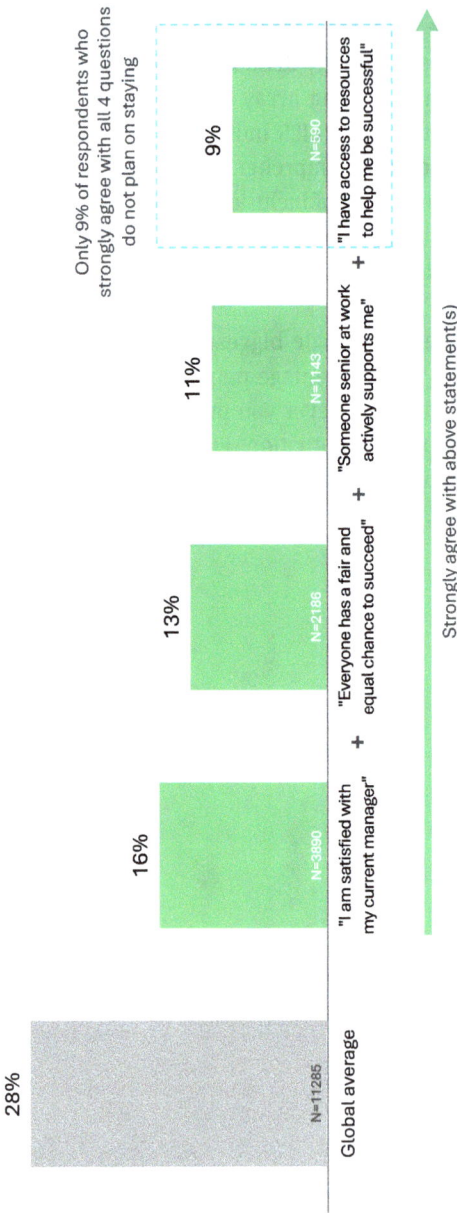

Only 9% of respondents who strongly agree with all 4 questions do not plan on staying

28%	16%	13%	11%	9%
N=11285	N=3890	N=2186	N=1143	N=590
Global average	"I am satisfied with my current manager"	+ "Everyone has a fair and equal chance to succeed"	+ "Someone senior at work actively supports me"	+ "I have access to resources to help me be successful"

Strongly agree with above statement(s)

"at risk" of leaving is defined as answering "maybe", "unlikely", or "definitely not" to the question: Do you see yourself working at your current organization in 1 year? Four factors survey questions: "How much do you agree with following statements?": I am satisfied with my current manager, At my organization everyone has a fair and equal chance to succeed regardless of their background, There is someone senior at work who actively supports me and has my back, I have good access to resources to help me be successful (e.g., financial, personal connections) - Answers include "Strongly Agree"

Source: BCG Employee Sentiment Survey, October 2023 (N = 11,285 across the US, Canada, UK, France, Germany, Australia, Japan, & India)

What happens if these levers get worse? We looked at the impact on retention risk. Our analysis reveals that strong dissatisfaction with managers was linked to doubling of retention risk. Attrition risk for employees whose manager satisfaction falls goes from 28% to a whopping 56% attrition risk.

Figure from prior page

Strongly agree with above statement(s)

16%	13%	11%	9%
N=3890	N=2186	N=1143	N=590

"I am satisfied with my current manager" + "Everyone has a fair and equal chance to succeed" + "Someone senior at work actively supports me" + "I have access to resources to help me be successful!"

28%
N=11285
Global average

74% of respondents who strongly disagree with all four questions do not see themselves staying

+28pts

Strongly disagree with above statement(s)

74%	66%	61%	56%
N=88	N=212	N=362	N=903

"I have access to resources to help me be successful!" + "Someone senior at work actively supports me" + "Everyone has a fair and equal chance to succeed" + "I am satisfied with my current manager"

% who do not see themselves at current organization in 1 year

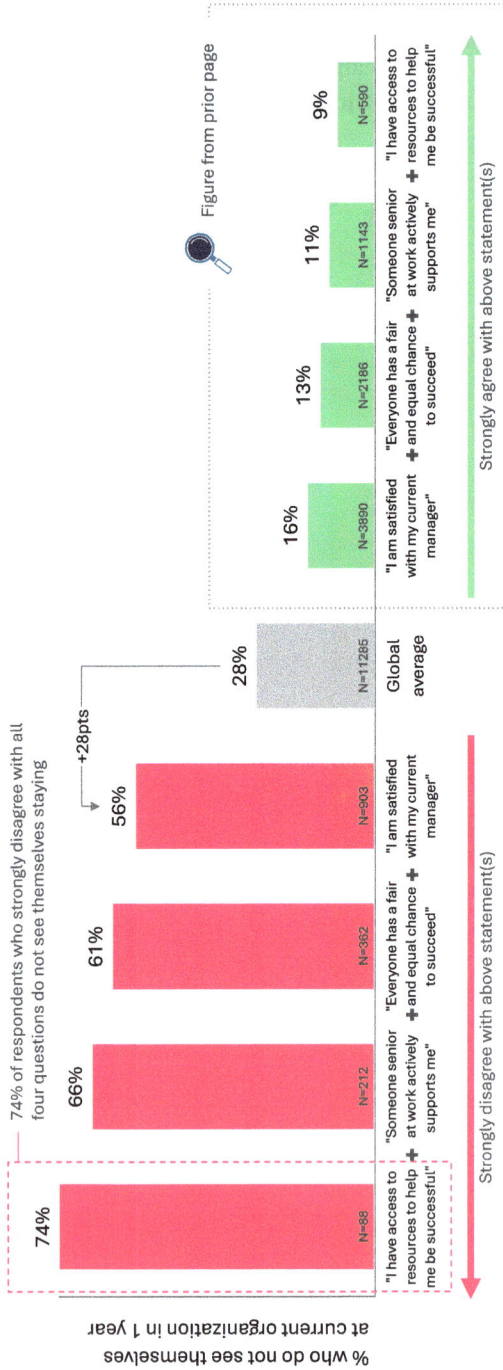

"At risk" of leaving is defined as answering "maybe", "unlikely", or "definitely not" to the question: Do you see yourself working at your current organization in 1 year?
Four factors survey questions: "How much do you agree with following statements?": I am satisfied with my current manager, At my organization everyone has a fair and equal chance to succeed regardless of their background, There is someone senior at work who actively supports me and has my back, I have good access to resources to help me be successful (e.g., financial, personal connections) · Answers include "Strongly Agree" or "Strongly Disagree"
Source: BCG Employee Sentiment Survey, October 2023 (N = 11,285 across the US, Canada, UK, France, Germany, Australia, Japan, & India)

While leaders don't knowingly hire poor managers, or try to make their managers worse, certain circumstances can put manager quality at risk in a significant way. For example, implementing new technologies and strategies could stress managers depending on their existing capabilities. High manager turnover requiring newly promoted employees and new hires can also impact manager quality. It's important to pay attention to manager quality, and reported stress and burnout across managers, particularly in these situations.

Where to Start

Now that we know investing in managers is the most critical lever for promoting strong retention outcomes, how should organizations think about hiring and developing excellent managers? What makes a good manager so good that their employees will overwhelmingly want to stick around?

One thing you can do is upskill managers on many dimensions of their leadership – from domain expertise to delegation skills to delivering clear feedback. Looking again at the quantitative findings from our 11,000-employee survey for insight into which characteristics correlated most highly with employee's reported satisfaction with their managers, we found the top characteristics encompassed interrelated themes, each of which can be addressed by senior leaders.

While the qualities addressed in this survey do not represent an exhaustive list of all possible qualities a manager could or should possess, they do provide a valuable place for senior leaders to begin seeking improvements from managers at all levels while they work to understand – with deep employee discovery tools – the needs (stated and unstated) of their own employee population and sub-segments within. The top three correlated manager characteristics we found in this part of the study included:

– *My direct manager creates a safe working environment.* Hazard-free and safe working environments are important for morale, productivity, and general employee wellbeing. Providing the appropriate resources and oversight to ensure workers have a safe place to work is imperative.
– *I feel comfortable sharing my views with my manager when I disagree.* Workers must feel safe voicing their opinions and making reasonable mistakes without fearing retribution. Process improvements often originate from frontline workers who should be empowered by their managers. Giving workers freedom and opportunities to collaborate and challenge established methodologies is a good first step.

— *My direct manager is committed to diversity, equity, and inclusion.* The benefits of a diverse workforce are well documented. Managers who not only work to build diverse teams but demonstrate continued commitment to these ideals, enable workers to feel more comfortable, and thrive in their workplaces.

Like Customers, Employees Are All Different

While addressing these four workplace characteristics is a great starting place, and a no-regrets move, specific populations have different needs. By segmenting our population of employees, we were able to identify some trends that provide insight.

For example, when segmenting the population for employees under 35, there are three key needs that hold paramount importance: continuous learning and personal growth, engaging in enjoyable work, and the prospect of career advancement. These elements are intricately interconnected and make this subgroup more inclined to envision themselves becoming an executive/leader in their organization. In general, those under 35 are more likely to leave within the next year (35%, versus 25% for their over 35-year-old counterparts). But when employees under 35 cannot see themselves becoming an executive, they're over 70% more likely to leave compared with employees over 35 who do not see themselves becoming an executive/leader.

% who do not see themselves at current organization in 1 year

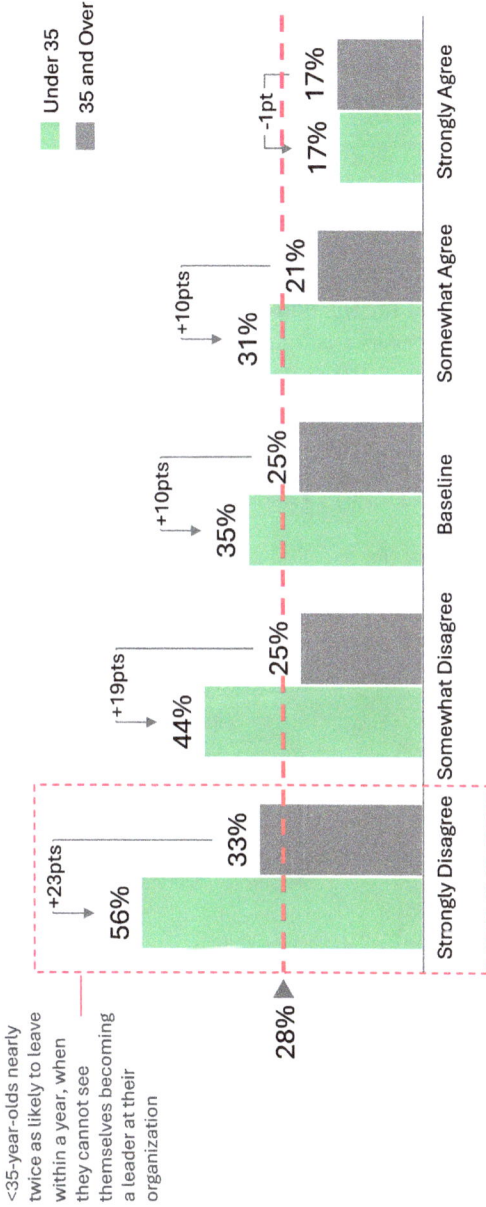

Legend: Under 35 / 35 and Over

<35-year-olds nearly twice as likely to leave within a year, when they cannot see themselves becoming a leader at their organization

28%

Strongly Disagree: Under 35 — 56%, 35 and Over — 33% (+23pts)
Somewhat Disagree: Under 35 — 44%, 35 and Over — 25% (+19pts)
Baseline: Under 35 — 35%, 35 and Over — 25% (+10pts)
Somewhat Agree: Under 35 — 31%, 35 and Over — 21% (+10pts)
Strongly Agree: Under 35 — 17%, 35 and Over — 17% (−1pt)

How much do you agree with the following statement?
"I can see myself becoming an executive/leader at my organization"

Sample size: Respondents who are under the age of 35 (N=3489), 35 and over (N=7796)
Source: BCG Employee Sentiment Survey, October 2023 (N = 11,285 across the US, Canada, UK, France, Germany, Australia, Japan, & India)

While there are overarching patterns at the workforce level that can help identify common needs, each organization is different. The distinctiveness is primarily shaped by the particular composition of its workforce, so it is imperative to gain a deep understanding of the organization's unique employee segmentation and distribution to best identify tailored strategies for intervention and improvement.

The Bottom Line

Our research highlights the current dynamic between employer and employee. Many employees are on the lookout for something better. It is therefore time to start thinking about your employees as customers. In any scenario, emotional needs dominate, and it is a no-regrets move to significantly invest in building better managers who can deliver the connection, support, appreciation, and motivation all employees – and frankly, all humans – crave.

✴✴✴✴✴✴✴✴✴✴✴✴✴✴✴✴✴✴✴✴✴✴✴✴

Can Management Be Beautiful?

Madeleine Michael, Martin Reeves, Claus Dierksmeier, and Georg Kell

Bertrand Russell, the Nobel laureate, logician, philosopher, and humanitarian, insisted that "mathematics, rightly viewed, possesses not only truth, but supreme beauty – a beauty cold and austere, like that of sculpture, without appeal to any part of our weaker nature . . ." and this is the view that propelled his life.[29] So passionate was his pursuit of beauty that he described a six-month prison sentence for conscientious objection as "agreeable," as it allowed him to work undisturbed, writing the entirety of *Introduction to Mathematical Philosophy* from his cell.[30]

Many of us have fleetingly felt the inspiration that drove Russell – watching our children thrive or being fully absorbed in a passion project. But most are rarely motivated this way in their work. Instead, we are more likely driven by obligation or financial rewards. Whether we do it knowingly, we rely on the business philosophy called scientific management. Formulated in the early 1900s by Frederick Winslow Taylor, scientific management is about the maximizing efficiency and measurability of work. He believed that managers ought to specify "not only what is to be done but how it is to be done and the exact time allowed for doing it."[31]

Taylor believed that agency and control should remain with managers as much as possible. To do this, work would be subdivided, standardized, and measured. Each task was codified, and workers were trained to execute them as specified. Finally, managers were to ensure that every step could be observed and measured for further optimization.

Scientific management is a product of its time, conceived when a significant amount of work took place in factories. It is a powerful approach for optimizing physical production, at least in part because it minimizes the quirky and unpredictable human aspects of work. Scientific management loses its power when applied to work where it is precisely these human elements that are critical. Specifically, scientific management is less effective in the following contexts.

- **Problems of cooperation.** Effective cooperation between humans cannot be readily compelled or mandated. Likewise, no KPI can completely measure its

---

29 https://users.drew.edu/~jlenz/br-ml-ch4.html

30 https://www.openculture.com/2020/02/bertrand-russells-prison-letters-are-now-digitized-put-online-1918-1961.html

31 Taylor FW. *The Principles of Scientific Management.* Harper & Brothers, 1911, archive.org, https://archive.org/details/principlesofscie00taylrich/mode/2up

success, or properly incentivize its implementation. To cooperate effectively, we need to share common aspirations and values with others and no amount of automation or standardization can ensure this.

- **Creative or empathic work.** Work that can be easily standardized is becoming less important for humans to execute. Over time, routine work, from bus-driving to copyediting, will be automated using artificial intelligence. As routine work disappears, we will be left with work which depends upon more uniquely human traits and abilities like empathy, creativity, and ethics. These are not the skills scientific management was designed to support.
- **Inspiring the next generation of employees.** Young people today want their jobs to be personally and socially meaningful. According to a recent Gartner Research poll,[32] more than half of respondents reported that the COVID-19 pandemic had "made [them] question the purpose of [their] day-to-day job". It is not enough for companies to have a purpose statement. Employees increasingly want to believe in the companies and work which absorb the major portion of their waking hours. The tools of scientific management – goals, quotas, evaluations, monetary incentives, and the threat of being fired – are insufficient to motivate today's knowledge workers.
- **Continuous transformation.** The pace of business change is accelerating to keep pace with technology and shifting societal expectations, such as decarbonization. As the pace increases, scientific change management approaches, which tell us what to change but not why, leave employees exhausted. Classical approaches rely on top down prescription, overwhelming employees with a sense that any change is an alien event happening to them, rather than a forward-looking opportunity they are a part of and have ownership over.

In short, there is a limit to how far we can stretch the paradigm, and we are reaching it. Leaders implicitly know that we need to better inspire and use human talent, hence our collective obsession with purpose. These attempts often fall short however, as author Ranjay Gulati implies[33] in his need to distinguish "deep purpose" from mere "purpose".

Instead, we need a new paradigm to stand beside scientific management. We need a paradigm which holds our humanity as the central ingredient in solving human problems. We need a more humanistic approach to management.

---

32 https://www.gartner.com/en/articles/employees-seek-personal-value-and-purpose-at-work-be-prepared-to-deliver
33 https://bcghendersoninstitute.com/deep-purpose-with-ranjay-gulati/

Frank Knight, a leading economic and business thinker of the 20th century, balked at the notion of managing human tasks with 'scientific management' alone. In his words:

> *A large part of economic activity, of the task of making a living for society, consists of converting material things into forms which can be scribed and standardized. The process of such transformation can be reduced to rule and specification, that is, they can be treated "scientifically." But the larger and more difficult part of the work of the world consists either of working things into forms which we can only characterize by such vague terms as beauty . . . or else in working with human beings themselves and bringing them into relations which are agreeable and effective. Just what it is that makes human relations agreeable and effective baffles scientific statement just as obstinately as that which makes an esthetic object beautiful.*[34]

What could "beautiful" management, better able to inspire the full potential of human creativity and cooperation, look like? We must look further back for inspiration. Since antiquity, philosophers, artists, and clergymen alike have studied beauty for its ability to inspire, and for the almost gravitational pull it has[35] on us.

The ancient Greeks believed that beauty, truth, and goodness were closely related. In fact, the word for beauty common in Plato's time was *kalos*, meaning noble or fine. In addition to beauty, it designated something moral beyond duty or obligation. Importantly, it was understood that neither beauty nor this elevated morality can be compelled – both must come from an intrinsic motivation. To do something beautiful, in that Greek sense, is to do something good, out of motivation simply to do that good thing, rather than because of an ulterior motive.

The Greeks also believed that beauty was a path to understanding something beyond the finite – giving us the ability to see beyond ourselves and beyond the moment toward some greater common purpose. This was echoed by many medieval thinkers, who described all beauty, whether natural (say, that of a flower), manufactured (say a painting), or intellectual (a well-ordered mathematical proof) as an emulation of God's perfect beauty. Later philosophers severed the connection between beauty and the divine but continued to insist that beauty gave access to a greater truth. Good aesthetic taste was seen as a path to empathy and improved judgment, and as such as a conduit for the moral betterment of humanity.

The power that beauty has isn't a dusty relic or a philosophical whimsy. Bertrand Russell lelt it. And no doubt many of us have felt it fleetingly too in those moments when our work seemed noble and infinite, more of a privilege than a duty.

34 Frank H. *Knight in Iowa City, 1919–1928*. Emerald Group Publishing Limited, 2011. https://www.google.com/books/edition/_/FQ0zqzbhbMgC?hl=en&gbpv=0
35 https://renovatio.zaytuna.edu/article/why-beauty-is-indispensable-to-common-good

Then we sense that beauty is a miraculous motivator. When we have distilled some of this power, inside or more likely outside of work, we know that it is noninstrumental, that it helps us see beyond ourselves, often to a common higher purpose.

The future of work has become a fashionable topic, with discussion largely focused on how to reorganize existing activities temporally and spatially in the current management paradigm. But we are also free to imagine more substantially new ways of working and managing. What would it take to inspire people's best efforts without compulsion, to engage their curiosity and imagination, to awaken higher aspirations, and to illuminate common purpose, engaging the full potential of human talent? We don't have all of the answers, but our investigations provide some clues on how to materialize "beautiful management".

Pursue Infinite Goals
Tactical goals are undoubtedly useful in many contexts. But where appropriate, dare to treat such goals as an oblique result of pursuing excellence. Imposing finite goals provides collective consistency and protection for near-term priorities, but sometimes at the expense of autonomy, aspiration, or personal meaning.

Allow People to Work on Whole Problems
Encourage curiosity and ownership of whole problems, from inception to completion. It may be more efficient to subdivide and parcel out tasks, but less likely to inspire. For those that must naturally be subdivided, develop narratives that show how all activities are essential parts of the whole, encouraging ownership and cohesion across the firm.

Pursue Prosocial Effects
Beauty is not just seen or heard; it is also felt. It reaches for the heart, so to speak. Because it is so personal, beauty can also be a powerful interpersonal agent. To consider beauty together, or better, to create beauty together, is to build a lasting understanding and a common purpose. Through beauty, we learn to embrace causes larger than ourselves. We learn also to take joy in others' success – the hallmark of lasting social collaboration. And so caring for others in and through one's work turns from a duty to a voluntary commitment.

Inspire, don't Compel
When is the last time you put your all into something you were told to do, or incentivized to do, as opposed to something chosen as meaningful to you? It rarely

happens, and though to compel is simpler as a manager than to inspire, efforts toward the latter are undoubtedly more effective.

Encourage Alignment with Excellence, not Hierarchy

Goals may be best identified from the mountain top, tasks not so much. The more creative, adaptive, and fast-paced the work, the greater the need for individual autonomy. Even so, employees need an orientation that integrates diverse approaches into a harmonious whole. Aesthetic excellence provides that self-steering orientation toward the larger cause. It is also, in many ways, less arbitrary and more convincing than a principle of because-I-said-so.

Take inspiration from great craftsmen and women, such as carpenters, architects, and ceramicists, who, without prescriptive direction, conceive work that brings joy to many. Apple's key industrial designer, Jony Ive, watched his father work as a silversmith during his childhood and reports that the hands-on process of making was an important influence.

Cultivate Pride in Your Workplace

Recall the first home you had that you were proud of. How did your experience of that space differ from your experience in a college dorm, or childhood home? You likely made sure you actually liked the art you hung and took much more care cleaning. Similarly, when we take pride in something, especially something we believe to be beautiful, we take more care in preventing corrupting forces. In your first home, the corrupting forces were likely dust bunnies and dirty dishes; in the workplace, corrupting forces are apathy, corporate decline, harassment, and corruption itself.

Facilitate Individual Journeys

Scientific management tries to distill individuality out of the workplace. But for some jobs, especially those that are more creative in nature (including, as Frank Knight insisted, management), to standardize is to obstruct excellence.

From manager to creative designer to data scientist, moments of excellence and inspiration can only come when an employee applies the best of her specific abilities, whether that means following the handbook or not.

This list is not comprehensive – it can't be, since unlike scientific management, inspiration and beauty have no simple universal formulae. But hopefully, it can help us to peep beyond the constraints of scientific management and help us to tap into a neglected part of human potential. Neither is the implied approach a panacea. We don't suggest that anyone practice only 'beautiful management', but that the scientific and the beautiful serve managers as complements. If we are optimizing a production line, scientific management will likely provide the best approach. But it will serve us well to give the engineers doing that optimization the space, agency, and inspiration to do work that is truly their best.

✳✳✳✳✳✳✳✳✳✳✳✳✳✳✳✳✳✳✳✳

How People Can Create – and Destroy – Value with Generative AI

François Candelon, Lisa Krayer, Saran Rajendran, and David Zuluaga Martínez

Key Takeaways

A first-of-its-kind scientific experiment finds that people mistrust generative AI in areas where it can contribute tremendous value and trust it too much where the technology isn't competent.

- Around 90% of participants improved their performance when using GenAI for creative ideation. People did best when they did not attempt to edit GPT-4's output.
- When working on business problem solving, a task outside the tool's current competence, many participants took'GPT-4's misleading output at face value. Their performance was 23% worse than those who didn't use the tool at all.
- Adopting generative AI is a massive change management effort. The job of the leader is to help people use the new technology in the right way, for the right tasks and to continually adjust and adapt in the face of GenAI's ever-expanding frontier.

Generative AI will be a powerful enabler of competitive advantage for companies that crack the code of adoption. In a first-of-its-kind scientific experiment, we found that when GenAI is used in the right way, and for the right tasks, its capabilities are such that people's efforts to improve the quality of its output can backfire. But it isn't obvious when the new technology is (or is not) a good fit, and the persuasive abilities of the tool make it hard to spot a mismatch. This can have serious consequences: When it is used in the wrong way, for the wrong tasks, generative AI[36] can cause significant value destruction.

We conducted our experiment with the support of a group of scholars from Harvard Business School, MIT Sloan School of Management, the Wharton School

---

36 https://www.bcg.com/capabilities/artificial-intelligence/generative-ai

---

Note: In addition to the collaborators from the academic team listed above, the authors would like to thank Clément Dumas, Gaurav Jha, Leonid Zhukov, Max Männig, and Maxime Courtaux for their helpful comments and suggestions. The authors would also like to thank Lebo Nthoiwa, Patrick Healy, Saud Almutairi, and Steven Randazzo for their efforts interviewing the experiment participants. The authors also thank all their BCG colleagues who volunteered to participate in this experiment.

at the University of Pennsylvania, and the University of Warwick.[37] With more than 750 BCG consultants worldwide as subjects, it is the first study to test the use of generative AI in a professional-services setting – through tasks that reflect what employees do every day. The findings have critical implications across industries.

The opportunity to boost performance is astonishing: When using generative AI (in our experiment), OpenAI's GPT-4) for creative product innovation, a task involving ideation and content creation, around 90% of our participants improved their performance. What's more, they converged on a level of performance that was 40% higher than that of those working on the same task without GPT-4. People best captured this upside when they did not attempt to improve the output that the technology generated.

Creative ideation sits firmly within GenAI's current frontier of competence. When our participants used the technology for business problem solving, a capability outside this frontier, they performed 23% worse than those doing the task without GPT-4. And even participants who were warned about the possibility of wrong answers from the tool did not challenge its output.

Our findings describe a paradox: People seem to mistrust the technology in areas where it can contribute massive value and to trust it too much in areas where the technology isn't competent. This is concerning on its own. But we also found that even if organizations change these behaviors, leaders must watch for other potential pitfalls: Our study shows that the technology's relatively uniform output can reduce a group's diversity of thought by 41%.

The precise magnitude of the effects we uncovered will be different in other settings. But our findings point to a crucial decision-making moment for leaders across industries. They need to think critically about the work their organization does and which tasks can benefit from or be damaged by generative AI. They need to approach its adoption as a change management effort spanning data infrastructure, rigorous testing and experimentation, and an overhaul of existing talent strategies. Perhaps most important, leaders need to continually revisit their decisions as the frontier of GenAI's competence advances.

---

37 We designed the study with input from Professor Karim R. Lakhani, Dr. Fabrizio Dell'Acqua, and Professor Edward McFowland III of Harvard Business School; Professor Ethan R. Mollick of the Wharton School at the University of Pennsylvania; Professor Hila Lifshitz-Assaf at the University of Warwick; and Professor Katherine C. Kellogg at the MIT Sloan School of Management. Our academic colleagues analyzed our data. Please see our scholarly paper for more details.

The Value at Stake

Our findings make clear that generative AI adoption is a double-edged sword. In our experiment, participants using GPT-4 for creative product innovation outperformed the control group (those who completed the task without using GPT-4) by 40%. But for business problem solving, using GPT-4 resulted in performance that was 23% lower than that of the control group (see Figure 4.1).

Difference in individual performance with GPT-4
compared to control group (%)

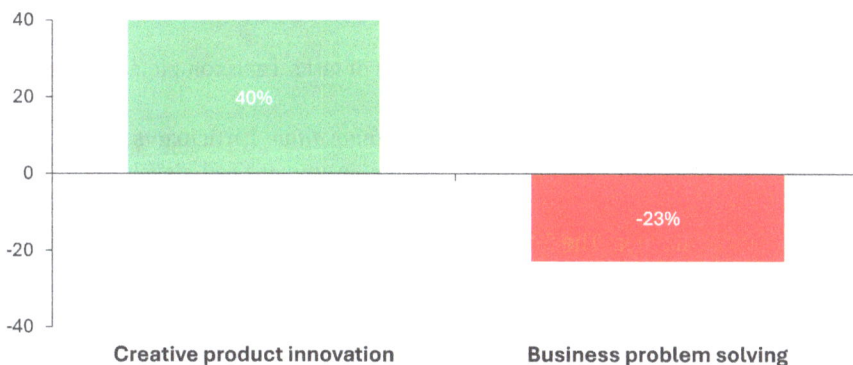

Figure 4.1: Generative AI Significantly Boosts or Hurts Performance, Depending on the Type of Task.

The creative product innovation task asked participants to come up with ideas for new products and go-to-market plans. The business problem-solving task asked participants to identify the root cause of a company's challenges based on performance data and interviews with executives. (See "Our Experiment Design and Methodology.") Perhaps somewhat counterintuitively, current GenAI models tend to do better on the first type of task; it is easier for LLMs to come up with creative, novel, or useful ideas based on the vast amounts of data on which they have been trained. Where there's more room for error is when LLMs are asked to weigh nuanced qualitative and quantitative data to answer a complex question. Given this shortcoming, we as researchers knew that GPT-4 was likely to mislead participants if they relied completely on the tool, and not also on their own judgment, to arrive at the solution to the business problem-solving task (this task had a "right" answer).

***

Our Experiment Design and Methodology

A total of 758 junior individual contributors in BCG's client-facing consulting business from across the world volunteered for the experiment; they all had at least an undergraduate degree and up to four years of work experience, on average. All results presented in this article and in the scholarly paper controlled for the more than 20 factors commonly used in the social sciences, such as gender, educational attainment, English language proficiency, geography, previous generative AI experience, views about generative AI, and several self-reported personality traits.

Task Design

Our experiment was designed around two sets of tasks, each completed by a separate group of participants.

The first set focused on *creative product innovation*. Participants were asked to brainstorm ideas for new products to solve an unmet need, develop the business case for each, create testing and launch plans, and write memos to persuade others to adopt the idea. The following are some of the questions that participants had to answer:

- *You are working for a footwear company in the unit developing new products. Generate ideas for a new shoe aimed at a specific market or sport that is underserved. Be creative and give at least ten ideas.*
- *Come up with a list of steps needed to launch the product. Be concise but comprehensive.*
- *Use your best knowledge to segment the footwear market by users. Develop a marketing slogan for each segment you are targeting.*
- *Suggest three ways of testing whether your marketing slogan works well with the customers you have identified.*
- *Write marketing copy for a press release of the product.*

The second set focused on *business problem solving*. Participants were asked to identify channels and brands in a fictitious company to optimize its revenue and profitability, based on interview notes with (fictitious) company executives and historical business performance data. The following are some of the questions that participants had to answer:

- *The CEO, Harold Van Muylders, of Kleding (a fictitious company) would like to understand the performance of the company's three brands (Kleding Man, Kleding Woman, and Kleding Kids) to uncover deeper issues. Please find attached interviews from company insiders. In addition, the attached excel sheet provides financial data broken down by brands.*

- *Using this information, if the CEO must pick one brand to focus on and invest in to drive revenue growth in the company, what brand should that be? What is the rationale for this choice? Please support your views with data and/or interview quotations.*

The two sets of tasks were deliberately designed to resemble some of the work that participants perform as management consultants.

The creative product innovation task was designed to play to GPT-4's strengths as an LLM, primarily because it involved creativity, refinement, and persuasive writing, which are within GPT-4's frontier of capability. The business problem-solving task was explicitly designed to be difficult for GPT-4 to complete. This task, which contains a clear right answer, was designed to be complex enough to ensure that GPT-4's answer on a first pass would be incorrect. Participants could solve the business problem-solving task either by relying on their own judgment to tease out the nuances in the questions and data provided or by prompting GPT-4 to better "think through" the problem.

Measuring Baseline Proficiency

Before attempting the experimental task, each participant also solved a baseline task without the use of any AI tool. This task was designed to be very similar to the experimental task in terms of difficulty and the skills it tested for.

By evaluating performance on this baseline task using the same grading rubric as the experimental task (see below), we were able to create a sense of each participant's baseline proficiency in the specific task type. This then enabled us to understand how GPT-4 use affected relative performance across individuals with different levels of baseline proficiency.

Grading Rubric

Each set of tasks had its own grading rubric:

For *creative product innovation,* participants were graded on a scale of 1 to 10, on four dimensions: creativity, persuasive writing, analytical thinking, and overall writing skills. Overall performance was calculated as the average of the four dimensions.

For *business problem solving*, participants were graded on the correctness of the response (that is, which channel or brand is most likely to boost revenue or profitability for the fictitious company). Performance was assessed as a binary grade (correct or incorrect).

Experimental Treatment Design

Each of the 758 participants in the experiment was randomly assigned to one of the two sets of tasks (creative product innovation or business problem solving), controlling for key demographic variables. Within each set of tasks, participants were then randomized into three groups:

- Group A: Those who used GPT-4 to solve the task after a 30-minute training on best practices on GPT-4 use (see the sidebar on training).
- Group B: Those who used GPT-4 to solve the task without any training.
- Group C: Those who did not use GPT-4 to solve the task (control group).

Once sorted into groups, participants were asked to complete two tasks: a baseline task (which they all carried out without GPT-4) and the experimental task (which groups A and B completed with GPT-4, and group C without). In total, 99% of participants in groups A and B – those with access to GPT-4 – did in fact use the tool to complete the tasks.

Incentive Structure

A cornerstone of this experiment is its proximity to real-world tasks performed by business professionals. For this experiment to fully capture how participants may behave in the real world, a substantial incentive structure was put in place to ensure that participants would do their best to solve each task.

To ensure this, participation in this experiment was noted in participants' bi-annual performance reviews. Successful completion of the experiment was tracked and ultimately factored into participants' annual performance bonuses. In addition, top 20% of performers were specifically called out to their managers to further incentivize high performance.

Grading Methodologies

For both the baseline and the experimental tasks, the output from participants was graded by humans (a combination of BCG consultants and business school students with experience grading academic assignments). The human graders were "blinded," in that they did not know whether the output was from participants who used GPT-4 or not. Furthermore, grading assignments were made in such a way that grader-specific fixed effects (some graders are naturally harsher than others) were controlled for, ensuring that the results were not biased in that way.

We also used GPT-4 to independently grade performance on all tasks, using the same rubric as the human graders. Human-generated grades largely coincided with GPT-4 grades, leading to the same takeaways from the experiment. In line with standard academic practice, we primarily relied on human-generated grades for the analyses presented here, except for those that concern changes in distribution between baseline and experimental tasks. For the latter analyses in particular, we relied on the GPT-4 grades to maximize consistency across baseline and experimental tasks (in the human-generated grading system, different graders may have scored the baseline and experimental submissions for the same participant).

For a more detailed description of the experimental design, please see our scholarly paper[38] on the topic.

∗∗∗

We also knew that participants were capable of finding the answer to the business problem-solving task on their own: 85% of participants in the control group did so. Yet many participants who used GPT-4 for this task accepted the tool's erroneous output at face value. It's likely that GPT-4's ability to generate persuasive content contributed to this result. In our informal conversations with participants, many confirmed that they found the rationale GPT-4 offered for its output very convincing (even though as an LLM, it came up with the rationale after the recommendation, rather than creating the recommendation on the basis of the rationale).

The double-edged sword effect holds across all levels of baseline proficiency. (At the start of the experiment, participants completed a baseline task without using GPT-4 that we then graded and ranked; see the sidebar on our design and methodology). This has an important caveat: The lower the individual's baseline proficiency, the more significant the effect tended to be; for the creative product innovation task, these individuals boosted performance by 43%. Still, the effect was material even for the top-ranked baseline performers, among whom the upside and downside of using GPT-4 on the two tasks were 17% and –17%, respectively (see Figure 4.2). (Throughout, our discussion of participants' performance is not indicative of their absolute levels of competence and talents with respect to these or other tasks.)

The strong connection between performance and the context in which generative AI is used raises an important question about training: Can the risk of value destruction be mitigated by helping people understand how well-suited the technology is for a given task? It would be rational to assume that if participants knew the limitations of GPT-4, they would know not to use it, or would use it differently, in those situations.

Our findings suggest that it may not be that simple. The negative effects of GPT-4 on the business problem-solving task did not disappear when subjects

---

38   https://papers.ssrn.com/sol3/papers.cfm?abstract_id=4573321

Average change in performance with GPT-4 (%)

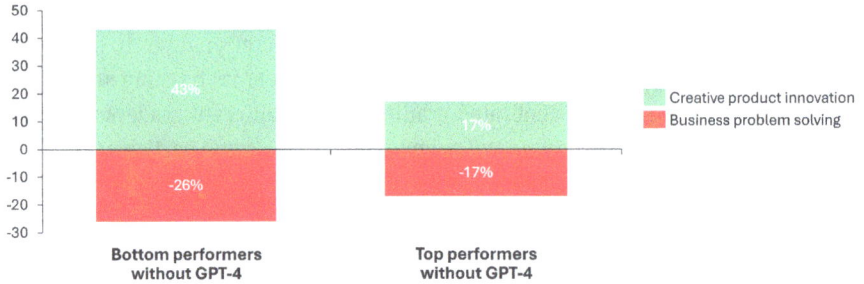

Sources: Human-Generative AI Collaboration Experiment (May-June 2023); BCG analysis.
Note: Bottom and top performers are identified on the basis of baseline proficiency (performance on baseline task, without the use of GPT-4). For creative product innovation, % change refers to the average change in individual performance relative to the baseline task. (Note that the change in performance for the average participant as presented in Exhibit 1 is not an arithmetic average of the figures in Exhibit 2.) For business problem solving, % change reflects the performance difference between the treatment and the control groups.

Figure 4.2: Generative AI's Performance Effect Is Strongest When Baseline Proficiency is Lowest.

were given an overview of how to prompt GPT-4 and of the technology's limitations. (See "Our Use of Training in the Experiment.")

✳✳✳

Our Use of Training in the Experiment

The training provided to a subset of respondents lasted for approximately 30 minutes and was designed as a "tell, show, and do" crash course on how best to use GPT-4 for the task that participants were about to execute. During the tell phase of the training, participants were told about the best practices for using GPT-4. The show phase provided an example that illustrated how these concepts could be applied to a sample task. Finally, in the do phase, participants were given the chance to test their learning by using GPT-4 on a baseline task they had just completed, in preparation for the experimental task.

Participants in the business problem-solving task were informed of the challenges and pitfalls of using GPT-4 in a problem-solving context. They were shown an example of how GPT-4 can fail at reasoning and cautioned against relying heavily on GPT-4 for such tasks.

✳✳✳

Even more puzzling, they did considerably worse on average than those who were not offered this simple training before using GPT-4 for the same task (see Figure 4.3). This result does not imply that all training is ineffective. But it has led us to consider whether this effect was the result of participants' overconfidence in their own abilities to use GPT-4 – precisely because they'd been trained.

Average change in individual performance with GPT-4
compared to control group (%)

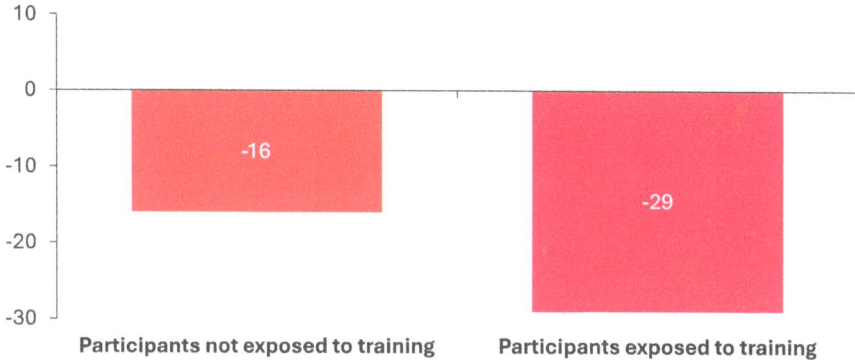

	Participants not exposed to training	Participants exposed to training
	-16	-29

Sources: Human-Generative AI Collaboration Experiment (May-June 2023); BCG analysis.
Note: The simple (30-minute) training program that participants received provided a high-level overview of good prompting practices for GPT-4, along with a note on shortcomings in the technology's reasoning capabilities.

Figure 4.3: Simple Training Compounds the Performance Decline for the Business Problem-Solving Task.

New Opportunities for Human Talent

Effects at the group level, like the ones discussed above, aren't necessarily indicative of how generative AI impacts individuals. When we look behind the averages, we find that the use of GPT-4 has two distinct effects on individual performance distribution (see Figure 4.4). First, the entire distribution shifts to the right, toward higher levels of performance. This underscores the fact that the 40% performance boost discussed above is not a function of "positive" outliers. Nearly all participants (around 90%), irrespective of their baseline proficiency, produced higher-quality results when using GPT-4 for the creative product innovation task. Second, the variance in performance is dramatically reduced: A much higher share of our participants performed at or very close to the average level.

In other words, participants with lower baseline proficiency, when given access to generative AI, ended up nearly matching those with higher baseline proficiency. Being more proficient without the aid of technology doesn't give one much of an edge when everyone can use GPT-4 to perform a creative product innovation task

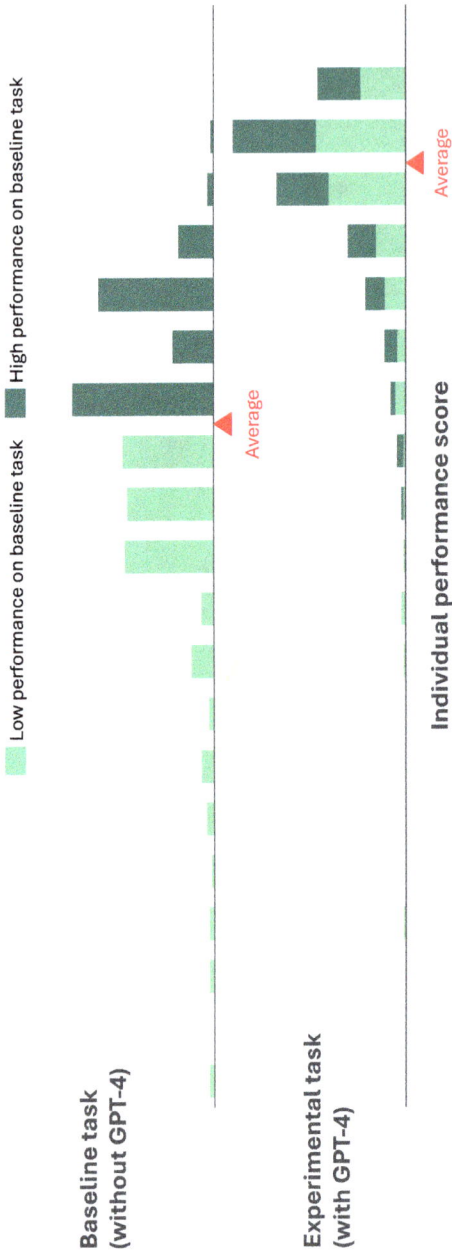

Figure 4.4: Generative AI Is a Powerful Leveler of Performance.

(see Figure 4.5). The fact that we observed this effect among our well-educated, high-achieving sample suggests that it may turn out to be even more pronounced in contexts that are more heterogenous, with a wider spread in proficiency.

Average individual performance

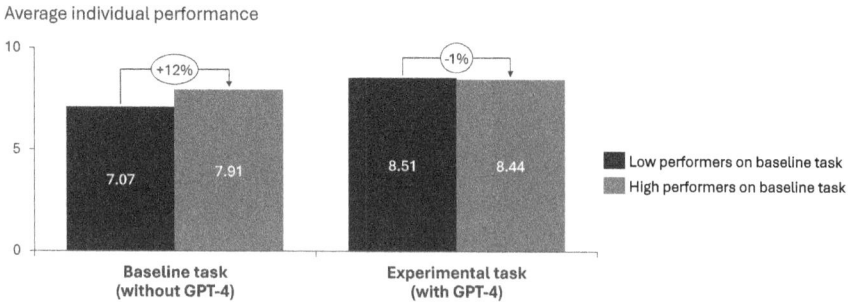

Sources: Human-Generative AI Collaboration Experiment (May June 2023); BCG analysis.
Note: Findings reflect results (on a 10-point scale) for the creative product innovation task only. Baseline task performance was used as a proxy for proficiency on this type of task. Both distributions reflect GPT-4-based performance grades rather than human grades for greater consistency of within-subject analysis.

Figure 4.5: Generative AI Eliminates the 12% Baseline Proficiency Gap.

Digging deeper, we find that because GPT-4 reaches such a high level of performance on the creative product innovation task, it seems that the average person is not able to improve the technology's output. In fact, human efforts to enhance GPT-4 outputs decrease quality. (See the sidebar on our design and methodology for a description of how we measured quality.) We found that "copy-pasting" GPT-4 output strongly correlated with performance: The more a participant's final submission in the creative product innovation task departed from GPT-4's draft, the more likely it was to lag in quality (see Figure 4.6). For every 10% increase in divergence from GPT-4's draft, participants on average dropped in the quality ranking by around 17 percentile points.

It appears that the primary locus of human-driven value creation lies not in enhancing generative AI where it is already great, but in focusing on tasks beyond the frontier of the technology's core competencies.

Interestingly, we found that most of our participants seemed to grasp this point intuitively. In general, they did not feel threatened by generative AI; rather, they were excited by this change in their roles and embraced the idea of taking on tasks that only humans can do. As one participant observed, "I think there is a lot of value add in what we can do as humans. You need a human to adapt an answer to a business's context; that process cannot be replaced by AI." Another noted, "I think it's an opportunity to do things more efficiently, to stop wasting time on things that are very repetitive and actually focus on what's important, which is more strategic."

Quality of output

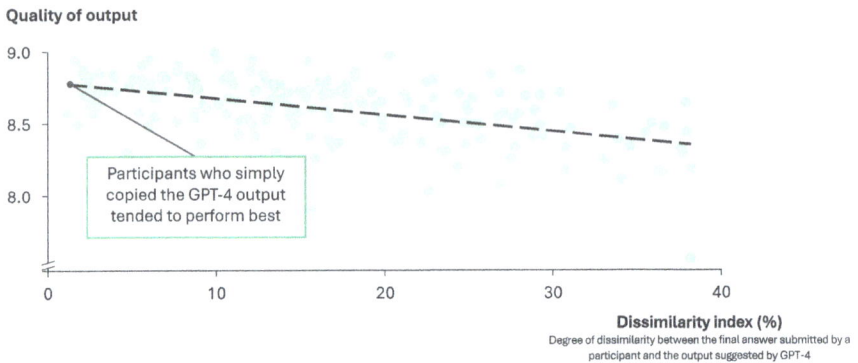

Participants who simply copied the GPT-4 output tended to perform best

Dissimilarity index (%)
Degree of dissimilarity between the final answer submitted by a participant and the output suggested by GPT-4

Sources: Human-Generative AI Collaboration Experiment (May-June 2023); BCG analysis.
Note: Findings reflect results (on a 10-point scale) for the creative product innovation task only. Outliers have been removed for readability, without impacting results.

Figure 4.6: On Tasks Where GenAI Excels, Human Attempts to Modify the Output Decrease Its Quality.

However, it is worth keeping in mind the population of this study: highly skilled young knowledge workers who are more likely to be able to make this transition easily. Other professionals may feel greater fear or experience more difficulty adapting their role to the new technology.

The Creativity Trap

Even if you use GenAI in the right way, and for the right tasks, our research suggests that there are risks to creativity.

The first risk is a tradeoff between individual performance gains and collective creativity loss. Because GPT-4 provides responses with very similar meaning time and again to the same sorts of prompts, the output provided by participants who used the technology was individually better but collectively repetitive. The diversity of ideas among participants who used GPT-4 for the creative product innovation task was 41% lower compared with the group that did not use the technology (see Figure 4.7). People didn't appreciably add to the diversity of ideas even when they edited GPT-4's output.

The second risk is drawn from a sample of our interviews with participants. Roughly 70% believe that extensive use of GPT-4 may stifle their creative abilities over time (see Figure 4.8). As one participant explained, "Like any technology, people can rely on it too much. GPS helped navigation immensely when it was first released, but today people can't even drive without a GPS. As people rely on

Individual performance

Difference in individual performance with GPT-4
compared to control group (%)[1]

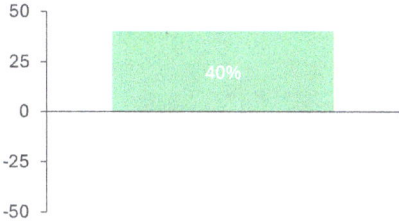

Collective diversity of ideas

Total change compared to control group (%)[2]

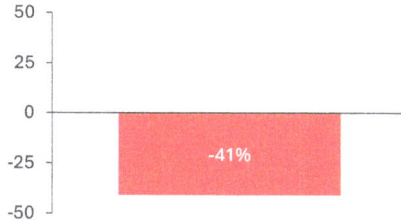

Sources: Human-Generative AI Collaboration Experiment (May-June 2023); BCG analysis.
[1] Findings reflect results from the creative product innovation task.
[2] Diversity of ideas was measured using TF-IDF and cosine similarity methodologies.

Figure 4.7: Generative AI's Boosts to Individual Performance May Undercut Collective Creativity.

a technology too much, they lose abilities they once had." Another participant noted, "This [phenomenon] is definitely a concern for me. If I become too reliant on GPT, it will weaken my creativity muscles. This already happened to me during the experiment." Businesses will need to be mindful of their employees' perceptions of and attitudes about generative AI,[39] and how those might affect their ability to drive innovation and add value.

Share of participants (%)

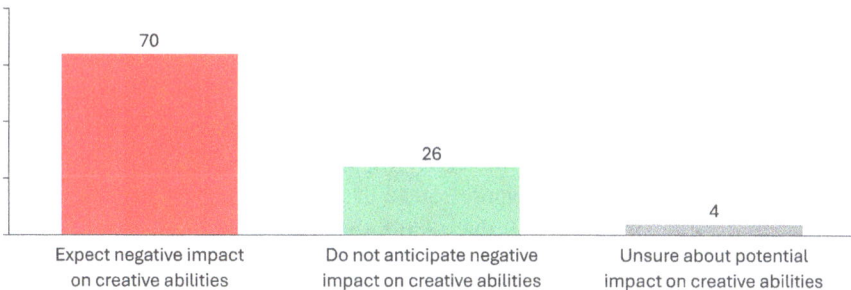

Sources: Human-Generative AI Collaboration Experiment (May-June 2023); BCG analysis.
Note: Based on a sample of 60 one-on-one interviews with participants who completed the creative product innovation (generative AI-friendly) task using GPT-4. The analysis focuses on the 46 participants who, in response to open questions, explicitly referred or alluded to the impact of generative AI on their creative abilities.

Figure 4.8: Participants Believe that Use of GenAI May Stifle Their Creativity Over Time.

---

39 https://fortune.com/2023/09/01/ai-artificial-intelligence-employees-professional-identity/

We don't yet have data to confirm our participants' perceptions; this is a topic for further study. But if employees' concerns bear out, it could compound the group-level risk. Specifically, the loss of collective diversity of ideas may be exacerbated if employees experience some atrophy of individual creativity.

The Generative AI Change Imperative

Inspired by the findings from our research, we envision a series of questions, challenges, and options that can help business leaders make generative AI adoption a source of differentiation – and, as such, an enabler of sustained competitive advantage.

Data Strategy. Any company that incorporates GenAI can realize significant efficiency gains in areas where the technology is competent. But if multiple firms apply the technology across similar sets of tasks, it can produce a leveling effect among organizations analogous to the pattern observed among participants in our experiment. As a result, one of the keys to differentiation will be the ability to fine-tune generative AI models with large volumes of high-quality, firm-specific data.

This is easier said than done. In our experience, not all companies have the advanced data infrastructure capabilities needed to process their proprietary data. Developing these capabilities has been a key focus of AI transformations, but with the arrival of generative AI, it becomes all the more important: As we have argued elsewhere,[40] the power of GenAI often lies in the identification of unexpected – even counterintuitive – patterns and correlations. To reap these benefits, companies need a comprehensive data pipeline, combined with a renewed focus on developing internal data engineering capabilities.

Roles and Workflows. For tasks that generative AI systems have mastered – which, of course, is an ever-expanding list – people need to radically revise their mindset and their approach to work. Instead of the default assumption that technology creates a helpful first draft that requires revision, people should regard the output as a plausible final draft that they should check against firm-established guardrails but otherwise largely leave as is.

The value at stake lies not only in the promise of greater efficiency but also in the possibility for people to redirect time, energy, and effort away from tasks that generative AI will take over. Employees will be able to double down on the tasks that remain beyond the frontier of this technology, reaching higher levels of proficiency.

---

40 https://sloanreview.mit.edu/article/ai-is-helping-companies-redefine-not-just-improve-performance/

Turning the lens on ourselves, we can already envision our employees spending less time manually summarizing research or polishing slides and instead investing even more effort in driving complex change management initiatives. The impact of generative AI's disruption will of course vary dramatically across job categories. But at least some workers – including the majority of our participants – are confronting this prospect with optimism.

Strategic Workforce Planning. To get the AI–human dynamics right in complex organizations, leaders must grapple with four questions that have no easy answers:

–   **Which capabilities will you need?** As with any other technology, it will take people to define what and how generative AI will be used. But it isn't obvious which human capabilities are best suited to maximizing the tool's value or how often these capabilities will change. We're seeing this uncertainty play out in real time with respect to LLMs: The role of "prompt engineer" didn't exist a year ago, but demand for this role during Q2 2023 was nearly seven times higher than it was in Q1.[2] (GPT-4 was launched toward the end of Q1, on March 14, 2023.) And yet, prompt engineers may no longer be needed once generative AI itself has mastered the task of breaking down complex problems into optimal prompts (as it appears it soon will with autonomous agents). Even the selection of optimal LLMs for specific business applications, which is largely done by humans at present, may in the future be outsourced to AI systems themselves.

–   **What is your hiring strategy?** Because generative AI is a great leveler of proficiency on certain tasks, raw talent may not be a good predictor of high performance in a world of widespread GenAI use. For example, some people may have lower baseline proficiency for a type of task while being quite capable of partnering with generative AI to outperform peers. Finding these individuals will be an important goal for future talent strategies, but the underlying traits are not yet clearly identified.

–   **How will you train people effectively?** As our findings indicate, straightforward training won't be sufficient. Effective training will likely need to explicitly address any cognitive biases that may lead people to over-rely on generative AI in situations where the technology has not yet reached the right level of competence.

    We also see a potentially deeper issue: Even as certain tasks are fully handed over to GenAI, some degree of human oversight will be necessary. How can employees effectively manage the technology for tasks that they themselves have not learned how to do on their own?

–   **How will you cultivate diversity of thought?** Our results suggest that GenAI detracts from collective creativity by limiting the range of perspectives that individuals bring to the table. This loss in diversity of thought may have ripple effects beyond what we can currently envision. One plausible risk is that it could shrink the long-term innovation capacity of organizations – for example, by making ideation more homogenous. It's a slippery slope, as a decline in innovation capabilities means less differentiation from competitors, which could impede growth potential. The good news is that the ideas that humans generate on their own and the ideas that they generate when assisted by generative AI are vastly different. Setting aside the degree of diversity in each group, when we compared the output of the control and experimental groups, the overlap (semantic similarity) was less than 10%. The key for leaders will be to use both approaches to ideation – which ultimately will create an even wider circle of ideas.

Experimentation and Testing. Generative AI systems continue to develop at a stunning rate: In just a few months between the releases of OpenAI's GPT-3.5 and GPT-4, the model made huge performance leaps across a wide range of tasks. Tasks for which generative AI is ill-suited today will likely fall within its frontier of competence soon – perhaps in the very near future. This is likely to happen as LLMs become multimodal (going beyond text to include other formats of data), or as models grow larger, both of which increase the likelihood of unpredictable capabilities.

Given this lack of predictability, the only way to understand how generative AI will impact your business is to develop experimentation capabilities – to establish a "generative AI lab" of sorts that will enable you to keep pace with an expanding frontier. And as the technology changes, the collaboration model between humans and generative AI will have to change as well. Experimentation may yield some counterintuitive or even uncomfortable findings about your business, but it will also enable you to gain invaluable insights about how the technology can and should be used. We put our feet to the fire with this experiment – and we believe all business leaders should do the same.

∗∗∗

Generative AI will likely change much of what we do and how we do it, and it will do so in ways that no one can anticipate. Success in the age of AI will largely depend on an organization's ability to learn and change faster than it ever has before.

∗∗∗∗∗∗∗∗∗∗∗∗∗∗∗∗∗∗∗∗∗∗∗∗

How Employees Feel About Their Jobs Can Make or Break a Company's AI Transformation. Here's How Leaders Should Handle It

François Candelon, Lisa Krayer, and Saravanan Rajendran

Artificial intelligence is upending not just how people work, but how they relate to their jobs – their professional identity. AI uniquely impacts white-collar workers in a way no technologies have before.

In the past, automation technologies focused on automating portions of physical tasks performed by humans. The rise of robotics did just that, displacing low-skilled workers from the manufacturing process of goods like cars. The development of software, on the other hand, affected middle-skilled workers, by automating more complex tasks. AI is now coming for white-collar skills – decision-making and intellectual abilities – that up until recently, we thought were uniquely human.

The new frontier of generative AI encroaches even further than prior AI systems on the work done by white-collar workers. This is because, as Microsoft[41] CEO Satya Nadella outlined in his recent company keynote,[42] there are two layers that drive generative AI's capabilities: First, an advanced reasoning engine that can be both pretrained with general information and then re-trained on company-specific data to provide custom insights; and second, a natural language interface that makes English "the hottest new programming language." The result is that generative AI can provide sophisticated insights, but also do so in an accessible way. That capability resembles the work of a high-level employee, upsetting the professional identity of white-collar workers.

Proactively addressing these professional identity concerns is vital for organizations because employees who feel their professional identities are threatened by AI are more resistant to its adoption, and less likely to use and derive value from it. This ultimately hurts the company overall. Our research shows that organizations with employees who personally get value out of AI are nearly six times more likely to reap significant financial benefits than organizations where employees don't see the value of the technology.

---

41 https://fortune.com/company/microsoft/
42 https://www.youtube.com/watch?v=RhwVMt_XCUE

There are a number of schools of thought on the elements that make up an individual's unique sense of professional identity, and how it evolves over time. According to self-determination theory, there are three key components of professional identity: a sense of competence (importance of role and belief in one's expertise), autonomy (level of discretion to make decisions), and belonging (connection to a wider group that generates meaningfulness). To address AI's impact on employees' professional identity, executives will need to address each of these three elements.

Redesign Roles to Allow Humans to Go Beyond AI

When AI assumes a task previously performed by humans, it has the potential to damage employees' sense of competence. For example, AI can now outperform radiologists in diagnosis accuracy. As a result, many medical students are turning away from a potential career in radiology because AI's superior performance in the field diminishes their sense of competency. The rapid advance of generative AI in the workplace is having a similar effect on employees' sense of competence across a growing number of industries.

What constitutes meaningful work for humans in this new reality? To create a new sense of purpose, organizations will need to identify what tasks humans are uniquely suited for, distinguishing them from the tasks AI excels at. Deploying AI to tackle these distinct tasks frees human workers to assume roles where they have the capacity to go above and beyond AI This allows human workers to add value in the presence of AI, enabling them to derive a renewed sense of competency in their work.

When H&M deployed AI to make its yearly purchasing decisions on how many and what types of clothes to buy for its markets around the world, the retailer's buying team first decried the move – and then resisted it. While the purchasing task itself was tedious, involving hundreds of thousands of hours of manual work now automatable by AI, the feeling of being replaced impacted how the workers perceived themselves and their work, fundamentally changing their professional identity. H&M buyers' resistance hindered AI adoption, potentially wiping out the financial benefits of the technology for the company.

To help overcome their opposition to the move, H&M helped its employees find a new sense of purpose. The company redefined workers' roles to accentuate what they did best. No longer were these employees manually calculating discounts on declining products; now they were engaged in sophisticated merchandizing work for new products and analyzing customer behavior. To further cement these changes, the company renamed its teams to reflect new roles, paving the way for workers to forge new professional narratives. Buoyed by these changes, H&M employees felt empowered, regained a sense of competency, and invested in the use of AI.

Restore Employee Autonomy by Making AI "challengeable"

Unlike previous advances in automation, AI has a unique ability to make decisions or, at the very least, provide guidance on what decisions should be made. This makes employees feel reliant on a machine for making decisions, fundamentally threatening their autonomy. The ever-expanding decision-making prowess of generative AI has only heightened this threat, particularly with the rise of autonomous agents, like AutoGPT and BabyAGI, that don't just make decisions but independently plan, problem-solve, and perform entire tasks, to get to a particular goal.

This encroachment on employee's autonomy has several negative consequences. For instance, according to a recent study by the IT research firm Gartner,[43] increased autonomy improves employee performance and retention, while lowering worker fatigue. How, then, can leaders restore their employees' sense of autonomy?

First, it is critical for leaders to ensure that AI implementations allow for override privileges. This restores a sense of agency and creates a virtuous feedback loop, making employees more likely to adopt AI in the first place. For example, a well-known bias among humans is "algorithmic aversion," where people distrust and refuse to use AI, even if it is high-functioning, when it does not operate to absolute perfection. Academic research has shown that giving participants the ability to modify AI outputs overcomes this aversion – regardless of how extensively or how frequently participants modified the outputs. Override privileges also perform a critical function, allowing well-trained expert humans to correct AI mistakes when the technology goes off-track.

Second, leaders must highlight to their employees how using AI may allow for less oversight from managers, which improves employees' sense of autonomy. At Walgreens, for instance, managers initially controlled how pharmacists filled prescriptions through strict guidelines designed to ensure patient satisfaction. With the adoption of AI, a new system was put in place: AI would predict when pharmacy orders would be ready in a bid to reduce customer wait times. This meant that fewer interventions, like fulfillment guidelines, were needed from management. In fact, in one instance, a manager called to congratulate the pharmacists for reducing customer complaints and ultimately gave individual phar-

---

43 https://fortune.com/company/gartner/

macists more agency to run their own operations as they see fit. This greatly boosted the sense of autonomy felt by pharmacists at Walgreens.

Rebuild the Sense of Belonging by Fostering New Types of Connections

AI can negatively impact an individual's sense of belonging by reducing human-to-human interactions around tasks now automated by AI. This has already happened in factories where the few remaining employees work mostly in tandem with machines – yet in isolation from one another – to ensure quality control.

Generative AI, with its ability to conduct lifelike chatbot conversations, makes this threat even more pervasive. Within companies, some human-to-human interactions are already being replaced with chatbot interactions. The shift away from these small workplace interactions adds up to a big problem: It lowers employees' sense of belonging, which jeopardizes their wellbeing, and, in turn, hurts business performance. A 2019 survey by BetterUp[44] found that a strong sense of belonging in the workplace led to a 56% increase in job performance, a 50% drop in employee turnover, and a 75% reduction in sick days taken by employees.

One solution to employee isolation is to redesign a company's workflows. A call center at a US bank, for example, created "squads" or teams of operators who support similar customers and leveraged an AI-powered software to generate more opportunities for interaction – virtual channels, synchronization of breaks, and tracking of common goals at team-level. One year after the bank implemented this software, its call centers reported a 23% increase in productivity and a 28% increase in employee retention. These squads go well beyond mere efficiency gains. At Oomph, a digital services company, the results have been dramatic: team happiness, productivity, and success have soared since the creation of squads. Squads improved Oomph's culture, which has trickled down generating numerous benefits both at the employee and organizational level.

Conclusion

There is no doubt that AI, especially with the advent of generative AI, is a technological revolution. As organizations look to reap the full benefits of this technological revolution, however, they must now turn their attention to the human impact

---

44 https://www.betterup.com/press/betterups-new-industry-leading-research-shows-companies-that-fail-at-belonging-lose-tens-of-millions-in-revenue

of this revolution. As AI entrenches itself deeper in the workplace, it poses unique challenges to workers and their professional identities. The key is to recognize the importance of this professional identity threat and create an environment where humans can thrive alongside AI. Doing this will require action not just from executives at the very top, but managers at all levels of an organization.

Chapter 5
Establishing New Models of Leadership and Culture

The Case for the Intergenerational C-Suite: Why Companies Need More Age Diversity in Their Leadership Ranks
Martin Reeves and Adam Job

Every year, Fortune publishes the Future 50,[1] a ranking of the world's largest public companies by their long-term growth prospects, codeveloped with Boston Consulting Group. In this series, we assess trends related to the future growth potential of businesses.

Societies around the globe are aging, as birth rates decline and lifespans increase. This is expected to result in significant economic and societal challenges – driven by a shrinking labor force,[2] increased health expenditures, and more pressure on social safety nets.

Businesses will feel these effects in several ways. For one, the demographic shift will induce a change in demand. In Japan, for example, the domestic diaper market has shifted[3] from the traditional target group (parents of young children) to older adults, who use the products for incontinence control. As wealth becomes concentrated with the elderly,[4] companies must actively pursue opportunities to develop new products and services tailored to older people.

Moreover, there will be a significant change in the composition of the workforce – as younger age groups shrink (see Figure 5.1), and as increasing health spans as well as changes to retirement regulations mean that older people work for longer. With a 60-year-old in the Western world now likely to live another 17

---

1 https://fortune.com/ranking/future-50/2023/
2 https://www.cgdev.org/publication/global-mobility-confronting-world-workforce-imbalance
3 https://www.bcg.com/publications/2020/challenge-of-slow
4 https://www.forbes.com/sites/neilhowe/2018/03/16/the-graying-of-wealth/?sh=696a37d4302d

---

https://doi.org/10.1515/9783111369921-006

years[5] of healthy life, it will be crucial for firms to improve their inclusion of more experienced workers.[6]

Global population by age groups, 1950 to 2100

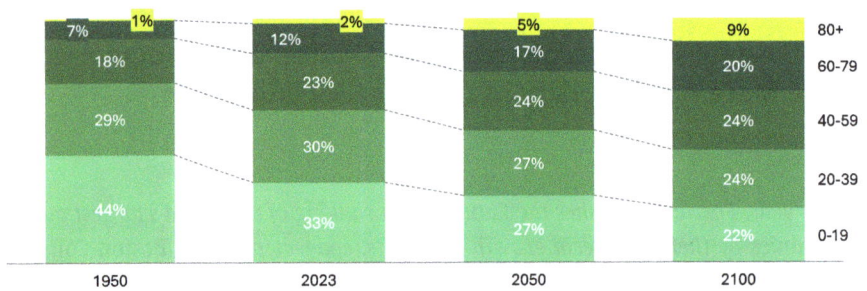

Sources: United Nations, Department of Economic and Social Affairs, Population Division. World Population Prospects: The 2022 Revision.

Figure 5.1: Major Shift in Demographic Composition Towards Older Age Groups Projected.

The Age of Company (and Political) Leaders Is Increasing Rapidly

There is, however, one area where business is racing ahead of the demographic shift: Company leadership. The average hiring age of CEOs at Fortune 500 and S&P 500 companies has risen dramatically over the past two decades – from 46 years old to 55 years old.[7] Several of the world's largest companies are now helmed by executives that are significantly older than this, including Warren Buffett (age 93, Berkshire Hathaway); Seifi Ghasemi (79, Air Products & Chemicals); and Bob Iger (72, Disney). Rupert Murdoch (92, Fox Corp.[8] and News Corp.) retired from the chairman role in September, but noted in his farewell memo[9] to staff that he would continue to "be involved every day in the contest of ideas" at the company.

5 https://www.census.gov/content/dam/Census/library/visualizations/2021/comm/healthy-life-expectancy.pdf
6 https://hbr.org/2022/03/work-in-the-era-of-no-retirement?ab=seriesnav-bigidea
7 https://static1.squarespace.com/static/62164a05607c3e5978f251ec/t/63d4519fd948164d83bfd602/1674858912116/V.+Report+22+Winter+FINAL.pdf
8 https://fortune.com/company/fox/
9 https://fortune.com/2023/09/21/rupert-murdoch-retires-succession-fox-news-corp-92-years-old/?queryly=related_article

The aging trend is also playing out in political leadership: The average age of a US Senator has increased steadily since 1980[10] – from 54 then to 63 now – and the likely candidates for next year's US Presidential election are 81 and 77 years old.

As a result of these developments, questions have arisen about how old is too old to lead,[11] with some commenters worrying about a perceived frailty or potential cognitive decline of the oldest leaders. Others point out that research shows no relation between age and individual job performance[12] and that aging may have positive effects on leadership capabilities by increasing experience, warmth, and empathy. The departure of many young founder-CEOs of tech companies – such as Aporva Mehta of Instacart,[13] or Ben Silbermann of Pinterest – during the 2022 "tech crash" has shown that having a visionary at the company's helm is not a panacea,[14] as navigating companies through troubled times requires extensive experience and operational skills.

The debate, thus, should not focus on questioning the capabilities of more seasoned leaders or of less experienced talents. Rather, we believe it should focus on how businesses can balance perspectives across different time scales.

Age Diversity in Leadership Is Crucial for Overcoming Today's and Tomorrow's Problems

Businesses need to juggle the execution on their current business model and the exploration of options that could form the basis for future growth and advantage. Achieving the required ambidexterity[15] is harder than ever: With rising interest rates, investors are increasingly demanding short-term payoffs rather than trusting long-term promises. At the same time, companies must contribute to solving humanity's thorniest problems – such as climate change and biodiversity loss[16] – which are unfolding over the long run. Doing so is not just a moral imperative; rather, finding solutions to these challenges is key to achieving a sustainable competitive advantage.[17]

---

10 https://www.nbcnews.com/data-graphics/118th-congress-age-third-oldest-1789-rcna64117
11 https://fortune.com/2023/09/23/rupert-murdoch-retires-at-92-get-ready-for-the-100-year-old-ceo/
12 https://www.scinapse.io/papers/1979028850
13 https://fortune.com/company/instacart/
14 https://www.nytimes.com/2022/08/10/business/silicon-valley-boy-boss.html
15 https://www.bcg.com/publications/2018/2-percent-company
16 https://bcghendersoninstitute.com/biodiversity-the-next-arena-in-sustainable-business/
17 https://bcghendersoninstitute.com/winning-through-the-great-climate-upheaval/

With the rapid aging of company leaders, there is a danger that the balance between these different time scales may be lost, at a cost to companies and to society. The Future 50 ranking provides some evidence of this: The average age of CEOs of the top 50 firms with the greatest long-term growth potential is markedly lower (52 years) than in the roughly 1,700 companies that make up the rest of the sample (58 years). Moreover, there is a statistically significant, negative relationship between corporate vitality (our measure of long-term growth potential) and CEO age, which continues to hold even after controlling for firm size and age (see Figure 5.2). Indeed, the age of the top executive is the fourth-biggest factor (of a list of 19) in terms of its predictive power for vitality.

Corporate vitality score

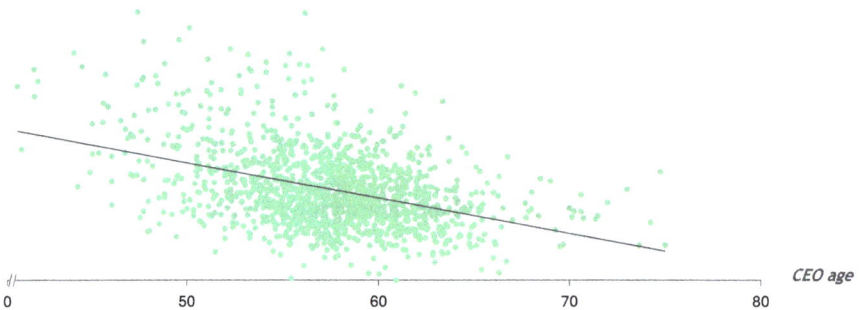

Notes: Corporate vitality score is calculated based on two pillars: Top-down, market-based assessment of revenue growth potential and bottom-up analysis of a firm's capacity to deliver (based on financial and nonfinancial metrics – including long-term strategic orientation, technology and investments, people, and structure; these factors are weighted based on their contribution to long-term growth using an AI model); sample includes over 1,700 publicly listed companies with at least $10 billion in revenue in 2022 or $10 billion in market value at year-end 2022;
Source: BCG Henderson Institute analysis

Figure 5.2: Corporate Vitality is Negatively Linked to CEO Age.

We believe this loss of balance can be addressed by striving for more age diversity in leadership ranks, i.e., a better inclusion of younger talents. Studies show, for example, that age-diverse leadership teams are better positioned to drive the adoption of sustainable business model innovations[18] and achieve superior CSR performance.[19] More generally, bringing together diverse but complementary perspectives, skills, and networks in teams has been shown to lead to better decision making, more productive collaboration, and improved overall performance.[20]

---

18 https://www.sciencedirect.com/science/article/pii/S004016252300094X
19 https://link.springer.com/article/10.1007/s11301-022-00294-5
20 https://journals.aom.org/doi/10.5465/AMBPP.2021.62

So how can businesses achieve a better balance of experience and curiosity in their upper echelons?

Toward Intergenerational Leadership

Achieving intergenerational leadership is not yet a well-codified area of business. Below, we outline four potential paths that companies should explore to harness the benefits of age diversity.

Consultation: One approach involves consulting younger leaders on strategic direction-setting. This may be accomplished by establishing a shadow board, in which younger talents team up with more experienced executives. This can help overcome generational divides[21] and bring new perspectives to established leaders. Companies including Gucci, Mövenpick Hotels & Resorts, and TotalEnergies[22] have established such boards and are reporting positive results.[23]

Another type of consultation is mentoring. For example, Chip Conley, who joined Airbnb in 2013[24] as head of global hospitality and strategy at age 52, quickly became one of the most trusted advisors[25] to CEO Brian Chesky (then aged 31) and eventually mentored more than 100 people at the company, being affectionally called it's "modern elder."[26] Conley points out that a crucial part of successful cross-generational mentorship is for it to be mutual – with wisdom being shared in both directions.

Coleadership: A more formalized model would be to install top leadership with shared decision-making responsibilities – e.g., a co-CEO model, which research indicates can yield positive impact on shareholder value.[27] A well-known example of coleadership was put in place at Google[28] in 2001, when Larry Page and Sergey Brin (both 28 at the time) convinced Eric Schmidt (then 48) to join up as CEO and chairman, providing "adult supervision"[29] to the founders, who took on the roles of president of products and president of technology, respectively.

---

21 https://hbr.org/2022/03/how-shadow-boards-bridge-generational-divides?ab=seriesnav-bigidea
22 https://fortune.com/company/total/
23 https://hbr.org/2019/06/why-you-should-create-a-shadow-board-of-younger-employees
24 https://fortune.com/2022/09/09/generation-gap-at-work-chip-conley-modern-elder-academy/
25 https://www.fastcompany.com/3027107/punk-meet-rock-airbnb-brian-chesky-chip-conley
26 https://www.fastcompany.com/90255475/airbnbs-chip-conley-is-doubling-down-on-being-a-modern-elder
27 https://hbr.org/2022/07/is-it-time-to-consider-co-ceos
28 https://fortune.com/company/alphabet/
29 https://www.wired.com/story/at-google-eric-schmidt-wrote-the-book-on-adult-supervision/

Another example is that of the cofounders of Workday, Dave Duffield and Aneel Bhusri,[30] who, at the time of their company's IPO (in 2012) were 72 and 46 years old, respectively. The two applied the co-CEO model successfully – growing Workday's valuation eight-fold between the IPO and Duffield's retirement in April 2021.

Separation: Another route to strengthening the voice of the next generation is to install separate decision-making bodies. This may be done vertically, by implementing a bicameral governance setup (like in many governments), in which a chamber of less experienced talents could propose strategic moves for a separate chamber of more experienced executives to approve (or vice versa).

An even further-reaching idea is to construct different "temporal business units" focused on developing capabilities or offerings on different time horizons. For example, in the Alphabet portfolio, Google is responsible for making breakthroughs in machine learning and AI development to enhance the firm's core search product in the short run, while DeepMind's main mission is to develop an artificial general intelligence in the longer term.

Substitution: Finally, and most boldly, paving the way for the next generation may also take the form of creating space for more junior leaders by imposing term limits or other retirement rules for leaders, or defining quotas for age diversity. More than half of S&P 1500 companies have put in place mandatory retirement policies for CEOs and directors based on age, while rules based on tenure remain rare.[31] Crucially, these leadership decisions should not be made based on age alone but be paired with regular performance assessments and succession planning.

✳✳✳

Companies are confronted with heightened pressure on both short-term execution and on finding solutions to long-term problems like climate change. The rapid aging of company leadership may lead to a loss of balance of short- versus long-term perspectives at this critical juncture. To counteract this, firms should strive toward intergenerational leadership models to achieve an improved balance between experience and curiosity.

✳✳✳✳✳✳✳✳✳✳✳✳✳✳✳✳✳✳✳✳✳✳✳✳✳✳✳

---

30 https://www.forbes.com/sites/georgeanders/2013/09/16/snubbed-by-oracle-workdays-duffield-and-bhusri-hit-jackpot/?sh=13f40a7c1412
31 https://www.prnewswire.com/news-releases/companies-are-moving-away-from-mandatory-director-retirement-policies-and-pursuing-other-ways-to-achieve-board-refreshment-301601561.html

Winning the Ecosystem Game: The Leadership Gap

Martin Reeves, Michael G. Jacobides, and Ulrich Pidun

The Leadership Gap

One of the defining business changes of the dawn of the 21st century has been the meteoric rise in importance of business ecosystems. Enabled by digitization and the growth of modular technologies that have redefined the nature of possibility, such ecosystems have transformed sectors, redrawn the boundaries of markets, and challenged the existing industrial order. Ecosystems have fueled the ascent of many Big Tech firms, each of which draws on their own and others' platforms to build collaborative ecosystems, transforming business strategy, and also potentially policy as well. With AI-enabled ecosystems being the latest manifestation of ecosystem power, the topic rightly remains hot.

As ever, though, excessive enthusiasm and hype cut two ways. On the one hand, they raise awareness and help us focus on new possibilities. On the other hand, hype means hyperbole, and some of the would-be innovators are quick to adopt the label, without necessarily having a solid plan, much less capabilities and implementation skills that can back up the claims they make. Business ecosystems are no exception. Even firms that proudly speak of their ecosystem achievements have private worries about getting their strategy right, and even more so, getting organizational design and leadership right as well.

This should not be a surprise. Ecosystems are often misunderstood. They may have become a focus of academic work and practitioner excitement, but the way they add value is elusive and confusing to many, especially as firms are mired in delusions of grandeur, often wasting valuable resources in unrealistic attempts to become orchestrators rather than participate as partners.

One of the less discussed reasons for ecosystem failure is that the attitudes of leaders seem to be stuck in the previous era. Ironically, the very forces that have brought about ecosystems – the opportunities of collaborating and leveraging complementors, the possibility to experiment and quickly scale new solutions, and the ability to do this outside a firms' boundaries – are the forces that undermine ecosystem development within firms, when they are stuck to an outdated model of managing and leading, which is maladapted to winning the ecosystem game.

What matters, then, is the attitude and leadership skills that underpin success in the ecosystem game. This is why most of the (spectacular) success stories tend to either be new firms (mostly digital natives), and firms that are open to experimenting and have been born with the systems, structures, principles, and values congenial to ecosystems. Both types of firms have developed the leadership orientation that is required to make the successful in this new game.

From Intuition to Evidence

Our article is informed by our research over the last few years. We have independently engaged in research, joining forces to consider what ecosystems are and how they operate, including a compendium of ecosystem research. This, on the BCG/BHI side, draws on more than four years of dedicated research on business ecosystems and from our experience as strategy consultants to more than 50 companies building ecosystems. We studied over 100 failed ecosystems and compared them to their successful peers. Results were substantiated through 20 targeted interviews with a diverse set of executives from startups, big tech, and global corporations. On the Evolution Ltd/London Business School side, in addition to academic research and work on regulating ecosystems we engaged in research with a dozen organizations and in-depth work with four of them, speaking with over 150 executives in considering success and failures in ecosystems, and explored in detail how to approach ecosystems.

Solving a Different Problem

Ecosystems, by their nature, have emerged to solve the problems of organizations working in silos, to offer creative new solutions that spread outside the organization. They require us to rethink how we add value to the customers, and require we find ways to collaborate and draw on the initiative of partners, be they complementors (those working in our ecosystem) or orchestrators (those whose ecosystem we work with). Whatever our role is, successful strategy in ecosystems requires us to think and act differently. Success in the ecosystem game is not akin to implementing a pre-set plan, and showcasing robust progress along a well delineated, predictable path. It consists of getting the right approach to either participate in or build a set of alliances and links that will excite customers and partners alike. This means they are distinct from other, traditional forms of organization:

- Ecosystems are most effective in unpredictable but highly malleable business environments that require "shaping" strategies, which disrupt and recast an industry.
- Ecosystems cannot be entirely planned and designed, have emergent properties and thus require adaptive strategies, flexibility and willingness to pivot.
- This is further complicated by the limited hierarchical control in a business ecosystem and the need to inspire and persuade partners to voluntarily participate, which poses specific governance challenges.
- Once launched, ecosystems can scale very fast and experience exponential growth, mainly driven by network effects and increasing returns on data. The resulting winner-takes-all dynamics and potential market dominance can lead rapidly to increased public and regulatory scrutiny.
- Building an ecosystem requires high and sustained upfront investments with comparably long payback times. And success is not guaranteed: our research showed that 85% of ecosystems are not sustainable in the long run, and they tend to fail rather late after having spent substantial amounts of investment, for a predictable set of reasons.

Ecosystems, then, require a different approach, as they solve a different problem, using distinct approaches. While the exact prescriptions may differ depending on whether it is advisable for a firm to build its own ecosystem (NB: more infrequently than one might expect) or participate in existing ecosystems through a portfolio-of-efforts way (more often than not), there are some common issues for leadership and leadership development.

Leadership is particularly important in an ecosystem world because success requires changes to a firm's traditional operating model and management mindset, creating a tough change management challenge for legacy firms. At the same time, the particular characteristics of business ecosystems pose many new leadership challenges that executives may not be well prepared for, based on their traditional management education. Successful ecosystem leaders need distinct leadership traits in terms of their thinking model, strategic style, mindset, and behaviors, the four steps that need to all change and be aligned for a firm to win the ecosystem game.

Step One: Get Your *Thinking Model* Right

Ecosystems require a fresh mental model, where the focus shifts from the product to the needs of the customer, and where the purview shifts from what happens within the boundaries of the firm to consider context and partners/those that are complementors. Granted, this will not come free – ecosystems need to solve big enough problems to justify their sustained investment. By their very nature, to succeed and disrupt industries, they require a systemic approach, as well as imaginative counter factual thinking as opposed to incremental improvements to longstanding business models.

System Thinking

- Ecosystem success depends on the performance of the entire system, not of its individual contributors, individually considered.
- Ecosystem design thus requires a true systems perspective. It is not sufficient to design a single firm value creation and delivery model, success also depends on, for instance, explicitly addressing the co-innovation challenge, adoption risk, and value distribution among ecosystem members as well as understanding and influencing regulation. As CEO Stephen Elop rightly observed when commenting on Nokia's demise in mobile phones: "Our competitors aren't taking our market share with devices; they are taking our market share with an entire ecosystem!"

Counterfactual Thinking (Imagination)

- To identify opportunities for ecosystem business models, leaders must focus less on optimizing current operations, exploiting existing capabilities, and expanding present positions and more on uncovering unmet customer needs and imagining new solutions, beyond the scope of their current activities.
- One of the strengths of a business ecosystem is that it can address challenges and enable value propositions that no individual company could achieve alone. Finding such opportunities requires counterfactual thinking and imagination, "the ability to create a mental model of something that doesn't exist yet."

Step Two: Recalibrate Your *Strategic Style*

Ecosystems also represent a different style of strategic choice, requiring new approaches to strategy and therefore also to leadership. Two of the defining characteristics of ecosystems strategy are that they reshape strategic environments and also need to be adaptive in responding to unpredictable and rapid shifts.

Shaping Strategy

- To shape the future of an industry, build an ecosystem and motivate partners to join requires visionary leadership and commitment, combined with long range communication skills.
- Studies in cognitive science show that the most important leadership traits in shaping environments include: reciprocity (willingness to give as well as to take), deliberateness (acts consciously and intentionally), and at ease with ambiguity (able to act and decide on partial information).
- Such unpredictable and malleable environments require mutual trust and reciprocity among stakeholders. Though the foundation for productive ecosystems must be laid carefully and deliberately, ecosystems evolve organically, requiring leaders to be comfortable with the ambiguity that comes from having only partial control and constant evolution.

Adaptive Strategy

- Ecosystem leadership thus needs to balance shaping strategy with adaptive strategy. More important, though, most organizations should aim to develop a portfolio of ecosystem plays where they are partners and not orchestrators, and this means they need to be adaptive as the context they are embedded in evolves.
- Studies in cognitive neuroscience indicate that the most important leadership traits in adaptive environments include: multitasking (capable of handling several tasks simultaneously), dynamic evaluation (able to assess situations quickly), and openness to trial and error (willing to try different actions despite understanding that failure may occur). This becomes all the more important in the context of ecosystems whereby a firms' role requires fluidity: Should a firm be a partner or orchestrator? Act in one or multiple ecosystems? How can it manage opposing requests by multiple stakeholders, who are outside a firms' boundaries and act independently?
- In such unpredictable and difficult-to-control environments, leaders must be able to stay flexible. As new opportunities emerge and new information about them is revealed, effective leaders quickly select and scale the successful ones in a process of trial and error. Consider Airbnb's shift of emphasis from urban to rural locations and offering online events, retailers offering kerbside pickup and home delivery, e.g., at the same time, flexibility does not mean that leaders cease measuring and evaluating outcomes.

Focus on Value Creation (not only value capture)
- The best way to create value as an ecosystem player is not to focus so much on value capture and on growing one's own share of the pie at the expense of others, but to grow the pie together, so that everybody benefits. The failure of the metaverse to live up to its promise so far is partly the result of leading firms such as Meta spending too much time divvying up the pie and setting up expectations of outlandish share of revenue, while at the same time not considering the real use cases for the customers, who, given the lackluster performance of immersive technologies, were broadly unconvinced.
- This requires a long-term perspective and may involve co-investing in the ecosystem beyond the boundaries of one's own firm and supporting or even subsidizing partners that are bottlenecks to improving the overall customer value proposition. Alibaba, for instance, invested heavily to support the many small sellers on its B2B marketplace with tools and data to run their online stores, partner with manufacturers, coordinate with logistics partners, and arrange online payments. Similarly, Airbnb focused early on providing professional support for hosts on its platform, such as photography and cleaning services, linen delivery, and tools to simplify property listing and guest check-in.

Step Three: Adjust Your Mindset

Ecosystems strategies require a different orientation to traditional alternatives. In particular, they require a more external orientation, a more collaborative mindset, a greater tolerance of ambiguity, and also patient investment to secure long term rewards.
- *Outward (not inward) focus:* As the locus of value creation and innovation moves from the company to the ecosystem, leaders must look beyond the boundaries of their own firm to explore business opportunities and secure the required resources and capabilities. Too often ecosystem thinking is still dominated by what a firm can offer – especially if it is dynamic and diversified. This, though, misses the point. Leaders must be more receptive to ideas and impulses from the outside world and beyond their own industry.
- *Collaborative (versus purely competitive) mindset:* Traditionally, most firms are successful because they are better than their competitors and beat them in the market. However, to be successful in an ecosystem world, leaders need to move from a purely competitive to a more collaborative mindset. To create an effective ecosystem, not an "*ego*system", they need to be reciprocal, compromise and fight the temptation to misuse their position of power as an

orchestrator, or even the temptation to default for orchestrating an ecosystem as opposed to partnering with someone else's.
- *At ease with ambiguity:* Ecosystem leaders must embrace the uncertainty related to the evolutionary development of business ecosystems. They must be ready to confront dilemmas, such as between shaping and adaptive strategies, value creation and value capture, openness and control of ecosystem governance.
- *Patience and stamina:* Given the need for high and sustained upfront investments for building an ecosystem, and their typically long payback time, orchestrators cannot expect instant gratification and need their leaders to signal strong commitment, patience, and stamina.

Step Four: Change Your Behaviors

All of the above require new leadership behaviors, including leading from behind, trust based leadership and humbleness.
- *Leading from behind:* Business ecosystems are based on voluntary collaboration between largely independent partners. Ecosystem leaders must accept that they will not be in full control. They must lead in less formal ways through active influencing, networking and moderating. This also involves taking responsibility beyond the boundaries of the firm, for example, for partner behavior that cannot be fully controlled.
- *Trust-based leadership:* Effective leadership in a business ecosystem cannot be based on power because the orchestrator cannot force partners to join and contribute to the ecosystem. Instead, ecosystem leaders need to convince partners based on a strong vision, evidence, credibility, and honesty, and they need to create trust and enthusiasm among partners. This is, for example, why many tech players (such as Google, Amazon and Apple) struggled to establish themselves as orchestrators in the health care space.
- *Humbleness:* Effective leaders in business ecosystems need to spearhead all the required changes in leadership characteristics and behavior listed above. We found that this is facilitated by certain personality traits and manners that contradict the popular image of an omnipotent leader. Successful ecosystem leaders tend to be more curious than determined, more humble than assertive, better at listening than presenting, and they exhibit strong empathy and are willing to admit mistakes and make compromises. Indeed, one of the key strategic choices when designing an ecosystem – whether to orchestrate or play the role of a contributor – is an act of humbleness. We observe that almost all companies considering building an ecosystem assume that they can

play the orchestrator role, although arithmetically few can eventually do so. Furthermore, we have shown that complementors can be highly successful.

Indeed, most examples of successful incumbent transformations from individual performer to ecosystem player have been led by visionary CEOs. Think of Sam Allen at John Deere, Zhang Ruimin at Haier, Ma Mingzhe at Ping An, Piyush Gupta at DBS, and Satya Nadella at Microsoft. Microsoft is itself a fantastic take of a firm that, under Gates, played the ecosystem game like a pro, teaming up with Intel to dominate the world, but later, as it became successful and cash-focused lost its ability to support, inspire trust, and be humble. Windows Mobile was thus a spectacular failure, which, however, led to reflection and change – shifting away from its hardball past to a more collaborative approach, by opening its interfaces for integration with other platforms, and no longer trying to dominate its ecosystems, leaving room for others to lead.

Digital ecosystems have already transformed the corporate landscape starting with B2C businesses, and this dynamic seems set to continue as the new choice spreads to B2B businesses, more regulated industries like insurance and health care, and to the public sector.

The choice is very different from traditional structural and strategic options and requires different leadership behaviors and ways of thinking. One of the most important but also under appreciated risks for legacy companies embracing ecosystems is that existing leaders transfer traditional leadership approaches and skillsets to situations where they will not work. Conversely, the opportunities for firms in all sectors who want to go beyond their traditional recipes to find dynamic, collaborative ways to grow abound, provided they get their strategy and leadership skills right. Time to retool.

✶✶✶✶✶✶✶✶✶✶✶✶✶✶✶✶✶✶✶✶✶✶✶✶

Why the World Needs Generative Leaders

Jean-Michel Caye, Jim Hemerling, Deborah Lovich, Marie Humblot-Ferrero,
Fanny Potier, and Robert Werner

Today more than ever, we are relying on our leaders to deliver. We're asking more of them than we have in decades.

Put yourself in the shoes of a business leader – or, if you happen to be one, keep those shoes on. Here are some of the daunting priorities and concerns likely to occupy your mind every day:

– Short-term results	– Climate and environmental footprint
– The great resignation	– Employee safety and mental health
– Speaking out on societal issues	– Employees' demands for more flexibility
– Artificial intelligence	– Shrinking competitive advantage
– Geopolitical risk	– Ecosystem collaboration
– Customer journeys	– Always-on transformation

Each of these issues is complex and high stakes. And as if that weren't enough, when not on the job, leaders are also worrying about the COVID-19 pandemic's impact on their own families.

But here is some good news. We ran a year-long research project to examine how business leaders are currently performing and what people want and expect from them. Notably, 75% of the 9,000 employees who responded to our survey said they were satisfied with how leaders performed during the first wave of the pandemic. [1] In that uncertain and frightening time, leaders *did* rise to the occasion. They were creative and flexible because they had to be.

Generative Leadership

Our research suggests that what worked during the pandemic can form the basis for an approach to leading that we call generative.[2]

Generative leaders strive to leave the world a better place than they found it. With so much at stake, they are seizing a rare opportunity to do better not just for their shareholders, but for their customers, for their teams, for society, and

Note: The authors would like to thank the following colleagues for their valuable contributions to the development of this article: Cailin Ahern, Vikram Bhalla, Divya Chanana, Kristy Ellmer, Wanjun Fang, Grant Freeland, Brittany Heflin, Bill Higgins, Philippine Leccia, and Mickey McManus.

for the planet as well. Shareholders are of course vital stakeholders, because as one client told us, "You don't get to have a long term without a short term." But shareholders sit alongside a set of other stakeholders whom generative leaders view as vital to the future. Generative leaders believe that their obligation to society and the planet is at the core of their businesses, not just an afterthought. (For an example, see the sidebar, "Generative Leadership Up Close at Microsoft.")

∗∗∗

Generative Leadership up Close at Microsoft
In 2014, when Satya Nadella became Microsoft's CEO, the company was in solid shape, with healthy revenues and margins and $76 billion in cash and equivalents. Yet its share price had stagnated, and future prospects were unclear. An insular, arrogant, and internally competitive culture and obsession with its Windows operating system cash cow was preventing Microsoft from aggressively entering new markets.

"The company was sick," Nadella wrote in his 2017 book, *Hit Refresh*. "Employees were tired. They were frustrated. They were fed up with losing and falling behind despite their grand plans and great ideas."

Nadella and his leadership team embraced a generative approach to leadership that has led to a remarkable transformation. Guided initially by a new "mobile first, cloud first" vision, Nadella and his team shifted investments away from Windows toward Azure, Microsoft's cloud offering. The company also made bold bets on the future, such as investments in AI. As stated in its 2017 annual report, "Our strategy is to build best-in-class platforms and productivity services for an intelligent cloud and an intelligent edge infused with artificial intelligence."

These big changes in direction and priorities required a more engaged, empowered, and inspired team. Nadella moved to transform Microsoft's adversarial, competitive culture into one focused on a growth mindset, collaboration, an obsession with the customer, and diversity and inclusion – while also making a difference to society. Instead of a company of "know-it-alls," as Nadella put it, Microsoft endeavored to fill itself with "learn-it-alls" – and to transform its leadership team to reflect this learn-it-all culture, as well.

Microsoft became more dynamic and entrepreneurial, breaking down stifling product and leadership silos, modernizing engineering practices, and turbocharging its go-to-market capability. The company abandoned its harsh rivalries with competitors and forged partnerships with Apple, Google, and Salesforce, contributing to a collaborative ecosystem. As Nadella said, "It is incumbent upon us, especially those of us who are platform vendors, to partner broadly to solve real pain points our customers have."

The company's financial results have been extraordinary. Since 2014, Microsoft's market capitalization increased seven-fold, from around $300 billion to more than $2.1 trillion in early March of 2021.

Microsoft generated this wealth for shareholders at the same time that it was pursuing social goals. Its mission "to empower every person and every organization on the planet to achieve more" has encouraged the company to address big problems like climate change. In 2020, Microsoft cut its carbon emissions by 587,000 metric tons, purchased the removal of 1.3 million metric tons of carbon, and committed to match 100% of its electricity consumption with zero-carbon energy purchases by 2030.

Microsoft is also partnering with governments to solve a variety of social challenges by leveraging the company's financial resources, technologies, and AI capabilities. It has undertaken initiatives to make broadband affordable, established a $1 billion Climate Innovation Fund, and developed a Planetary Computer to help manage and protect Earth's natural systems. "The most useful thing I have done is to anchor us on the sense of purpose and mission and identity," Nadella said. "There is a reason we exist."

✳✳✳

Many leaders labor under the false impression that there must be a tradeoff between doing good for society and the planet and delivering returns to shareholders. But studies consistently show a strong positive correlation between companies' commitment to environmental, societal, and governance (ESG) concerns and financial performance. And this outperformance grows over time – by as much as 40%, according to one study. Research also suggests that the best talent, especially among younger workers, increasingly chooses employers with social and environmental policies that match their own personal values.

Take Ikea's leadership team, for example. Ikea has a long history of steady and profitable business, but its leaders have never rested on past successes. In 2011, when they decided to fundamentally change their company's relationship with the environment and society, they took immediate and concrete measures. The company started to carefully measure and report on its carbon emissions and those of its thousands of suppliers, and it rolled out stringent ethical and sustainable sourcing policies. Once Ikea's leaders had a better view of the company's entire supply chain, they set goals to keep improving over time. They linked those goals to their own annual bonuses and made sustainability a critical criterion in every new business case. And, importantly, they made all these changes while continuing to deliver steady returns to their shareholders. (For another example, see the sidebar, "L'Occitane Group's Triple Bottom Line.")

✳✳✳

L'Occitane Group's Triple Bottom Line

L'Occitane Group, a retailer of beauty and home care products, is embedding generative practices throughout the organization. In 2020, the company announced that it was pursuing B Corp certification, a status that reflects strong social and environmental performance. B Corp aligns with the company's pursuit of its "triple bottom line: financial, people, nature," explained Adrien Geiger, L'Occitane's group sustainability officer and global brand director.

"One of our key societal challenges is how to move from consuming to regenerating," Geiger told us. "And the solution lies in nature itself. Nature gives so many examples of how to solve this tension between consuming and regenerating at the same time. The key is to create a sense of purpose for people and at the same time to provide them with the means to be autonomous in action and find solutions on their own. A strong purpose enables projections and dreams. People need to see in it something positive for themselves and for society."

In the last several years, L'Occitane has adopted more environmentally sustainable practices, such as more responsible sourcing and recycling and "eco-refill" programs for its products. "My dream is to throw my shower gel bottle into the sea and make it consumable by fishes," Geiger said. "We're trying to climb Everest in flip-flops. I don't know if we'll make it in my lifetime. But that doesn't mean we should stay and enjoy the weather in Kathmandu."

Geiger said that the focus on GDP has distracted companies from other critical yardsticks. GDP "cannot be the only measure of our reality," he said. There "is a disconnect between the story we tell ourselves and reality."

***

The generative approach comprises three interconnected elements. First, generative leaders look to reimagine and reinvent their businesses. They think expansively about the future they want to create and focus on the right strategic priorities to reach it. Second, generative leaders create an inspiring and enriching human experience for their people – including outside of work. They lead with purpose, and they work to inspire and empower people at all levels of the organization.[32] Third, generative leaders find ways to execute and innovate through supercharged teams that work with agility across boundaries. They align their people effectively around the work to be done.

In other words, generative leaders lead equally with their head, their heart, and their hands.[33] While these are distinct elements of leadership, they come together to

---

32 https://www.bcg.com/capabilities/organization-strategy/overview
33 https://www.bcg.com/publications/2018/head-heart-hands-transformation

Head

Reimagining and reinventing the business to serve all stakeholders

Vision
- Be bold yet sustainable, define and seize opportunities to solve big global problems
- Find partners to help your organization do more
- Make big bets on new technology

Transparency
- Be clear, open, and fact-based all the way to the frontline, listen across the organization

Prioritization
- Streamline and simplify big goals so everyone can easily align behind them

Stakeholder inclusion
- Insist on having and hearing diverse voices and balance impact on all stakeholders

Reflection
- Deliberately pause and intentionally entertain opposing views before acting

Creativity
- Foster and reward imagination

Heart

Inspiring and enriching the human experience

Purpose-driven
- Foster people's sense of belonging to something bigger than themselves

Recognition
- Inspire people to believe they can do the remarkable and that their contribution matters

Care
- Connect deeply, empathize, and give without expectation

Empathetic listening
- Be present and listen without an agenda

People coaching and development
- Coach and provide feedback to help others discover and realize their potential

Celebration
- Celebrate success and progress rather than perfection

Hands

Executing and innovating through supercharged teams

Super-teaming
- Align people across and beyond your organization; use technology to enable them
- Enlist the right technology so that people can focus on doing the things that only humans can do

Resilience
- Adapt as you go; make space for recharge and recovery

People empowerment
- Cede decision-making as much as you can

Courage
- Make and own the tough decisions, sometimes in the absence of consensus

Role modeling
- Help solve problem; be open, curious and humble; seek out and act on feedback

Experimentation
- Cultivate learning from risk-taking and trial and error

Sources: BCG and BVA Group leadership survey, October 2020 and JULY 2021: BCG analysis

Figure 5.3: The Elements of Generative Leadership.

reinforce one another (see Figure 5.3). Our data shows that organizations unlock the greatest value when these three complementary elements are working together in balance. But it's rare to find an organization whose leadership team excels at leading with all of them. It requires self-awareness and humility and a hunger to keep growing and improving. Let's examine what generative leadership looks like in practice.

The Head: Reimagining and Reinventing the Business to Serve All Stakeholders

Generative leaders have bold visions for the future. They seek to reimagine and reinvent their business for the benefit of all stakeholders. For a generative leadership team, ESG is not a token gesture subordinate to the core business. Sustainable practices are essential to how the business makes money.

Generative leaders not only reimagine their own company's products and services. They lead the way across organizations to reinvent their industries. They cultivate and reward creative thinking in their teams. They pursue new technologies and realize ideas that once seemed impossible.

Consider the efforts of Pfizer and other organizations to produce a billion doses of a COVID-19 vaccine in record time. To achieve this breakthrough, Pfizer deployed cutting-edge technology and rigorously prioritized work. Pfizer also engaged in radical transparency, so that all employees understood the vision and what they needed to do to achieve it. In a generative organization, transparency works in both directions, ensuring that the leadership team understands and responds to the perspectives of people on the frontline. The best generative leaders achieve the same transparency, alignment, and feedback with respect to stakeholders outside the organization, too.

Enel, an Italian energy utility, is a powerful example of what can happen when leaders take a generative approach. Francesco Starace became CEO of Enel in 2014. When he and his leadership team decided to move their staid industry into renewable energy, they made some remarkably bold and transformational bets over the course of six years:

– They invested in 1,000 startups after reviewing more than 16,000 ideas and pitches.
– They encouraged team members to spend 20% of their time on innovative projects in order to build a culture of innovation and sustainability.
– They introduced a "my best failure" initiative to promote creativity and encourage team members to take risks.
– They rolled out a crowdsourcing platform that allowed outsiders to propose solutions to different innovation challenges; the platform now includes 500,000 participants from more than 100 countries.

To implement these initiatives, Enel reinvented its approach to leadership. It advocates and celebrates *team* leadership, not heroic individual leaders. In 2021, Guido Stratta, Enel's head of people and organization, published an essay on "soft leadership," writing, "We will move from 'me' to 'we.'" This leadership model, he continued, "is attentive to relationships, trust, and respect for each person's talents, while continuing to focus on achieving objectives."

Six years after it began this program of reinvention, Enel became the world's largest supplier of renewable energy. Its bold and creative vision paid off handsomely for shareholders: in those six years, Enel increased its market value by 2.6 times.

The Heart: Inspiring and Enriching the Human Experience

Generative leaders seek to inspire and enrich the human experience by building great cultures and workplaces where people can do their best work.[34] Employees value recognition and a sense of belonging and a clear purpose that is bigger than themselves. In fact, in our survey, the top four qualities that employees said they seek in their leaders relate to the heart (see Figure 5.4).

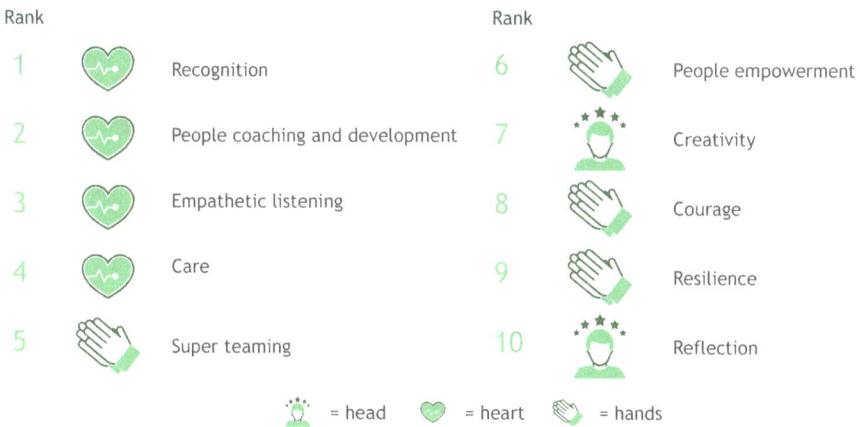

Rank			Rank		
1	♡	Recognition	6	✋	People empowerment
2	♡	People coaching and development	7	☺	Creativity
3	♡	Empathetic listening	8	✋	Courage
4	♡	Care	9	✋	Resilience
5	✋	Super teaming	10	☺	Reflection

☺ = head   ♡ = heart   ✋ = hands

Sources: BCG and BVA Group leadership survey, October 2020 and JULY 2021; BCG analysis

Figure 5.4: The Leadership Qualities That Employees Value Most Relate to the Heart.

Generative leaders achieve these goals by investing in relationships with people. They're empathetic and give of themselves without any expectations, especially

---

34 https://www.bcg.com/capabilities/organization-strategy/organizational-culture

during difficult times. Rather than standing apart, they engage with their teams. They prioritize coaching and development in order to help people realize their full potential. And they push upskilling and reskilling so people can meet the demands of always-on transformation. They also insist on celebrating success, learning, and progress – progress, not just perfection.

Above all, generative leaders genuinely care about people – and that extends beyond the workplace. As Francine Katsoudas, Cisco's executive vice president and chief people, policy, and purpose officer, told us, "We care about our people even on the weekends." Consistent with this 24/7 caring philosophy, she alerted her leadership team to managers' need for more support early in the pandemic, leading Cisco to significantly expand access to mental health resources.

Cisco cares about its people because it's the right thing to do, Katsoudas told us. And what's right also happens to be good for business. Cisco was named the best company to work for by *Fortune* in 2021.

Best Buy has likewise done an exceptionally good job on the heart dimension of leadership. Under former CEO Hubert Joly, the company undertook a successful turnaround that emphasized the employee experience, while its stock generated annual returns of around 20%. "Everybody was saying, 'You better cut, cut, cut, close stores, fire a lot of people,'" Joly told *Harvard Business Review* in 2021. "The usual recipe of turnarounds. No, it started with listening to the frontliners. They had all of the answers. And I spent my first week in a store in St. Cloud [Minnesota] with my blue shirt and my khaki pants, the badge called 'CEO in Training,' to just listen to the frontliners."

"Headcount reduction is the last resort," Joly said. Rather than increasing value by extracting personnel costs, Joly and his leadership team pushed to find generative solutions. "Everybody wants to do something good to other people, and see how it connects to their work. Create an environment that's very human. Where there's genuine human connection. Where you can focus on creating the environment where they can become the best, biggest, most beautiful version of themselves."

However, improving the human experience is where leaders are most likely to fall short. Our work with clients undergoing major transformations suggests that leaders devote the least amount of time and energy to those qualities (see Figure 5.5).

Interestingly, our survey also suggests that employees in advanced economies value the heart dimension more than those in other parts of the world (see Figure 5.6).

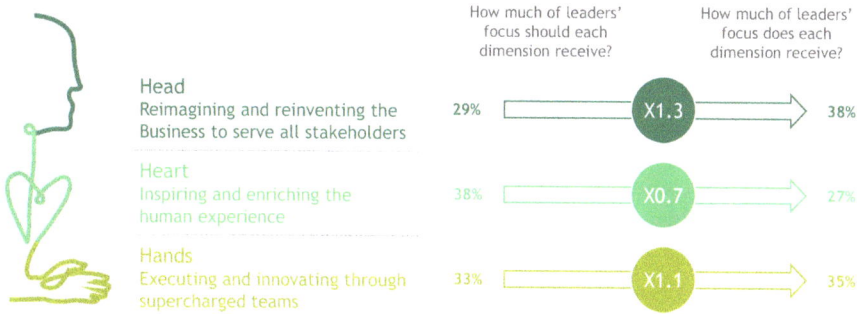

	How much of leaders' focus should each dimension receive?		How much of leaders' focus does each dimension receive?
Head Reimagining and reinventing the Business to serve all stakeholders	29%	X1.3	38%
Heart Inspiring and enriching the human experience	38%	X0.7	27%
Hands Executing and innovating through supercharged teams	33%	X1.1	35%

Sources: BCG and BVA Group leadership survey, October 2020 and JULY 2021: BCG analysis

Figure 5.5: Leaders Fall Short on the Heart Dimension of Leadership.

The Hands: Executing and Innovating through Supercharged Teams

Generative leaders reimagine leadership as a team sport. It's no longer possible, if it ever was, for the hero CEO to grapple alone with the complexity of our constantly and exponentially changing world. Instead, generative leadership calls on leaders to form teams of people with different perspectives within and across organizations, making sure that they don't neglect a key voice or stakeholder. They create high-functioning, empowered, cross-functional "supercharged" teams that execute and innovate with agility. These teams can move quickly and in unison, anticipating where the ball will land rather than focusing on where it is today. They adapt to changing conditions. Their members' primary allegiance is to the team, not to whatever part of their organization they come from. Generative leaders build resilience in their teams by ensuring a balance between sprints and recovery.

Generative leaders build these teams and organizations in several ways. First, they engage directly with team members, showing up at team events and on video calls and other occasions. They even work on the frontline, as Joly did, to see things from the bottom up.

Second, generative leaders ensure that teams work together in the service of the overall purpose and strategy, so that the organization functions as a single entity. They see their role as removing roadblocks. They are willing to dirty their hands to help solve problems.

Third, they cede decision making to their teams without passing the buck. They have the courage to make and own tough decisions, sometimes in the ab-

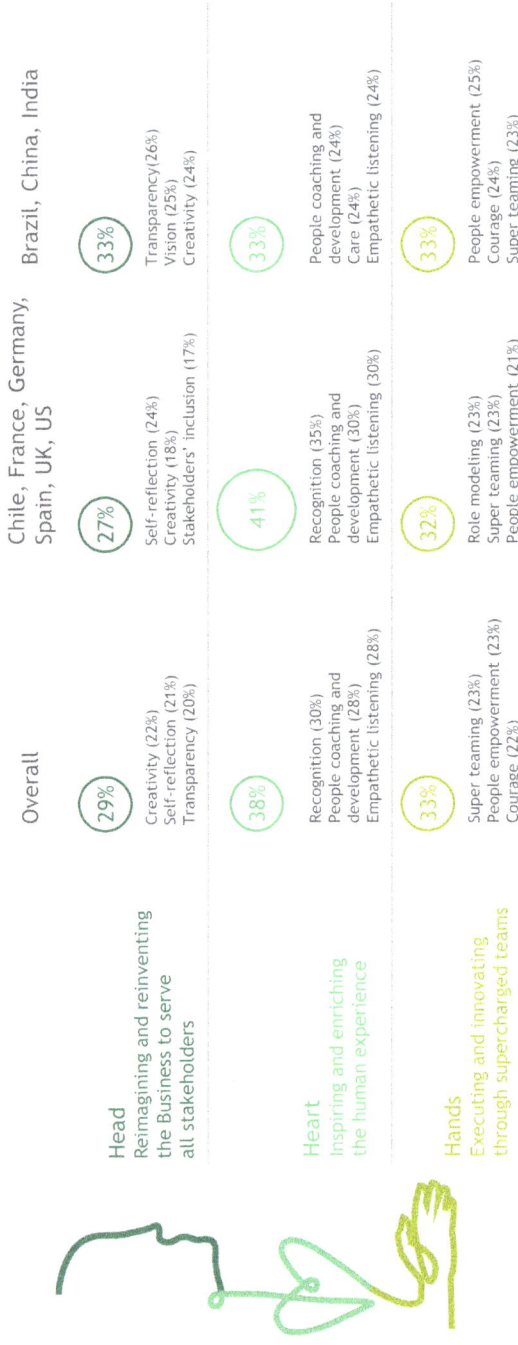

	Overall	Chile, France, Germany, Spain, UK, US	Brazil, China, India
Head Reimagining and reinventing the Business to serve all stakeholders	29% Creativity (22%) Self-reflection (21%) Transparency (20%)	27% Self-reflection (24%) Creativity (18%) Stakeholders' inclusion (17%)	33% Transparency (26%) Vision (25%) Creativity (24%)
Heart Inspiring and enriching the human experience	38% Recognition (30%) People coaching and development (28%) Empathetic listening (28%)	41% Recognition (35%) People coaching and development (30%) Empathetic listening (30%)	33% People coaching and development (24%) Care (24%) Empathetic listening (24%)
Hands Executing and innovating through supercharged teams	33% Super teaming (23%) People empowerment (23%) Courage (22%)	32% Role modeling (23%) Super teaming (23%) People empowerment (21%)	33% People empowerment (25%) Courage (24%) Super teaming (23%)

Sources: BCG and BVA Group leadership survey, October 2020 and July 2021: BCG analysis

Figure 5.6: Employees in More Advanced Economies Place Special Value on the Heart Element of Leadership.

sence of consensus. They incorporate AI[35] and other new technologies into core workflows to speed up processes and free up people to do the things that machines can't do.

Generative leaders also seek to be role models: they are open, curious, vulnerable, and humble, and they seek out and act on feedback. They encourage learning through experimentation, and they reward risk taking and continuous improvement.

Finally, generative leaders embrace ecosystems of partners, especially those that augment AI and other digital capabilities.[36] These ecosystems require leaders to exert influence over people outside of their direct control. For many leaders, this may mean developing a new muscle.

More broadly, generative leaders are engaged with the outside world. They demonstrate connection and influence with outside stakeholders. They are proficient in the world of social-media.

Pfizer is a powerful example of executing and innovating at lightning speed as a united team. Early in 2020, Pfizer began a company-wide push to produce a vaccine against COVID-19. Critically, it formed a supercharged team with Germany's BioNTech, a specialist in the development of mRNA vaccines, and a network of academic experts. Michael Dolsten, Pfizer's chief scientific officer and president of its worldwide research, development, and medical organization, told us that employees were galvanized to solve this pressing global problem. "Everyone felt that an individual person could make a big contribution to the team effort," he said. Dolsten credits CEO Albert Bourla with rallying the entire team to do what had never been done before. The sense of shared purpose broke down silos. Pfizer became "an unstoppable team," he said. "We needed R&D, manufacturing,[37] everybody to perform at the highest possible level."

To reach this goal, Pfizer created multidisciplinary teams among R&D, manufacturing, and other parts of the business. It also inverted the traditional project timeline, imposing a deadline of eight months instead of determining the timeline by working backward from each step in the process. Each step was allocated a time slot within those eight months. Serial processes became parallel whenever possible. These measures allowed Pfizer to have its vaccine available by winter in the northern hemisphere. It's hard to overstate how ambitious the eight-month deadline was. Dolsten estimated that such a develop-

---

35 https://www.bcg.com/capabilities/artificial-intelligence
36 https://www.bcg.com/capabilities/digital-technology-data/build-operate-transfer
37 https://www.bcg.com/capabilities/manufacturing/overview

ment process would normally take seven or eight years. But Pfizer's teams "didn't want to let other teams down."

As we now know, these multidisciplinary teams succeeded in partnership with their collaborators. By the end of 2021, Pfizer had delivered more than a billion vaccine doses globally.

Putting Generative Leadership into Practice

Of course, leadership teams can't wait for a pressing global pandemic to help them break down silos and form teams of champions. What are leaders to do? Are they all in a position to reinvent their businesses, enrich the human experience of their employees, and execute and innovate through supercharged teams? If they're not close today, how do they get closer?

As we've said before, generative leadership is a team sport. It can't be pursued in isolation. The shift from a "me" sport to a "we" sport requires trust and team behavior across the organization, as well as continual feedback, reflection, and coaching. The path will be different for different leadership teams, because no two teams will have identical starting points or needs.

Becoming more generative is a long-term pursuit. Like healthy living or athletic conditioning, it requires fundamental and permanent lifestyle change rather than episodic training or dieting.

Whether you are already on the journey or just getting started, the following practices can help leaders and leadership teams become more generative. They will help clarify the mission of a leader and a team by focusing them on the head, the heart, and the hands of leadership.

Head. To help further develop these capabilities:
- Ask yourself and the members of your team what your organization would need to do to reduce its carbon footprint by half. How would the overall business operate? How long would it take? Could you do it in half the time?
- Set up a monthly sounding-board session with select customers, suppliers, employees, and societal stakeholders to solicit suggestions on how to further improve your organization's environmental and social impact. How could you achieve that impact while increasing profitability? Which disruptive technologies, such as AI and deep tech, could you leverage? With whom would you need to partner?

Heart. To help further develop this muscle:
- Reserve a few minutes at the end of team meetings to reflect on the purpose of your organization:
  - Recognize the achievements of your teams and how they contribute to your purpose.
  - Solicit feedback on how helpful the meeting you just had was – and how to improve it next time.
  - Try to make a habit of this. Do it weekly or monthly.
- Spend at least a few days each quarter with frontline employees in order to understand their daily work and listen to their concerns. It's not enough to shake hands or appear on occasional video calls with the team. "Being present" means more than meeting and greeting team members. It means spending enough time with them to understand their ideas about how things might be improved and where they need your help.
- Create a plan to make your benefits and support for team members and their families best in class. Start by finding out what your team members truly need and value. Understand how those needs vary across different groups of employees. Then identify a set of actions you can take to improve support immediately.
- Block out an hour a week to check in one-on-one with team members – junior people, peers, or partners – about how they and their families are doing and how they feel about their work. Throw away the agenda and listen; these conversations build heart.

Hands. To help further develop supercharged teams and other capabilities:
- Ask yourself which of your priorities could be better achieved by increasing cross-functional teaming both inside and outside of your organization. Where do you need more people working across current team boundaries? How can you help them to do so?
- Invite a different set of team members monthly to provide feedback on how they can better leverage technology to supercharge their work. Do your team members have the right set and amount of data to make informed decisions? Are their tech tools helping or hindering their ability to create supercharged teams?
- Upskill yourself in one or two areas, such as AI, big data, or virtual collaboration tools. Then talk about what you are learning whenever you can.

Throughout the world, we are starting to see generative leadership teams emerge. These teams are pursuing a better vision for the workplace, for society, and for the planet. Their view of the future is bright and optimistic, and they are committing their companies to renewing the earth's depleted resources. In this moment of tremendous and accelerating change, the world is calling for leaders who can stand up and make a lasting difference. Generative leaders are answering the call.

✶✶✶✶✶✶✶✶✶✶✶✶✶✶✶✶✶✶✶✶✶✶✶✶✶✶✶✶

Beyond "Agree to Disagree": Why Leaders Need to Foster a Culture of Productive Disagreement and Debate

Julia Dhar, Sana Rafiq, and Kateryna Gudziak

"You don't bring bad news" explained a former WeWork employee. [1] As outsiders shared skepticism about WeWork's business model and a series of red flags sprang up in the months prior to the organization's implosion in 2019, disbelieving senior employees remained silent. They did not want to be the bearers of bad news to their CEO at the time. Although the organization has since moved on under new leadership, the WeWork story is emblematic of a broader trend: In this era of polarization and rancorous discourse in all realms of society, it is increasingly difficult to have open and productive disagreements at work.

A survey of 6,000 tech employees[38] found that 17.5% of them do not speak up at all to their managers. Situations like this are particularly unfortunate because team and corporate performance are contingent upon a culture in which employees feel free to communicate their ideas and opinions as they work together and solve problems. While many organizations may not view their culture as one that actively suppresses disagreement, few foster a culture in which open and productive debate is a cornerstone. As a result, it becomes ever harder for senior leaders to get the full, unvarnished truth from employees, and they can end up making big decisions based on half-truths or incomplete data.

Why Encourage Debate?

Failure avoidance is only one reason why leaders should prioritize open disagreement. Healthy debate also amplifies innovation. In 1921, when William Knudsen, one of Ford Motor's top engineers and a leading expert in flexible mass production, offered Henry Ford his sketches for producing customized Model Ts, the company's autocratic founder simply walked away. Ford paid a costly price for not engaging in a debate with a subordinate; soon after, Knudsen joined General Motors and implemented his ideas as the head of Chevrolet, narrowing the Model T-to-Chevy sales ratio from 13:1 to 2:1 in just five years.[2]

Repressing alternative opinions also hurts employee engagement and retention. Just as Knudsen promptly left Ford, employees who do not feel comfortable speaking up at work are less likely to want to stay with their company. By repel-

---

38 https://sloanreview.mit.edu/article/when-employees-speak-up-companies-win/

ling employees who think differently, organizations can inadvertently create a consensus-driven culture and fall prey to group think.

Organizations that inhibit debate are also vulnerable to "decision spin"[39] – a costly phenomenon wherein decisions bounce around the company, from group to group and up and down the hierarchy, frequently accompanied by requests for more analysis or options. Decision spin reduces productivity and the quality of output. Executives leave meetings in apparent agreement to a proposed plan of action, but nothing is done. Oftentimes it is not unexpected factors that hamper success[40] but known factors that were either not surfaced or not taken seriously.

The business imperative of nurturing a culture of productive disagreement is clear. The good news is that senior leaders can play a highly influential role in this regard. By integrating the concepts of openness and healthy debate into their own and their organization's language they can institutionalize new norms. Their actions can help to further reset the rules of engagement by serving as a model for employees to follow.

We propose a series of tactical strategies and offer a three-part Disagreement Temperature Checklist that senior leaders can employ to encourage employees to speak truth to power and to each other. To help promote a culture based in truth, evaluate the prevalence of debate in your organization's culture and team dynamics. Ask yourself the questions in the following checklists on a weekly or monthly basis to assess whether you and your team embody and actively instill the values of debate in your organization.

Institutionalize: Make Debate a Core Tenet of Your Organization

In 2018, a BCG study[41] of 100,000 corporate filings revealed that companies that described themselves using humanistic language including words that support debate and diverse opinions, such as truth, true, fact, and transparency, enjoyed a 0.7% premium in annual growth and a 0.6% premium in annual shareholder returns over a three-year period, as well as enhanced employee engagement and management diversity. Yet few companies have explicitly stated organizational values around upholding and seeking truth, respecting facts, and encouraging debate.

---

39 https://www.forbes.com/sites/ronashkenas/2015/12/17/to-avoid-decision-spin-managers-need-to-embrace-conflict/?sh=1f818943484b
40 https://www.bcg.com/publications/2021/how-companies-implement-successful-transformation
41 https://www.bcg.com/publications/2018/humanization-corporation

Leaders should incorporate the concept of productive debate into corporate value statements and the way they address colleagues, employees, and shareholders. Michelin, for example, built debate into its value statement. One of its organizational values is "respect for facts," which it describes as follows: "We utilize facts to learn, honestly challenge our beliefs . . . ." Another company that espouses debate as value is Bridgewater. Founder Ray Dalio ingrained principles and subprinciples such as "be radically open-minded" and "appreciate the art of thoughtful disagreement" in the investment management company's culture. The company's website states, "Bridgewater's competitive edge is our pioneering workplace culture that relies on truthful and transparent communication to ensure the best ideas win out."

Leaders should also highlight – and repeat often – values such as "truth seeking" and "debate" as priorities when undertaking major initiatives and as part and parcel of the desired end state in transformation efforts. Before the invasion of Normandy, Dwight D. Eisenhower told his senior commanders, "I consider it the duty of anyone who sees a flaw in this plan not to hesitate to say so. I have no sympathy with anyone, whatever his station, who will not brook criticism. We are here to get the best possible results." [3]

Disagreement Temperature Checklist Part I – Institutionalize

- Do your corporate statements (mission, vision, and values) reflect the importance of debate, diverse opinions, and seeking truth?
- Is a broad set of voices engaged in developing the company's most recent initiatives?
- Have you incorporated the language of productive disagreement into the way you speak about the company's growth strategy, both publicly and internally?
- Is productive disagreement embedded within individual performance reviews? Is it directly and indirectly rewarded?

Characterize: Talk the Talk, Walk the Walk

Value statements won't mean much unless they are reflected in everyday actions. Employees take cues from senior leaders. This starts with leaders exemplifying values in their behavior. Leaders, for example, should openly admit to mistakes and be willing to publicly change their minds when presented with better evidence. Leaders should also seek to create an environment of psychological safety. Acknowledging and recognizing who or what led to their own changes of perspective signals that employees are not only safe to share but also incentivized to share alternative opinions.

Harrah's grew to become the largest casino operator in the world thanks in large part to former CEO Gary Loveman's commitment to evidence-based decision making. Loveman, a PhD in economics, modeled the behavior he sought to promote in his company. He admitted his mistakes openly when presented with facts and analysis and emphasized that his "insights were not privileged over anyone else's [regardless] of title, rank, or anything else." [4]

Disagreement Temperature Checklist Part II – Characterize

– Did you recently ask anyone for an alternative perspective or a reason why your perspective might not be right?
– Did someone disagree with you?
– Did you share a contrarian point of view?
– Did you and your team consider a different conclusion before the end of recent meetings?
– Did you see anyone change their mind?
– Have any strategies been challenged or rethought?

Standardize: Make It the Norm, Not the Exception

Finally, leaders should formally incorporate the values of productive disagreement into the organizational fabric and ways of working. This can be done in a variety of ways, such as establishing debate-friendly rules of engagement for meetings and employing digital tools (for example, Mentimeter, Slido, and Easy-Retro) that provide real-time feedback, help surface silent majorities, stimulate out-of-the-box thinking, and encourage more inclusive conversations and productive disagreements.

Another way to ensure that dissenting opinions are heard is to build them into the organizational structure.[42] In the early 1500s, Pope Leo X established the office of promotor fidei (promoter of the faith) headed by advocatus diaboli (the devil's advocate) to provide arguments against granting nominees sainthood. The US Army uses "red teams" that are specifically tasked with challenging high-stakes decisions and plans, such as the plan to capture Saddam Hussein.

The same effect can be achieved by building debate into processes. At Pixar, directors present their projects at specific development points to a formal team

---

42 https://www.bcg.com/capabilities/organization-strategy/organization-design

called "the Braintrust," which is composed of respected peers. Embedded in the team's name is one of the core tenants of its operation: the team and the director trust that their shared mission to improve the film will create a space in which unbridled feedback is openly received. As a counterbalance to blunt critiques, the Braintrust has no formal authority, so the director can receive feedback without being obligated to act on it.

Disagreement Temperature Checklist Part III – Standardize

– Do your teams have formal activities and processes in place to pressure-test current operating hypotheses and regularly solicit contrary opinions?
– Do you get the truth from employees without resorting to anonymous surveys?
– Did everyone share an opinion in recent meetings?
– Did you and your team openly acknowledge any mistakes? If not, did you brainstorm how to avoid this in the future or develop an appropriate mitigation plan?

***

How did your answers to the questions in the three parts of the Disagreement Temperature Checklist add up? If your weekly or monthly review does not consistently result in a string of positive responses, it is likely that your organization's culture is less open to debate and productive dissent than it should be. In that case, consider what caused you to respond "no" to a given question. Evaluate what is required to turn each answer into a "yes." Is it an action you can take alone, or does it require engaging your team? Or do you need to undertake a broader shift within the organization? It isn't always easy to instill a culture of productive disagreement and debate in your organization – you may not always like what you hear, but you're unlikely to regret it.

When Innovation Has No Borders, Culture Is Key

Johann D. Harnoss, Anna Schwarz, François Candelon, Martin Reeves, Ashley Grice, Ryoji Kimura, and Nikolaus Lang

New ideas often come from looking at the familiar with fresh eyes, connecting and combining what's previously been separate. Innovation is thus a product of people crossing boundaries and imagining new possibilities.

The power of such connections – of bringing people from different nations and cultures together and the creative spark it can enable – has been one of the guiding principles of the "Innovation Without Borders" series. In previous articles, we have argued that reducing the obstacles to global migration, and thus building bridges to opportunity for talented people regardless of where they were born or what their circumstances might be, is a moral cause that also has a strong business case. The war in Ukraine, along with ongoing conflicts in Afghanistan, Syria, and elsewhere, reminds us that not all migration is voluntary – which only makes the moral cause that much more urgent.

It is with those principles in mind that we present this third article in our series. Talented, creative people can be found in every part of the world – talent that could enable companies and countries to see things in a new way and ignite the much-needed innovative spark that drives sustainable growth. But whether because of restrictive immigration policies, skill mismatches, or cultural barriers, today only a small fraction of the world's skilled workers choose to live and work outside of their birth countries. Can we afford to keep overlooking this vast but latent creative potential?

We don't think so, and CEOs agree: 95% of senior executives we surveyed for this report say they plan to invest in building more globally diverse teams. Their rationale: closing talent gaps and fueling organic growth. Still, it's one thing to aspire to be a globally diverse company; putting those ideals into practice is another matter.

Our survey is the first of its kind. It explores the potential of globally diverse teams by probing the business strategies of executives in 20 industries and 10 countries, the personal beliefs that guide those executives, and the operational tactics they use. We found that even though executive awareness is high, corporate action is severely lacking. Only 5% of executives told us that their firms have successfully built globally diverse teams and won with them. That's a big disconnect between strategic intent and results. The root cause, according to many of our survey respondents: cultural obstacles.

In the pages ahead, we lay out a pragmatic way forward for business executives who intend to drive creativity and innovation and build a new performance culture through global diversity. We explore executive and societal beliefs about global migration and how executives can help lower the societal barriers that stand in the way of global diversity. And we share the multifaceted perspectives of executives from four continents to highlight the rewards of the journey to global diversity – and the struggles that can occur along the way. Finally, we present a deep dive into our research data to illuminate strategies and operational actions for readers, specific to their own country and industry contexts.

We are convinced that business leaders can create better companies – and societies – by actively embracing globally diverse teams and organizations and ensuring they generate visible benefits for all. The Greek philosopher Archimedes said, "Give me a lever long enough, and I can move the world." Diverse teams composed of local and global talent are such a lever. We believe it's time for business leaders to use it.

How to Create a Globally Diverse Organization (While Managing the Inevitable Culture Shock)

On March 1, 2010, Mickey Mikitani, founder and CEO of Rakuten, the Japan-based e-commerce firm, declared that from that day on, the company's 10,000-plus employees would all be required to use English as their official language. Any employee who didn't become proficient in English within two years would face demotion.

Mikitani said he was convinced that if Rakuten wanted to be a globally relevant innovator, it needed to increase communication and collaboration across the company, which included subsidiaries in Brazil, France, Germany, Indonesia, Taiwan, Thailand, and the US. And to bring together employees from so many different cultures, Rakuten needed a common language.

Companies that see global diversity as part of their DNA are...

2.2x more likely to be a world class innovator

2.5x more likely to be a fast growing company

The mandate applied throughout the organization, down to the menus in the cafeteria at the company's Tokyo headquarters. "Englishnization," as Mikitani called it, confused and irritated employees and executives alike, many of whom spoke little English at the time. Frustration ran deep as Mikitani insisted that board meetings be conducted in English even though they initially took twice as long while executives struggled with an unfamiliar language. Many employees considered leaving – at one point, 36% of Rakuten's engineers said they planned to re-sign before the two-year deadline.

But Mikitani stayed on course. He constantly communicated the importance of a common language in helping Rakuten reach its larger goals of attracting new talent, sparking creativity and innovation, and (ultimately) increasing growth and profitability. Policies were put in place to encourage frequent contacts between the company's far-flung divisions, enabling employees from different parts of the world to share knowledge and discover new ways of solving problems. Over time, the new corporate lingua franca began to break down the boundaries between Rakuten's headquarters and its previously siloed subsidiaries.

Today, Rakuten's staff is more international than ever, with one of the most globally diverse tech teams in Japan. The firm is now active in 30 countries and regions, but it thrives with a global "one team" culture. Rather than imposing a single point of view, Rakuten's common language levels the playing field for employees from different nations and cultures, allowing them to trade ideas, build empathy, and look at problems in a new way.[43] The success of this approach is undeniable: Rakuten's revenues grew from $3.9 billion in 2010 to $15.3 billion in 2021, a 13% annualized rate.

Rakuten's story illustrates the enduring benefits of building a globally diverse organization, one that is not just open to talented people from different nationali-ties but also more creative and innovative as a result. It also shows the struggles of an organization dealing with a disruptive change in culture.

So how can you build a globally diverse organization while avoiding such disruption?

To answer this question, we fielded a quantitative survey of 850 senior lead-ers in HR, R&D, and digital functions, and we interviewed 20 senior executives in startups, venture capital, and the corporate world. (See the sidebar, "About the Survey.")

Our study surfaced three key observations:

- The business case for globally diverse teams is clear: 95% of the survey's re-spondents said they intend to build globally diverse teams in order to address talent shortages, better meet the needs of global consumers, and generate the creative spark that drives innovation.

---

43 Neeley T. *The Language of Global Success: How a Common Tongue Transforms Multinational Organizations.* Princeton University Press, 2017. See also Neeley's "Why Global Success Depends on Separating Language & Culture." TEDxCambridge, October 2017. https://www.ted.com/talks/tse dal_neeley_why_global_success_depends_on_separating_language_culture

- Yet most pursue global diversity in ad hoc, not strategic, manner: nearly 80% of firms pull some of the operational levers in the four strategic plays associated with global diversity, but only 15% do so in in a comprehensive way.
- Finally, only 5% of respondents have fully scaled globally diverse teams throughout their organization, embedded the principles and values of global diversity in their corporate DNA, and captured convincing growth and innovation benefits from it.

That's a big gap between ambition and real-world results.

This gap is largely explained by one thing: culture. In times of talent scarcity, it isn't hard to make a convincing business case for global diversity – even putting aside the strong moral case for it. But senior executives, especially in large, established firms, worry about the soft side – namely the significant cultural change a globally diverse workforce brings with it. Leaders of large companies who express a strong intent to pursue global diversity (and many who already are) also voice a healthy skepticism that they can get thousands of employees to follow them without ruffling some feathers. As Sebastian Klauke, a member of Otto Group's executive board, told us, "I know lots of firms that are still hesitant to make that switch, partly motivated by an authentic worry that they'll leave lots of folks in teams and middle management behind." Our survey bears this out: While only 20% of respondents claim that "we don't know where to start" with global diversity, 38% cite "big language and cultural barriers" to it.

∗∗∗

Executive Perspective: Sebastian Klauke

Board Member, Otto Group

"Global talent changes the cultural mix and the performance of your organization."

Sebastian Klauke opened BCG's first Digital Ventures office in Germany and cofounded Autoda. de, the first German e-store for used cars, before joining the Otto Group as chief digital officer in 2017. He is currently a member of the company's executive board and is responsible for its e-commerce, technology, business intelligence, and corporate ventures. The Otto Group is a retail and services company with 50,000 employees, doing business in over 30 countries in Europe, North and South America, and Asia. With online revenues of approximately $11 billion, it is one of the world's largest online retailers.

How has Otto Group Approached Building a Culture of Innovation?

We've initiated a process of culture change, to first heal a few typical dysfunctionalities in large organizations, such as a lack of collaboration across teams and functions, and a tendency to look inward, not outward. We addressed those by introducing new agile ways of working, by reducing unnecessary frictions, and by flattening hierarchies where speed is critical. Now, we're starting to look at international hiring to mix up our teams and generate a new vitality impulse.

What's the State of Global Diversity at Otto Group?

We have very different dynamics in our portfolio. AboutYou, for example, has been very international since day one. To cope with the extremely high growth of the business, we took away all constraints in hiring and focused exclusively on finding the best talent. In our other businesses, digital transformation is on track, and we don't have a severe talent shortage issue. There, I see global diversity mostly as a lever to improve performance through deliberate culture change. It can help us build a culture of playful challenge, of reinvention through new people coming in, and overall, a somewhat more intense, dynamic organization.

How does Global Diversity Improve Performance?

There are two aspects to this. My thesis number one: diversity is a performance driver in teams. Opening up our teams to global talent brings in people with a fresh attitude who are hungry to learn and grow, and who believe they can make a difference. These people bring new perspectives that help us innovate better. Thesis number two: infusing global talent changes the cultural mix of your organization, to the point that it can elevate the performance level of your entire organization.

Why do so Many Firms Struggle to Embrace Global Diversity?

Starting from the top, there's a lot of "change angst" surrounding global diversity. Introducing English as a new means of communication sounds easy, but it is incredibly hard, even for top executives who fear that established teams will not be able to cope with the change. I believe this worry is genuine and well intended, but it also stands in the way of delivering on companies' growth and innovation ambitions.

How do you Overcome this "Angst" Around Global Diversity?

To kick this off, you need a compelling change impulse from the top. It needs to be supported by clear communication that fosters an environment of mutual trust – that is, trust in leadership and also trust that teams will embrace the change.

If you do it right, your organization will not just follow – you will discover that many people will enthusiastically lead the charge. It's really fascinating to see what global diversity does to your home-grown talent. I've often seen people briefly struggle first with the need to communicate in English and not being able to take established views for granted. But when you push through this, you get to this magic moment in which teams operate with a new mental agility that generates more productive frictions but also better outcomes.

How does Global Diversity Connect to Otto Group's Organizational Values?
Diversity is a core value, but we've not yet fully connected it with the moral cause of global equality of opportunity. However, you can already see it shining through. In our external communications, for instance, we celebrate equality of opportunity for people irrespective of background and national origin. Our employees enthusiastically, proudly support this. Me too!

✳✳✳

Is there a way to get to the benefits of global diversity without risking organizational upheaval? We think so. Becoming a globally diverse organization is a multiyear journey, but it can be managed without undue disruption by establishing a clear view of one's current starting position and then following a deliberate series of concrete steps and tactics. Here's how.

Getting to the Starting Line

It's easy to describe the markers of a globally diverse organization – management teams that bring a wealth of perspectives from different origin countries and a workforce that is similarly diverse down to the team level. It's harder to pinpoint the fundamental drivers of such diversity. Our survey results indicate that executive personal beliefs, executive priorities, and strategic objectives are among those drivers. They play an outsized role in explaining why some firms make the leap whereas others don't.

    Core Beliefs. Here's the finding from our research that surprised us most: there's a strong link between executives' personal embrace of global migration on a societal level and their companies' ability to embrace global talent. This suggests that executives' personal beliefs can not only help make their home countries more innovative and competitive (as we discuss later in this report) but also are foundational to organizational progress, perhaps because core beliefs drive executive priorities and strategic objectives. In our interviews we captured a wide range of core beliefs, starting from a healthy questioning of the economic value ("What's the business case here?") to a more instrumental, hard-nosed view ("We're hiring globally already, we have no choice") to a celebratory one ("We love our diversity") to the rare but strong values-based conviction ("We see the value of diversity every day, but we do it because it's right").

Executive Priority. Until a new idea becomes embedded in a company's DNA, it needs senior-level attention to survive – and global diversity is no exception. Asking if global talent and diversity are among the top five executive priorities is a great indicator of its strategic relevance within a company. Our data shows a robust link between the level of executive priority given to global diversity and innovation outcomes.

Strategic Objectives. There are essentially four reasons to embrace global diversity in a business context, translating to four corresponding strategic plays: the talent play, the ecosystem play, the innovation play, and the purpose play. (See the appendix, "Adoption of the Four Strategic Plays by Country and Industry.") Among those, the global talent and innovation plays tend to be the most salient, because they most directly tie to immediate profit-and-loss outcomes. Still, only few companies truly define a global talent strategy, let alone a strategy to systematically use global diversity to drive innovative thinking at scale.

Four Clusters of Maturity

When we analyzed the drivers above, we found that the firms in our survey fell into four distinct levels of global diversity maturity: companies we refer to as "question marks," companies that see global diversity as a tool, those who see diversity as a celebration, and those for whom diversity is a part of their DNA (see Figure 5.7). Half of the firms in our sample can be found in the first cluster, followed by 30% in the second and 15% in the third. Only 5% of our sample falls into the fourth cluster, which includes firms that are truly globally diverse and positioned to reap its highest benefits. Identifying the cluster a company occupies is a prerequisite for ambitious executive teams to drive action.

Question Marks. This was the largest cluster of the survey respondents. Leaders of firms in this cluster may know the theoretical case for global diversity, but they consider it unproven in their business context. (Granted, the business case may not be strong in firms with no talent shortages or limited digital transformation challenges.) As a result, they put little strategic emphasis on global talent diversity.

Firms in this cluster tend to be quite culturally homogenous, strongly reflecting the majority ethnic and racial profile of their home countries. They often deliver operational efficiencies because it can be easier to manage a homogenous workforce than a diverse one. But, as executives at one of the largest life and health insurance companies recently described to us, they also encounter obstacles, such as difficulties in hiring global tech talent and the regulatory demand that they set up national entities, which typically feature highly homogenous local teams. One German executive told us, "We are open to global talent as long as they speak our language quite fluently – not everyone here is comfortable in English, neither in IT nor in other functions that IT is serving." As a result, the company was unable to fill more than 100 jobs in digital and other areas.

While companies in all industries can be found in any of the four diversity clusters, industries with a strong national focus are often found in the question mark cluster. Insurance companies (64% of whom occupy this value cluster) are a good example, especially when regulators require them to operate dedicated entities to serve different national markets. A similarly high percentage of companies in the power and gas (70%) and transportation (67%) industries reside in this cluster.

Diversity as a Tool. This cluster encompasses firms whose leaders see global talent as an effective operational lever to address specific, persistent talent shortages. Firms in this cluster may not elevate global diversity to the overall HR agenda – placing strategic emphasis on it for specific teams, such as digital units or R&D hubs, instead.

We discussed this approach with a large European retailer that is building an omnichannel e-commerce experience powered by a personalized app. While the group language remains French, the firm has switched to English for most of its digital teams. A senior HR executive told us, "At first, we had to adjust to new virtual hiring processes, and introducing onboarding support for internationals was new for us. But our digital journey wouldn't be possible without international teams."

This digital-first dynamic is often at play in firms that are a few years into a digital transformation – and particularly in more global firms. Telecom (35%) and manufacturing (33%) companies are often found in this cluster, as well as companies pursuing initiatives that require skills in high demand.

Diversity as a Celebration. This includes firms that already have globally diverse workforces because they manufacture and source globally, have made recent foreign acquisitions, or sell in a global set of markets. These firms often run mainly on one shared language and have career paths that enable global talent to rise through the ranks to top management. They understand that, in addition to the instrumental value of broad-based talent pools, they need cross-cultural teams to ensure global operations run smoothly.

Global diversity	Question mark	Diversity as a tool	Diversity as a celebration	Diversity as part of DNA
1. Core belief	Unproven value	Instrumental value	Teaming value	Valuable & 'valued'
2. Executive priority	No priority	On Digital agenda	On HR agenda	On CEO agenda
3. Strategic objective	None	Limited	Talent Play	Talent + Innovation Play
% of large firms by cluster[1]	**50%**	**30%**	**15%**	**5%**

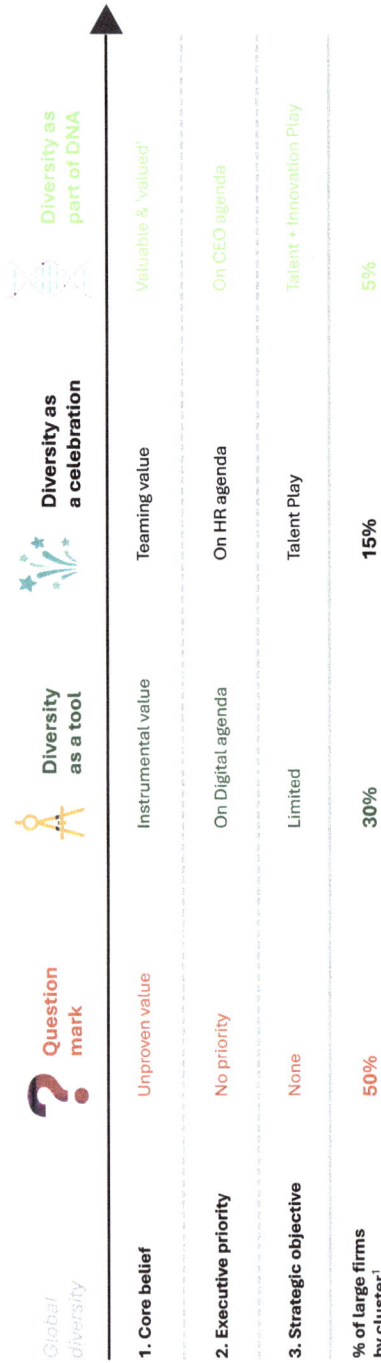

Source: BCG analysis.
[1]Firms with over $1 billion per year in sales.

Figure 5.7: What's Your Starting Point for Global Diversity?

Yet companies in this cluster tend to celebrate diversity more than fully make strategic use of it and reap competitive advantage. Reflecting this approach, the CTO of a global logistics unicorn told us, "Of course we're super diverse, but do we use this as an asset to drive cognitive diversity? We don't. Probably we would be so much better if we did.

Most of the companies in this cluster operate globally in one way or another: they have international business units, a global supply chain, or sell into global markets. This value cluster includes many global automotive (20%) and software and services companies (24%).

Diversity as Part of Your DNA. This last cluster includes the very few survey respondents who have embedded global diversity in their companies' DNA. The senior leaders of these companies strongly believe in and prioritize global diversity and pursue it as a strategic objective and purpose-driven priority. They consider it to be both a source of creative power and a potent force for talent attraction and retention.

The companies in this value cluster are translating global diversity into positive and enduring innovation outcomes: they are two times more likely to be world-class innovators than the rest. Zalando, the European e-commerce fashion platform, is one of these companies. Zalando was born global, but it also works hard to be "inclusive by design."[44] This effort starts at the top, where senior leaders pursue diversity in all its dimensions as a top priority and engage actively and transparently in advancing it. It cascades down through the workforce, which includes people from over 140 different countries and features various employee resource groups, which represent interest and origin communities. And it leverages their creative potential to develop or test ideas – such as in the development of its "Here to Stay" marketing campaign, which married Zalando fashion with the aesthetics and storytelling of global social justice activists.

Like Zalando, companies in this high-value cluster are often born global. Many are in the media and entertainment (13%) and high-tech industries (5%) but they also include some global players in manufacturing (8%) and consumer goods (6%).

---

44 "do.Better: Inclusive by Design." Zalando. 2022. https://corporate.zalando.com/sites/default/ files/media-download/Zalando-SE_D%26I%20Report%202022_Memo_English.pdf

Managing Three Moments of Culture Shock

The four clusters above serve as beacons in the journey to global diversity, with higher creativity, growth, and innovation output being the ultimate rewards. Each step on this journey offers benefits from a value creation perspective: firms that start as question marks can significantly increase their chances of becoming world class innovators by taking one or two steps in the journey to global diversity[45] (see Figure 5.8).

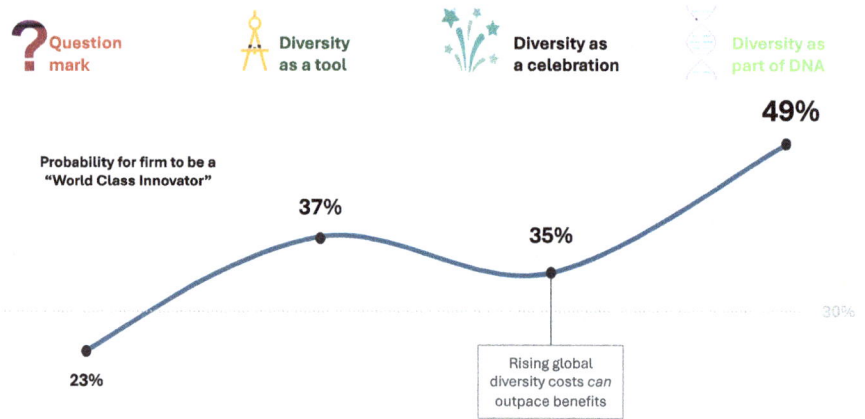

Source: BCG Analysis

Figure 5.8: Globally Diverse Teams Are More Innovative.

Our data confirms the well-known fact that global diversity and innovation are positively related, but it also shows that the path is not necessarily smooth. Clearly, there are quick wins associated with getting started on the journey, but there are also very real risks of getting stuck along the way. Firms in the middle of the journey face the biggest challenge: taking globally diverse teams out of the confines of digital units and driving toward a one-team agenda across the company, often introducing a common language to level the playing field. This produces friction before it shows results.

---

45 The relationship between global diversity and innovation is self-reported and correlational, and other factors may be in play. Firms that embrace global diversity today are likely to be different than firms that don't on many dimensions.

The core idea is that the journey does not require a large upfront commitment, but can be taken step by step (see Figure 5.9). While the journey is a team effort, each step has one clear owner within the senior leadership team.

First Step: Diverge

The goal in this step is to open up and bring global talent into your digital teams as a quick proof of the value of global diversity. The risk to manage is that some managers and teams are likely to oppose the prospect of integrating newcomers out of fear that they will upset established processes.

To avoid a broad-based culture shock, firms typically start small, with hard-to-fill roles in teams organizationally separate from the operational core. Once the value of such teams has been established, companies can start to showcase and broaden their efforts.

For any company hiring globally to drive digital transformations and products, chief digital officers or executives in charge of digital units are ideally suited to lead this first step, in partnership with HR. Here are some tactics that we have seen work well.

Make a strong case. Target hard-to-fill roles in your digital and/or product teams for a first foray into global diversity. Relieving severe talent constraints, especially in engineering, data science, and product management roles, helps sidestep resistance from team leaders and members (who are likely to welcome any help they can get) and deliver quick proof of the value of global talent. Because these teams tend to operate separately from the core business, there also is little chance of disrupting the workforce at large; in addition, such teams often are subject to fewer HR constraints, which can make hiring global talent easier. Once a likely team is identified, quickly compare the team's makeup and results to relevant peers (using sources such as LinkedIn analytics). The degree of diversity and results among peers can help bolster the case for change.

Keep the ambition front and center in daily operations. Simple heuristics, like "our digital teams should be as diverse as our customer base," can guide team leaders and HR scouts as they consider team composition and proceed through the hiring process.

Activate language bridges. It's paramount to identify one or two teams that are willing to switch to a common language in their work. If no team is willing, consider hiring from outside or "acqui-hiring" a small team that can form a nucleus to attract next hires. A leading European retail bank did this after finding it too difficult to repurpose an existing team to compete in fintech. "It was hard to develop the right culture from within," the company's chief financial officer told

Diverge
Open up (in digital)

Converge
Team better

Surge
See the outcomes

Tactics

Diverge
- **Make a strong case** in helping fill in-demand roles, i.e. for digital/ engineering talent
- **Set a first ambition**, e.g. "In Product, we must reflect our customer base"
- **Activate language bridges**, in selected teams to shape culture of openness

Converge
- **Switch to common language** in core functions, at least on HQ/Group level, give clear transition timeline
- **Fortune favors the cross-cultural,** avoid [nation]-only teams, ensure key teams are min-diverse
- **One team:** Create a culture that values differences & equality of opportunity

Surge
- **Publicly commit:** Set an unwavering innovation target - position global diversity as enabler
- **Foster culture** of cognitive diversity – create space for 'strong opinions weakly held'
- **Empower change makers** for globally diverse innovation teams & roadmap

Led by

Diverge: CDO/CTO or CHRO

Converge: CHRO

Surge: CEO

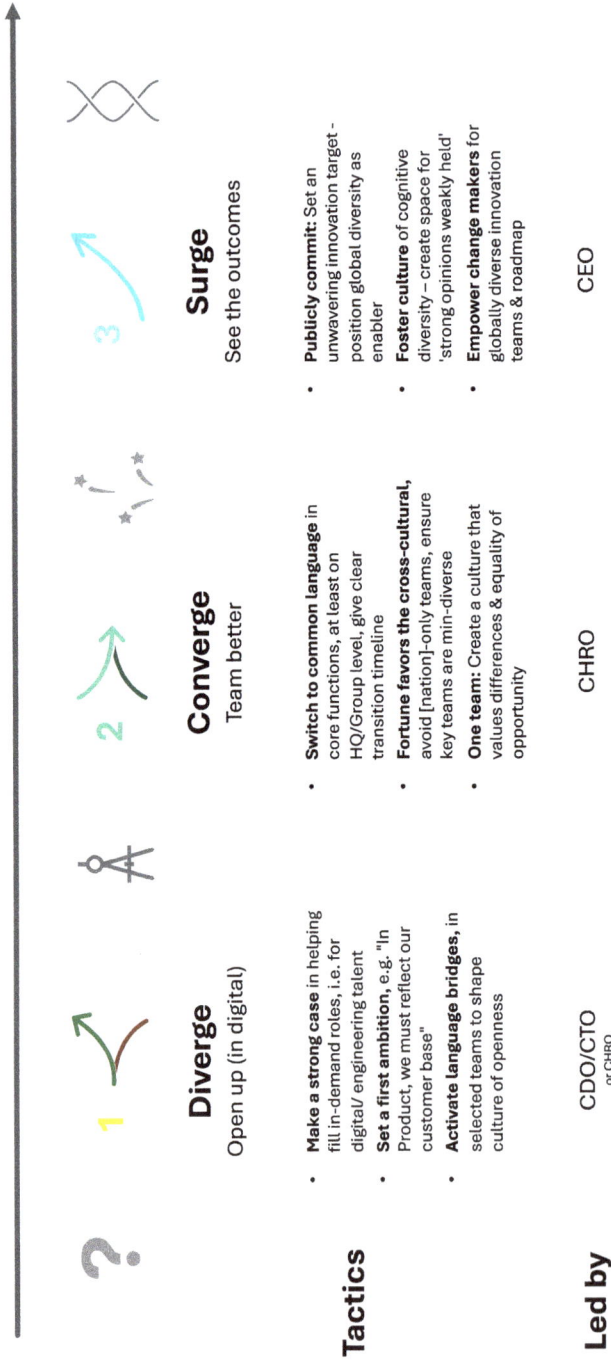

Source: BCG analysis

Figure 5.9: Leading Through Three Moments of Culture Shock.

us. "Ultimately we acqui-hired a small fintech team and built the entire unit around them." Today, the 100-plus employees in the unit represent more than 20 nationalities, communicate entirely in English, and serve more than 4 million customers.

Second Step: Converge

The goal of the second step in the journey is to scale global talent throughout the organization and establish the foundations for it to stick. The main risk in this step is the broader disorientation of employees and executives, especially when scaling requires new language requirements for thousands of employees. One way to manage this risk is to showcase the stories of teams that have already become globally diverse and use their experiences in overcoming disorientation to pave the way for this broader effort.

Chief people officers or HR officers are ideally suited to own this second step of the journey, teaming with a chief digital officer as needed. Siemens Healthineers provides a case in point. After the company acquired Varian, it hired a new CHRO, Darleen Caron. With 30 years of experience on both sides of the Atlantic, she brought the right background to the challenge Germany-based Siemens and US-based Varian faced in integrating diverse nationalities and mindsets. From the start, Caron made cultural transformation her top agenda item, both in its own right and also to drive multinational teams to achieve innovation excellence.[46] In acknowledging that this activity cannot simply be checked off a list within a post-merger integration, Siemens Healthineers prepared the ground for its teams to grow together in global diversity and drive toward its long-term innovation challenge: to eradicate cancer.

We've seen the following tactics work in this step.

Find a common language. To realize the full potential of global diversity, a company needs to be able to communicate effectively across borders – and that means establishing a common language. Many companies choose to adopt English; still, leaders must take steps to ensure that an English-first policy does not have the effect of enforcing Eurocentric cultural standards or create pressure on non-English speakers to conform to such standards.[47] English – or any common

---

[46] "Darleen Caron Appointed to Managing Board (CHRO) of Siemens Healthineers AG and Labor Director at Siemens Healthcare GmbH." Siemens Healthineers, February 21, 2021.

[47] The Rakuten example is instructive on this point; as Tsedal Neeley's research shows, rather than diluting the company's traditional Japanese culture, the English-only mandate helped spread that culture to its subsidiaries in other countries.

language – should merely be a conduit for helping organizations and individuals meet the challenge of maintaining effective communication channels.

And as the Rakuten example shows, leaders also should not underestimate the difficulties of learning a new language and the disruptions it can cause. With that in mind, Mickey Mikitani's drastic English-only mandate might not be the right path for some businesses. E.ON, the European electric utility provider, took a more moderate approach when it introduced English as the corporate lingua franca a decade ago, restricting the mandate to the employees in corporate head-quarters and directly associated units while giving its operating units the freedom to choose their preferred language.

Fortune favors the cross cultural. To avoid nationality siloes, start deliberately mixing the national composition of your teams. People of the same nationality tend to flock together quickly; it's easy to lose the benefits of diversity when you have a "Dutch" coding team or a "Brazilian" design" team, for instance. Specify minimum diversity levels and mandate regular staff rotations as a preventive measure. In the words of a serial entrepreneur we interviewed: "Avoid [nation]-only teams at all cost."

Promote a one-team culture. Subtle organizational norms can create obstacles to global diversity and negatively influence team performance. Sometimes these norms arise from cultural differences between individuals that are reinforced by language and communication differences. Indicating an acute awareness of the cultural bias at Rakuten, Mikitani felt obligated to say, "No Japanese [employee] is better than any other employee." And sometimes these differences arise from location – for instance, people who are located at or near centers of power in an organization can be perceived as more important than those working farther afield or remotely.

Companies can counter these issues by being extremely intentional in their internal communication. Levels, a fast-growing, remote-first health tech company, does this by providing online access to employees to all its communications, from core strategy documents to its video-based onboarding processes. The company has an extreme aversion to synchronous formats, like virtual meetings, and instead urges all team members to communicate asynchronously, rigorously documenting everything. Providing equal access to information helps the company reduce non-merit-based distinctions that stem from power, nationality, language, and other differences among its people. As a result, the company creates a more level playing field while upholding extremely high-performance standards.

Third Step: Surge

The last step is arguably the hardest. Its objective is to leverage global diversity and the cognitive diversity that comes with it to generate superior innovation outcomes. The inherent difficulty is that success is dependent on the creation and maintenance of a conducive work environment for global diversity. This takes a long time to cultivate and strong, consistent top-level support to maintain. In the words of Patrick Collison, cofounder and CEO of payment service provider Stripe: "If we can't build a culture in which people of any background can really thrive, I think we just have not achieved anything of value."[48]

The biggest risk at this step is, frankly, cynicism. If a company makes the sizeable effort involved in becoming globally diverse at the highest level but is not yet able to demonstrate significantly enhanced innovation outcomes, voices of doubt are sure to emerge. These can often be a source of new insights, but also risk stopping the journey just short of the finish line. To maintain a clear and unwavering commitment to global diversity, this step requires the direct involvement and leadership of the chief executive officer.

Here are the tactics that can help companies complete this final step:

Set an unwavering corporate purpose and innovation vision. Revisit the firm's ethos in light of its innovation ambitions – and explicitly embed the idea that innovation outcomes and products can only be realized if teams understand the company's role in the world and can muster the creativity that comes from global diversity.

Harness global diversity to foster divergent thinking. New and valuable insights are rarely the result of a singular individual's heroic insight, but often the result of intense, deliberate discussions within cognitively diverse teams. Especially in digital, product, market, and growth teams, aim to extract diverse perspectives to yield new valuable insights. As Mubarik Imam, former director of GAPS (growth, analytics, product, and strategy) and integrity at WhatsApp, told us, "If you are designing for two billion people, you want the most diversity you can have on your teams. When many voices and cultures are represented, you design better products."

Firms need to establish a culture with genuinely cognitively diverse teams. We've seen this in action at a renewable energy firm which aimed to reignite its teams' capacity for imagination. The firm runs ideation sessions open to any team member, with globally diverse idea teams forming on an ad hoc basis for

---

48 "Stripe Co-Founders John & Patrick Collison on Diversity in Tech." Bloomberg Markets and Finance/YouTube, May 30, 2018. https://www.youtube.com/watch?v=nsrYs-fyMuc

less than four weeks to develop projects that can compete for seed funding. This process has already surfaced ideas that could change the future trajectory of the company.

Firms need to establish a culture with genuinely cognitively diverse teams. We've seen this in action at a renewable energy firm which aimed to reignite its teams' capacity for imagination. The firm runs ideation sessions open to any team member, with globally diverse idea teams forming on an ad hoc basis for less than four weeks to develop projects that can compete for seed funding. This process has already surfaced ideas that could change the future trajectory of the company.

✳✳✳

Executive Perspective: Mubarik Imam
Former Director at WhatsApp

"Global diversity helped us have greater empathy for a global audience."

Mubarik Imam was born in the US and raised in Pakistan. She joined WhatsApp, the global messenger service, in 2013; she and her teams helped the company scale from 200 million to 1.9 billion users. Imam was director of GAPS (growth, analytics, product, and strategy) and integrity before leaving the company in 2019.

What Attracted You to WhatsApp?
My husband asked me an important question: "Where would you work, if you had to work for free?" My answer was simple: "WhatsApp."

WhatsApp helps us deepen our relationships with friends and families no matter the distance. It helps us fulfill a basic human need to communicate. Calling my future husband in Pakistan used to be my second highest expense after I moved to the Bay Area. WhatsApp is still how I connect with my family across six different countries.

I was drawn to [the company's] culture. It had mature founders who wanted to build a product for the world and an international team. I was actively looking for a team whose values aligned with mine and a place where I could be my full self.

How did Global Diversity Enable Product Innovation at WhatsApp?
Global diversity helped us have greater empathy and design our products for people with very diverse backgrounds. When building a product for very diverse people who will use it in very different ways, it is essential to have a microcosm of people from around the world who represent that diversity. I'll never forget the first time I walked into WhatsApp's office (when the entire company fit into a single room). It felt like a mini-United Nations.

Global diversity helped us have greater empathy and design our products for people with very diverse backgrounds. When building a product for very diverse people who will use it in very different ways, it is essential to have a microcosm of people from around the world who represent that diversity. I'll never forget the first time I walked into WhatsApp's office (when the entire company fit into a single room). It felt like a mini-United Nations.

Simplicity enabled us to make sure that people feel like our product was designed with an understanding of their context and culture. We always wanted to make sure the product was accessible to everyone, whether that person was a grandmother in Brazil or a first-time smartphone user in Pakistan.

We had firsthand experience with the challenges of weak network connectivity in different parts of the world, so we held ourselves to 99.9999% of deliverability (one message dropped in one million sent). Why is that important? Imagine how often displaced persons might find themselves without access to electricity – and then imagine someone needing to send one last message before their phone loses power. We really wanted to make sure that message got delivered. So, to us, reliability was not a vanity metric. It was a lifeline.

Privacy and security were a big part of our DNA. Protecting people's private communication was very personal for many of us who grew up in places where people couldn't speak freely. We built end-to-end encryption by default, because nobody (not even WhatsApp) should be in the middle of those messages.

How do you Reconcile the Different Views Produced in Globally Diverse Teams?
More perspectives will help you look at the world with slightly different nuances. But rather than trying to normalize these perspectives to a lowest common denominator, you should build on the nuances and see how they might create value.

In a world that is so centered around data and metrics, diverse perspectives also provide deep context to numbers. This context is often key to making informed decisions. When we were beta testing voice calling at WhatsApp, the metrics told us very little about the very real frustrations people had with calls dropping in low bandwidth settings. My personal experiences calling Pakistan, and then seeing my Turkish colleagues struggling with similar issues, really added flavor to the data and created an urgency that helped us address those frustrations head on.

How did WhatsApp Create a Culture that Supports Global Diversity?
I believe that culture is a reflection of the founders, particularly in early-stage startups. Jan Koum was from Ukraine. Together with Brian Acton, he not only actively sought to build global teams but also made sure that the teams' perspectives were heard and valued.

Now, the difference in a large company is that the distance between the people who understand the use cases and those who make the decisions sometimes becomes wider. So, the more diversity you have at the highest leadership levels of an organization, the more empathy those leaders are likely to have for the contexts relevant to core product decisions.

***

Empower the leaders of globally diverse innovation teams. Often, these people are rising figures in key technology, product, or market-facing functions who can orchestrate cross-functional, global teams and deliver meaningful new products or services. Such people are very hard to find, and they will move on unless they are truly empowered to make far reaching autonomous decisions on their projects. A clearly defined purpose – which underscores why their work matters to the whole of the organization – and a lean steering structure, which grants autonomy and offers a level of guidance that is based more on trust than control, is necessary for this to succeed. We have coined the term "imaginative listening" to describe this capacity of senior leaders to listen emphatically and jointly build upon ideas developed by these key team leaders.[49] If globally diverse teams are to muster the courage to voice ideas (and when necessary, dissent) and develop the resilience to see these ideas through the scaling phase – and ultimately to deliver innovation outcomes beyond expectations – an empowering environment is a must.

Innovation is about imagining new possibilities. In a time when much-needed sparks for innovation are scarce, the prospect of becoming two times more likely to be a world class innovator is by itself a compelling motivation for embarking on the journey to global diversity. And when you add in the human component – the chance to create opportunities for talented people from all over the world – the case for making that journey becomes too compelling to ignore.

Each step in this journey is likely to induce some temporary discomfort and disorientation in companies that already run under significant performance pressure. But strong, committed leadership can manage this challenge and successfully steer firms through it. Such leadership is a team effort that starts with the chief digital officer, needs the chief HR officer, and cannot succeed without masterful orchestration of the CEO.

Leaders who want to retain and bolster their companies' edge and creativity in the future should set off on the journey now. Their efforts at building globally diverse teams and organizations will deliver both corporate and social benefits for years to come.

$$***$$

About the Survey

Our survey provides a snapshot of the state of corporate global diversity across a variety of industries and geographies. It captures executives' personal beliefs, corporate strategies, and outcomes. It covers firms in more than 20 industries, ranging from asset-heavy cement production to knowledge-intensive software-as-a-service companies. It reveals that:

– Global diversity and workforce size are unrelated. Among companies with more than 10,000 employees, 34% have a highly homogenous workforce, with fewer than 10 nationalities represented. And only 7% have a highly globally diverse workforce, with more than 100 nationalities represented. Meanwhile, 10% of smaller firms report having a highly globally diverse workforce.

49 Reeves M, Fuller J. *The Imagination Machine: How to Spark New Ideas and Create Your Company's Future.* Harvard Business Review Press, 2021.

- Many leaders see global diversity as a source of strategic advantage: 45% of the survey respondents identified it as a source of strategic advantage for their companies; 38% indicate that it is already part of their corporate diversity agenda.
- Leaders see three principal benefits of global diversity: "improved global market access," "positively changing our culture," and "boosting our teams' creativity" were cited as key benefits by 40% of respondents.

While the survey was completed in September of 2021, the executives we have spoken with since then tell us that their belief in the importance of global diversity has only strengthened.

The BCG 'Innovation without Borders' Survey

850+
executive respondents

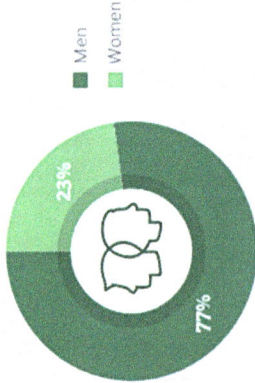

- Men
- Women

77%

23%

Responding firms covered the 10 largest destination and origin countries for global talent

Surveyed Countries
United States
Canada
Japan
United Kingdom
China
India
Germany
Nigeria
Brazil
United Arab Emirates

~ **$5.7T** combined revenues

>**6M** total employees

Full database: 20+ industries. The top 7 were:

124	107	94	78	61	61	50
Manufacturing	Finance	Technology	Energy	Automotive	Pharma	Software

Source: BCG research.

***

How Leaders Can Take a Stand for Global Diversity

Senior executives are almost always more conservative politically than society at large. But as a group, they make a hard left on the issue of migration. As Tuoyo Ebigbeyi, the COO of American Tower Corporation Nigeria, explained to us, "While there is certainly no shortage of talented, brilliant Nigerians, I believe there will be a net-positive multiplier effect to the broader economy by enhancing our perspectives through migration."

Fully 72% of 850 executives we surveyed agree with Ebigbeyi: They also believe that migration strengthens their countries. Unfortunately, only about 50% of their fellow citizens favor open immigration.

This relationship holds true even in the two countries most open to migration among those represented in our survey. In Canada, 69% of executives favor open migration policies compared to 61% in society at large. Similarly, in Germany, 70% of executives support open migration policies versus 64% of citizens overall, and 22% of executives favor of fully open borders as opposed to only 8% overall.

What makes this particularly striking is that the executives we surveyed tend to be more conservative politically than their compatriots. They are 24% more likely to self-identify as "center-right" or "right" than society at large – stances typically associated with support for more restrictive migration policies.

***

Executive Perspective: Tuoyo Ebigbeyi
COO of American Tower Corporation Nigeria

"Due to the shift to remote work, there's now an intense competition for Nigerian talent."

Tuoyo Ebigbeyi joined American Tower in 2016 and currently serves as the COO of its subsidiary in Nigeria. American Tower is a Fortune 500 provider of wireless infrastructure. Its global portfolio includes over 171,000 sites throughout the Americas, Europe, Africa, and Asia.

Why does Nigeria need Global Migration?

I believe migration is necessary for Nigeria because historically there has not been much socioeconomic upward mobility. The net effect is that relatively few Nigerians have left the country for schooling and work. As a result, only few have developed a global mindset through an exposure to different ways of thinking.

Migration is one way to broaden our talent pool – the pool of diversity in perspectives required to raise the level of critical thinking needed for effective business decision making. We need more repats,

Nigerians who go abroad and come back, and more expats, who are foreign born and come to Nigeria for work. While repats often have a higher likelihood of staying longer, both have their unique value.

One of the biggest challenges Nigeria faces today is getting the baseline right. By baseline, I mean the fundamental infrastructure, such as power, health care, and transportation, needed to stimulate sustainable macroeconomic growth. To do that, we need to successfully attract global talent to talent-scarce industries that are often capital intensive and infrastructure heavy.

How can Nigeria Attract Global Talent?

That's a challenge. In Nigeria, we are struggling with the macroeconomic headwinds of high inflation and currency devaluation. On average, wage growth has not necessarily increased in line with inflation. So, Nigerian firms can pay employees above market to attract global talent.

At the same time, with the rise of remote work, we are seeing global technology firms competing for Nigerian talent. Perhaps if that trend continues, it may lend itself to the repatriation of Nigerians expats who wish to return home.

Further, there are a lot of interesting and dynamic growth opportunities in the Nigerian entrepreneurial sector, especially in fintech startups, which are skyrocketing and drawing international attention. Look at Paystack, a Nigerian payment-service provider recently acquired by Stripe for more than $200 million. It is a firm whose mindset was global from day one and that helped them recruit their diverse talent base.

What does American Tower attract and retain global talent?

Of course, one baseline to attract and retain talent is to compensate employees fairly and competitively. But that is not enough. Attracting and retaining the best talent is about culture, too. While culture is very loosely defined, for us it means building an inclusive work environment that fosters diverse thinking. We want our employees to feel empowered and motivated. They are met with respect, and we do not use fear or micromanagement to drive results. It is also about good work. So, we try to give our teams projects that are mission based and allow for a high degree of purpose-driven work.

✳✳✳

What do these executives know? Almost all of them (95%) know that global diversity – that is, working with people from different countries and cultures – is an issue of strategic importance to their companies. This view squares with our research into the effects of global diversity on corporate innovation and business results. We found that companies with globally diverse workforces are 26% more likely to realize clear gains from the creative processes of their product and innovation teams and two times more likely to be innovation leaders than those with less diverse workforces. More broadly, the global movement of talent spreads ideas and helps countries attract capital. Economists peg the value of mobile talent to the global economy at $2.3 trillion annually. That's nearly the GDP of India.

The moral case and the business case for talent migration are both strong. Yet migration remains a highly politicized and polarizing issue. How then can leaders embrace and support global talent migration without becoming lightning rods for political controversy? Here are some ideas:

Lead by example. In 2015, in the face of skilled labor shortages, Kremer Machine Systems, a German specialist in industrial assembly, began hiring Syrian refugees. Though the firm had to invest at first to overcome language barriers, cultural differences, and improve the skills of the refugees it hired, the company found that those investments usually paid off in six months or less.

Rise to the occasion. In the wake of the war in Ukraine, civil society organizations, foundations, and corporate leaders in Europe sprang into action. Under the umbrella organization Alliance4Ukraine, NGOs, corporates, and startups came together to form an effective public-private ecosystem of funding partners, political support (including the German chancellor), and execution players. One of these players, a job-matching platform called Imagine Foundation, has managed to assemble a broad coalition of more than 800 corporate partners to form a hiring network for refugees from the war in Ukraine as well as those fleeing armed conflict and political oppression elsewhere.

Make successes public. GetYourGuide, the Berlin-based travel platform that reached unicorn status in 2019 and is now accelerating out of the pandemic, attributes much of its success to its ability to hire and leverage the talents of a global workforce. Just ask Tao Tao, the company's COO and cofounder. He is an enthusiastic advocate of open migration who often speaks publicly about its benefits for his company and Germany and the urgent need to embrace it at a policy level. His words carry weight because GetYourGuide is growing fast – and in no small part thanks to its high level of global diversity. Some of the ideas Tao champions, such as a points-based visa program for skilled talent, have found their way into the coalition agreement of the next German government.

Build a coalition of like-minded leaders. Chobani, the dairy produce manufacturer founded by Hamdi Ulukaya, a Turkish-born immigrant to the US, stands out for hiring 300 refugees (15% of the company's workforce). But Ulukaya, who is arguably one of the most outspoken corporate leaders on migration, leverages the company's efforts by enlisting other companies in the quest for global diversity. In September, he launched the Tent Coalition for Afghan Refugees, which brought together Amazon, Uber, UPS, Pfizer, Tyson Foods, and two dozen other companies to provide relocation services, training, and jobs for Afghanis who fled their country in the wake of US withdrawal.

None of the ideas above will produce an overnight change in how societies at large – and policy makers in particular – feel about global migration. But in tandem with the voices and support of the many organizations and citizens already in favor of more open borders, they can nudge politicians to reexamine immigration laws. The benefits of global diversity are created in large part by business. It's time for business leaders to act – for the benefit of global talent, local citizens, and our societies.

✳✳✳

Executive Perspective: Tao Tao
Cofounder and COO of GetYourGuide

"More open borders are a must-have for our future prosperity and economic growth."

Tao Tao is a native of Beijing. In 2009, he cofounded GetYourGuide, a travel site through which customers from over 170 countries have booked more than 45 million tours, activities, and attractions. GetYourGuide is headquartered in Berlin and has offices in 14 countries, staffed by a global team of over 550 travel experts and technologists.

Why does Germany need Global Migration?
Immigration is not only something that is nice to have – it is a must-have for our future prosperity and economic growth. Without it, stable net incomes in Germany will be hard to sustain. Just look at our slowing rate of innovation and aging population. Migration is not only about helping the people who come here. In fact, it is more about helping ourselves and preserving prosperity for future generations.

What can Germany do to Attract Global Talent?
I believe Germany – and Europe – offer great conditions for immigrants, but we are not marketing that fact. The US is still the number one country in terms of promoting inspirational immigrant stories of success. We need to change our narrative and broadcast it more actively. People all over the world should know that Germany and Europe are the best places to migrate to for people in pursuit of prosperous, free lives and exciting careers.

What roles does Global Talent Play at GetYourGuide?
I believe it is important that your workforce reflects the composition of your customer base. We are a travel platform used by people of all genders, religions, and ethnicities from all over the world. Our workforce and team composition must reflect that. We are a global firm and securing competitive advantage is in large part based on having a global team with a global mindset.

How do you Build a Global Team and get it to Work?
Often, the best talent in the world is located elsewhere, so we have no choice but to be open to talented people wherever they are. We see talented people in a customer-centric way. We have to offer them something valuable to ensure they will want to join our firm if we are going to compete with the many other firms that are making very attractive offers to great talent.

Once we attract talented people, we need to make sure we create the conditions that support them. As a firm, we've become expert at leveraging our culture and teams for social integration. Integration starts with an English-first policy in order to promote inclusion. We've also decided against remote work in favor of an in-person culture postCOVID-19 to capture the high levels of exchange and cooperation that are fueled by multicultural, onsite teams.

✳✳✳✳✳✳✳✳✳✳✳✳✳✳✳✳✳✳✳✳✳✳✳✳✳

An Innovation Culture That Gets Results

Justin Manly, Johann D. Harnoss, Hannah Lu Schmitt, Robert Werner,
David Blanchard, and Deborah Lovich

When interest rates rise, innovation budgets often fall. Yet preserving cash and fostering innovation are not mutually exclusive strategies. On the contrary, companies should embrace innovation even in challenging times. This principle held true during the Great Depression and in the aftermath of the 2008 financial crisis, as innovative companies thrived and outperformed their peers in both the short and the long term.[50]

Encouragingly, 86% of corporate innovation heads agree. As our Most Innovative Companies 2023[51] report reveals, leading companies have either maintained or substantially increased their investment in innovation this year. To reap the full benefits, however, companies need to promote a *culture* of innovation. Our research and survey results consistently show that companies with an innovation culture – those that embrace risk, foster collaboration, and grant autonomy to their teams – are 60% more likely to be innovation leaders.

In this article, we present some practical guidelines for executives seeking to design a high-impact innovation culture.[52] And we outline four areas of focus that offer a clear path for change, drawing on examples from leading innovators.

Culture, Innovation, and the Operating Model

First, what is culture? Essentially, it's the way people interact in an organization and the way work gets done. Culture is organic; it is as much shaped by the present as it is influenced by the organization's institutional memory and past behaviors.

An innovation culture is thus the collective behavior that shapes how new products and services get built and marketed to customers. To use an analogy, innovation culture is like software that runs on the "hardware" we generally associate with innovation: the strategies, governance, processes, organizational structures, metrics, and other aspects of the operating model.

All too often, we see a tendency to focus solely on the hardware of innovation. That's only natural, as organization structure, processes, and metrics are

---

50 https://www.bcg.com/publications/2020/six-moves-for-innovation-during-recovery
51 https://www.bcg.com/publications/2023/advantages-through-innovation-in-uncertain-times
52 https://www.bcg.com/publications/2022/innovation-without-borders

part of the standard tools of management. They are the tangibles that leaders can readily see, analyze, and implement.

Alas, this focus comes at the expense of the software – and this fundamental misunderstanding can trip companies up. (See "Why Companies Get Stuck.") Instead, hardware *and* software need to be seen as integral and foundational to innovation systems that drive real impact.

∗∗∗

Why Companies get Stuck

Some companies treat innovation as an abstract process, untethered to the market, to customer reality, or to avenues of opportunity. So they cannot figure out how to truly realize it. Many make primarily superficial efforts, what we call "innovation theater." This consists of such tactics as redesigning workspaces or offering kombucha on tap, moves that have little impact on their own.

Other companies cling to the "not invented here" mindset, an insular view that sees innovation in terms of proprietary technology and eschews externally developed ideas or resources. They think innovation happens only in the laboratory – and as a result they make no attempt to adopt new ways of working (such as an open-innovation approach that fosters diversity of thought, idea generation, and experimentation). Still others conceive of innovation as an innately risky activity that requires "permission" – one that depends on extensive business-case development, formalized stage-gate processes, and heavy-handed stakeholder management.

Leaders who overengineer with endless stage gates are like helicopter parents who hover over their children without allowing them the unstructured, unsupervised play so essential to creativity and cognitive development. Their intentions are good, of course, but by focusing only on the "hardware" part of the picture, they end up creating a culture (a "software") that does not foster the desired innovation outcomes. Both the software and the hardware are instrumental and must be in synch for the whole to work.

∗∗∗

It's the combination of a strong innovation culture and a lean operating model that makes a difference. As we've mentioned, companies with strong innovation cultures are 60% more likely to be innovators, while those with strong mechanisms in place (the hardware) are 35% more likely to be innovators. Those with both – we call them innovation culture leaders[53] – are nearly twice as likely to be a world class innovator (see Figure 5.10).

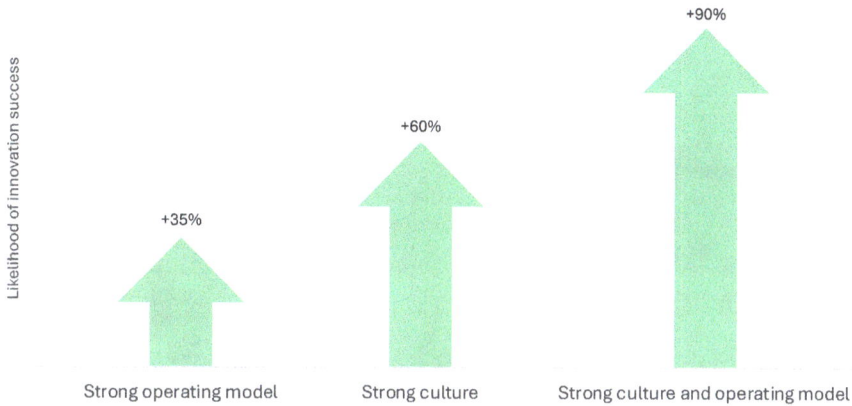

Sources: Global Innovation Survey, BCG i2i Team (n=3,236); BCG analysis.

Figure 5.10: Companies with a Strong Culture and Operating Model Are Nearly Twice as Likely to Win on Innovation.

Interestingly, innovation-culture leaders employ, on average, 10% fewer full-time people with formal innovation roles. What does this tell us? That culture does not have to be a costly endeavor – in fact, it can be a lever to run leaner, faster processes.

So how do you ingrain a culture of innovation? By changing the context in which people operate.

What Innovation-Culture Exemplars Focus On

From our experience, we've identified four aspects of innovation culture on which companies often focus: what successes you celebrate, how you create, how you lead, and how you team. Importantly, these aspects either add – or destroy – value, depending on *how* your teams work together.

Each aspect, when framed as a question, can help you determine what route to pursue to bolster your company's innovation culture. Zero in on one that offers the best opportunity for improvement and impact (see Figure 5.11).

Of course, culture change doesn't take hold overnight. But we've seen companies effect change fairly quickly. Every company has a different starting point

---

53 https://www.bcg.com/publications/2023/what-innovation-leaders-do-differently

	What do you celebrate?	How do you create?	How do you lead?	How do you team?
Typical levers	Purpose	Strategy	Governance	Agile teaming
	Metrics and KPIs	Customer insight	Portfolio management	New roles
	Rewards	Open innovation	Process	Cognitive diversity

Source: BCG Analysis

Figure 5.11: Four Guiding Questions.

and selects different aspects of their innovation culture to focus on, depending on that starting point and their strategy.

Fundamentally, though – and it bears repeating – to change culture, a company must build it into the operating model from the beginning. Fortunately, many such tactics are easy to implement, and quick wins invariably have a snowball effect.

What do you celebrate? What R&D and innovation outcomes does your company reward? What actions put the innovation team on the company's radar? What behaviors accelerate team members' promotions?

One example of a company that strongly believes in creating an environment conducive to innovation – and that encourages creativity and idea development from everyone, not just its official R&D team members – is 3M. The Minneapolis-based company hit a milestone in 2014, when it was granted its 100,000th patent; it remains a serial innovator, averaging 3,000 new patents each year. Indeed, some of 3M's greatest successes over the decades have come from experiments that didn't pan out but were given new life (such as Post-Its, which were discovered in the search for strong adhesives).

The company has long understood that one of the biggest impediments to innovation is the lack of time and space for employees to think beyond their current tasks. Another is the lack of a central hub where employees can share knowledge and jointly develop ideas. Performance management systems that do not recognize initiative, knowledge sharing, and achievements are a third obstacle.

Each of these impediments is relatively easy to address, however, and can yield quick results when redesigned in a way such that innovation-fostering behaviors are embedded into the company's operating system.

The "15% rule," which 3M has formalized, is one easy-to-implement policy. It gives employees the right to spend 15% of their time (also known as "magic time") on side projects. (Post-Its, in fact, were invented on one employee's 15% time.) At the company's Tech Forum – an informal organization similar to a university society – people can join a team to collaborate on a side project. Mentoring, teaching, and time spent developing others all count in formal performance reviews; in fact, they are requirements not only for promotion and incentives, but for advancement to the "Carlton Society," the company's highest technical career level.

3M understood earlier than most companies that it had to create a "pull" for innovation throughout the organization. While 3M rewards technical breakthroughs, the company steers its innovation efforts in part based on product vitality. These innovation efforts are succeeding: while 3M is best known for products such as Scotch tape, Post-Its, and Thinsulate, one-third of its sales come from products invented within the past five years. Purposeful choices like this – to reward innovation that promises to have impact rather than innovation for its own sake – have made 3M a serial innovator.

How do you create? How do you get new ideas? Do you introspect or interact with people outside of your company? What role do customer insights play in idea development?

Consider Unilever. The Foods R&D center of the consumer products giant was, until not long ago, located on the outskirts of Rotterdam, far removed from external influences and sources of inspiration. The company staffed its innovation teams almost exclusively with internal experts, which created a bottleneck when specific expertise was not available. It also slowed down innovation because highly qualified team members would get caught up in more transactional research activities. Finally, Unilever's in-house-only development process meant that new ideas were often latecomers to a trend.

To unlock an innovation culture with impact, the company decided to create an open innovation ecosystem. Step one was relocating the R&D group to an innovation hub on the campus of Wageningen University, Europe's foremost center for food and agricultural sciences research. The new location made it easier for the team to access a research network and cultivate partnerships.

Unilever augmented its in-house expertise with research contracts and joint initiatives with other local universities for more transactional work and new technologies such as high-throughput robotics and digital modeling capabilities. In this way, it expanded its access to talent while reducing its cost base. This model was replicated in the company's home and personal care unit with the creation of the Materials Innovation Factory at the University of Liverpool – today one of the largest centers for high-throughput robotics in material science.

One quick win Unilever scored was instituting a new approach to intellectual property (IP) rights. The company gained arising IP rights for its core categories only, agreeing to cede the rights to a project partner if it didn't use the result of the research within two years. This policy helped the team shift to an outward-looking culture while making partnering with the company even more attractive to external parties. Unilever also added digital skills to the job requirements for new hires, so that team members could work competently with the digital R&D model the company had adopted to speed collaboration and idea development.

How do you lead? Who makes what decisions on innovation? How broad are your project leaders' decision rights? Do you as a company lead by authority, or is leadership an activity anyone can participate in?

Take EDP (Energias de Portugal), a global green utility headquartered in Lisbon. Initially, the company's innovation model revolved around open innovation, an approach that relied predominantly on collaborations with startups through joint pilot projects and commercial contracts. This strategy produced the WindFloat project, a major success for EDP. The project developed an innovative technology that enables the company to explore wind potential at sea, at depths greater than 40 meters, without the need for towers.

To achieve a similar impact with even more projects – while better managing the significant risk inherent to any transformational innovation – EDP launched Innovation 2.0, a new approach to innovation that would also allow the company to replicate such success more systematically.

As part of Innovation 2.0, EDP unveiled the "Spiral" program, which had two objectives: spurring transformative ideas from those closest to the business needs and instilling a culture of innovation leadership among the company's up-and-coming talent.

It took many months for EDP to strike the right balance between empowering the teams while providing them with direction. An initial flurry of more than six dozen ideas was whittled down to the most promising ten. EDP arrived at a streamlined approach to vetting ideas, centered around four pivotal questions: Is the problem to be solved for significant? Can solving it have commercial impact? Is the innovation feasible? And can EDP succeed with it?

To this end, leaders crafted open-ended prompts, such as "How might we reduce energy losses from complex interference processes (the 'wake effect') in a wind park"? And they encouraged teams to think "problem first, and then solution" instead of starting with technology. The top ideas are now being developed, guided by project mentors, and funded with ad hoc, stage-gate budgets before the innovation board unlocks more significant development budgets.

This approach has created a culture of innovation at EDP that seeks to de-risk big ideas as early as possible, showing that precision guidance, empowerment, and ownership can lead to more projects that promise transformative impact.

How do you team? Do you enable everyone in your company to participate meaningfully in innovation? Do you draw on the most diverse perspectives when you form teams, or not?

At the dawn of the 2010s, Rakuten, the Japanese e-commerce company, was "lost in translation," literally losing days of work while translating documents between English and Japanese. Such slowdowns were putting the company at risk of losing its innovation edge. So one day, CEO and founder Mickey Mikitani instituted a bold new requirement: he declared that all company communications, from meetings and presentations to the canteen menus, would be in English. Mikitani gave employees two years to learn the language, offering free classes, e-learning tools, and one-on-one support. Employees who achieved the goal were eligible for promotion; those that did not risked demotion.

Understandably, the transition was stressful for many employees. But the "one common language" requirement transformed the company's innovation culture. Not only did it remove the language barrier that had impeded employee communication and prevented collaboration with global colleagues, but it allowed the company greater access to global talent.[54]

At Rakuten's corporate office today, there are employees who have migrated from Bulgaria, France, Indonesia, Germany, Iran, and elsewhere, and 80% of its new engineers hail from countries other than Japan – a total of 70 different nations in all. Thanks to this simple way of building a more collaborative work environment, Rakuten is now seen by many as an exemplar of the modern, digital, global Japan.

How to Rev Up Your Innovation Culture

These four examples offer inspiration to companies whose innovation culture needs a reset. But they represent merely a handful of ways in which culture leaders have fostered, pivoted, and sustained vibrant innovation cultures.

How can you build an innovation culture that will support your strategy? Start by looking at three things all culture leaders do well:

– **They clearly *articulate* the specific behaviors that are most critical to their innovation success.** Among them: striking a balance between freedom

---

54 https://www.bcg.com/publications/2021/virtual-mobility-in-the-global-workforce

and accountability; encouraging risk taking; and fostering playfulness while adhering to company standards. Companies that take their innovation culture seriously are crystal-clear about how these behaviors are defined: "freedom," for example, means seeking input, not consensus, while empowering decision making; "encouraging risk taking" means telling teams to dream big, learn from failure, and improve continuously. Companies that lead in innovation culture make sure to cultivate and reward those behaviors.

– **They *activate* these behaviors through the actions of their leaders**. An innovation culture is shaped from the top. Leaders articulate an innovation vision for their company and personally engage in key ecosystem outreach activities. They inspire innovation by providing the needed hardware to support the software: the incentives, platforms, and mechanisms for celebrating, cultivating, and rewarding new ideas; the accountability and ownership that teams need to operate unencumbered; and the freedom to collaborate with external partners. Put simply: leaders – from the C suite[55] to the front line – "walk the talk."

– **Most importantly, they *embed* the core behaviors into their operating model.** Innovation culture leaders know it takes more than setting up creative spaces with ping pong tables and espresso machines or laboratories segregated from the rest of the workforce and the company's day-to-day currents. Culture runs deep: it's embedded in a company's incentive systems, policies, processes, and practices. These companies also foster a strong innovation culture in their very hiring practices, seeking new employees that have an innovation mindset as well as those with diverse backgrounds, experiences, and ways of thinking.

✳✳✳

An Innovation Culture Barometer

How is your company performing in the three areas where innovation leaders excel? Here are some questions to ask.

Articulate

– How well have you identified the focused set of behaviors that your organization needs to spur innovation and support your strategy?
– How specifically and actionably have you articulated them?

---

55 https://www.bcg.com/publications/2020/why-it-is-time-to-bring-learning-to-the-c-suite

– How well do they serve as a guide for what "great" looks like in employees' and leaders' daily work?

Activate
– How effectively are your company's leaders role-modeling and supporting these innovation-fostering behaviors and activities?
– What could they be doing differently to become more effective role models? Are there any visible, symbolic moves that they could make immediately?
– What support might they need in order to get started, and to stay the course over the long haul?

Embed
– Which of your company's operating model elements might currently be quashing important innovation-fostering behaviors?
– What are the two or three changes you could make to your operating model that would best "hardwire" these behaviors?

***

Not long ago, Harvard Business School professor Gary Pisano observed that innovation leaders "have a tolerance for failure – but an intolerance for incompetence."[56] Innovation requires freedom to flourish, but boundaries and conditions in order to thrive. That's the essence of a high-impact innovation culture.

By focusing intently on these three areas – articulating, activating, and embedding the right behaviors – you'll be able to establish the best possible conditions for creating, teaming, leading, and celebrating innovation. Doing so thoughtfully and consistently will spark the innovation culture your company needs. Indeed, you'll be surprised by how quickly results accrue and sustain.

---

56 https://hbr.org/2019/01/the-hard-truth-about-innovative-cultures

List of Figures

https://doi.org/10.1515/9783111369921-007

Index

https://doi.org/10.1515/9783111369921-008

www.ingramcontent.com/pod-product-compliance
Lightning Source LLC
Chambersburg PA
CBHW061239220326

41599CB00028B/5479